Work

Work

*Theological Foundations and
Practical Implications*

Edited by

R. Keith Loftin
and
Trey Dimsdale

scm press

© R. Keith Loftin and Trey Dimsdale 2018

Published in 2018 by SCM Press

Editorial office
3rd Floor, Invicta House,
108–114 Golden Lane,
London EC1Y 0TG, UK
www.scmpress.co.uk

SCM Press is an imprint of Hymns Ancient & Modern Ltd
(a registered charity)

Hymns Ancient & Modern® is a registered trademark of Hymns Ancient
& Modern Ltd

13A Hellesdon Park Road, Norwich,
Norfolk NR6 5DR, UK

British Library Cataloguing in Publication data

A catalogue record for this book is available
from the British Library

978 0 334 05529 7

Typeset by Regent Typesetting
Printed and bound by
CPI Group (UK) Ltd

Contents

CONTENTS

Part 3 Practical Theology

Acknowledgements

A volume with the breadth of the present one represents a project that no editors could complete without the formal and informal assistance and support of many people. We owe a debt of gratitude to Dr Ethan Jones, Assistant Professor of Old Testament at Scarborough College, for his invaluable assistance in reviewing and editing the portions of the chapters requiring a sharp and thorough facility with the biblical languages. A version of Miroslav Volf's contribution to this book was previously published in his *Work in the Spirit*, and is here printed by the kind permission of Wipf and Stock Publishers (www.wipfandstock.com). Our own editors at SCM Press, David Shervington and Mary Matthews, have been helpful guides from start to finish. The Acton Institute for the Study of Religion and Liberty provided support and, through their flagship conference, Acton University, a platform for discussion, meeting, and growth for the editors and for many of the contributors.

Individually, I (Keith) am thankful to Dr Mike Wilkinson, Dean of Scarborough College, for providing encouragement and space for the pursuit of these important ideas in personal research and teaching in the classroom. Also, my students who have been engaged and curious have helped me to think about the ways in which these ideas matter in the world for which they are training to serve. As always, I am thankful to my loving wife, Julie, for her patience and encouragement.

I (Trey) am indebted to Fr Robert Sirico, Kris Mauren, David Milroy, and Paul Bonicelli, leaders at the Acton Institute, for cultivating the context to do such meaningful work with temporal and eternal significance. Dan Churchwell, my colleague in Program Outreach at Acton, is a helpful conversation partner for such projects. A special thanks is due to my hard-working, long-suffering, and very capable assistant Anna Kelly, without whom I would be far less productive.

We are both grateful for the careful, reflective, and insightful work of Mark Greene of the London Institute for Contemporary Christianity, who graciously wrote the Foreword. In truth, it is Mark who inspired this volume because of his many observations about the need to motivate academics to think and write about these topics. We can think of no better successor to the godly example of John Stott for how Christians should think winsomely and creatively about changing the world.

Contributors

Chris R. Armstrong (PhD, Duke University) is the Director of Opus: The Art of Work and serves as Professor of Church History at Wheaton College. Through Opus, Dr Armstrong works with Wheaton College faculty to help students to integrate their faith and their vocations. He is the author of *Patron Saints for Postmoderns* (IVP, 2009) and *Medieval Wisdom for Modern Christians: Finding Authentic Faith in a Modern Age with C. S. Lewis* (Baker, 2016).

John Bergsma (PhD, University of Notre Dame), Professor of Theology at the Franciscan University of Steubenville (Ohio), is the author of *The Jubilee from Leviticus to Qumran: A History of Interpretation* (Brill) as well as some two dozen peer-reviewed articles and chapters in such sources as *Biblica*, *Vetus Testamentum*, *The Journal of Biblical Literature*, and *Markets & Morality*. In addition to the PhD, he holds both the Master of Theology and Master of Divinity degrees from Calvin Theological Seminary.

Darrell L. Bock (PhD, University of Aberdeen) is Executive Director of Cultural Engagement and Senior Research Professor of New Testament Studies at Dallas Theological Seminary. He is a past Humboldt Scholar at Tübingen University, where he completed postdoctoral studies, as well as a past President of the Evangelical Theological Society. Among the dozens of books he has authored or edited are *Luke: Baker Exegetical Commentary on the New Testament* (2 volumes, Baker, 1994), *Acts: Baker Exegetical Commentary on the New Testament* (Baker, 2007), *A Theology of Luke and Acts* (Zondervan, 2012), and *Parables of Enoch: A Paradigm Shift* (Bloomsbury, 2014).

Darrell T. Cosden (PhD, St Andrews) is an independent scholar who has taught at schools in the United States, Scotland, Russia, and Ukraine. His doctoral work focused on the theology of work and eschatology, which culminated in two well-regarded books on the subject, *Theology of Work: Work and the New Creation* (Paternoster, 2004) and *The Heavenly Good of Earthly Work* (Paternoster, 2006).

Trey Dimsdale (JD, University of Missouri) is Director of Program Out-reach at the Acton Institute, as well as a Fellow at the Research Institute of the Ethics and Religious Liberty Commission of the Southern Baptist Convention. He sits on the Board of Directors for the National Faith and Work Association, for whom he is also an Academic Representative on the Board of Advisors.

Greg Forster (PhD, Yale University) teaches courses at Trinity Evangel-ical Divinity School in Chicago, where he also serves as director of the Oikonomia Network in the Center for Transformational Churches at Trinity International University. A highly sought after lecturer, Forster's books include *John Locke's Politics of Moral Consensus* (Cambridge, 2005), *The Contested Public Square: The Crisis of Christianity and Politics* (IVP, 2008), and *John Rawls and Christian Social Engagement: Justice as Unfairness* (Lexington, 2015).

Mark Greene is the Executive Director of the London Institute for Con-temporary Christianity (licc.org.uk).

Samuel Gregg (DPhil, University of Oxford), Director of Research at the Acton Institute, is the author of more than a dozen books, including *On Ordered Liberty: A Treatise on the Free Society* (Lexington, 2003), *Becoming Europe* (Encounter Books, 2013), *Economic Thinking for the Theologically Minded* (University Press of America, 2001), *Wilhelm Röpke's Political Economy* (Edward Elgar, 2010), and *For God and Profit: How Banking and Finance Can Serve the Common Good* (Cross-road, 2016). He was elected a Fellow of the Royal Historical Society in 2001 and a Member of the Mont Pèlerin Society in 2004. In 2008, he was elected a member of the Philadelphia Society and a member of the Royal Economic Society.

R. Keith Loftin (PhD, University of Aberdeen) is Associate Professor of Philosophy and Humanities at Scarborough College and Southwestern Baptist Theological Seminary. He is the editor of *God & Morality: Four Views* (IVP, 2012), co-author of *Stand Firm: Defending the Beauty and Brilliance of the Gospel* (Broadman & Holman, 2018), co-editor of *Christian Physicalism? Philosophical and Theological Criticisms* (Lexing-ton, 2018), and the author of numerous articles and reviews addressing topics both philosophical and theological.

Eugene Merrill (PhD, Columbia University and PhD, Bob Jones Uni-versity) was Distinguished Professor of Old Testament Studies at Dallas Theological Seminary for more than 35 years. Among his many books and articles are *A Historical Survey of the Old Testament* (Baker, 1991), *Everlasting Dominion: A Theology of the Old Testament* (Broadman & Holman, 2006), and *Kingdom of Priests: A History of Old Testament Israel* (Baker, 2008).

Michael Matheson Miller (MA, Nagoya University's Graduate School of International Development [Japan], MA in Philosophy from Franciscan University, and MBA in International Management from Thunderbird Graduate School of Global Business) is Research Fellow and Director of Acton Media at the Acton Institute. He is the director and producer of the award-winning film projects *PovertyCure* (Acton Media, 2012) and *Poverty, Inc.* (Acton Media, 2016).

Scott B. Rae (PhD, University of Southern California) is Professor of Christian Ethics and Dean of Faculty at Talbot School of Theology. A past president of the Evangelical Theological Society, he is the author of over a dozen books, including *Moral Choices* (Zondervan, 2000), *Biotechnology and the Human Good* (Georgetown University Press, 2007), and *Beyond Integrity: A Judeo-Christian Approach to Business Ethics* (Zondervan, 2012), he has also published dozens of peer-reviewed articles in the areas of ethics and Christian social issues.

Jay Wesley Richards (PhD, Princeton Theological Seminary) is Assistant Research Professor in the School of Business and Economics at The Catholic University of America, Executive Editor of *The Stream*, and Senior Fellow at the Discovery Institute where he works with the Center on Wealth, Poverty, and Morality. Prior to his doctoral studies in philosophy and theology, Richards earned both the Master of Divinity and Master of Theology degrees. He is the author of many books including *The Untamed God: A Philosophical Exploration of Divine Perfection, Simplicity and Immutability* (IVP, 2003) and *Money, Greed, and God* (HarperCollins, 2009).

John Taylor (PhD, University of Cambridge) is Professor of New Testament at Gateway Seminary.

Gabriela Urbanova (PhD, Bratislava) serves on the staff of Mr Branislav Skripek, Member of European Parliament and President of the European Christian Political Movement (ECPM). She also serves as the board of the ECPY, the youth movement of the ECPM.

Miroslav Volf (Dr. Theol., University of Tübingen) is the Henry B. Wright Professor of Systematic Theology and Founding Director of the Yale

Center for Faith & Culture. He is the author of some 100 peer-reviewed articles and chapters, as well as 17 books including *Work in the Spirit: Toward a Theology of Work* (Oxford, 1991), *After Our Likeness: The Church as an Image of the Triune God* (Eerdmans, 1998), *God's Life in the Trinity* (Fortress, 2006), and *Flourishing* (Yale University Press, 2015).

Jürgen von Hagen (PhD, University of Bonn) is Professor of Economics and Director of the Institute for International Economic Policy at the University of Bonn (Germany), and pastor of the Free Evangelical Church of Mülheim/Ruhr, Germany. He is the author of some 100 peer-reviewed journal articles and another 100 chapters in edited volumes, and his over 40 authored books include *The Economic Regulation of Broadcasting Markets* (Cambridge, 2007), *Fiscal Governance in Europe* (Cambridge, 2009), and *Money as God?* (Cambridge, 2014). He has taught previously at the Kelley School of Business, Bloomington, Indiana, where he maintains a visiting appointment, and the University of Mannheim, Germany. He is a member of the German National Academy of Sciences (Leopoldina) and has served as a consultant to numerous international organizations such as the IMF and the World Bank, and national governments in Europe and beyond.

Foreword: Good News for Work (and Beyond)

MARK GREENE

This important book is not just about work.

This book is about the future of mission, the scope of our discipleship, and the content of the invitation we make to those who don't follow Jesus. And it is vital for all three. And it is vital for our growing understanding of the purposes and potential of work.

Back in 1942, Dorothy L. Sayers, the great crime writer, forthright apologist, and pioneer workplace thinker, wrote:

> In nothing has the Church so lost Her hold on reality as Her failure to understand and respect the secular vocation. She has allowed work and religion to become separate departments, and is astonished to find that, as a result, the secular work of the world is turned to purely selfish and destructive ends, and that the greater part of the world's intelligent workers have become irreligious or at least uninterested in religion ... But is it astonishing? How can anyone remain interested in a religion which seems to have no concern with nine-tenths of his life?[1]

Indeed. Why would anyone remain interested or indeed become interested in a religion that ignores nine-tenths of their life?

Sayers's point was not just about work.

Her point was about Christianity as a whole.

And she had a point then, and she has a point now.

The reality in the UK, in the USA, and indeed globally is that over-all the religion we have been exhorting believers to follow and inviting non-believers to embrace is a religion that has inadvertently tended to be pietistic, leisure-time oriented, pastor-centric, and neighbourhood-centred. Yes, since John Stott, Billy Graham, Samuel Escobar, and Rene Padilla made such significant advances at the first International Congress

---

1 Dorothy L. Sayers, 'Why Work?'. in *Creed or Chaos?* (New York: Harcourt, Brace & Co., 1949), p. 56.

on World Evangelization in Lausanne in 1974, huge steps forward have been taken in embracing an active, purposeful, and sustained concern for the poor and in beginning to engage more proactively in the structures of society. However, their bigger holistic vision for gospel action in all of life has yet to find widespread, dynamic expression in the global church. It remains the case that the vast majority of lay Christians have no compelling, holistic vision for mission in their overall Monday to Saturday lives, and still less for their daily work.

Now, I believe that we will not see significant sustained, sustainable numerical growth in the church, Western or Majority World, or indeed transformation in our nations unless:

1 We disciple God's people for a dynamic, transformative relationship with God in every aspect of life.
2 We offer all those involved in daily work a rich biblical understanding of work.

We must help workers to see not only that work matters to God but *why* it matters; why their particular work matters; how work is central, not peripheral, to God's purposes in time and eternity – in blessing all nations, in witnessing to all nations, and in God's plan for reconciling and restoring all things.

The forces ranged against such a seismic shift in thinking and living are formidable and have been deeply embedded in the culture of denominations, training colleges, hermeneutics, homiletics, seminary training, publishing, hymnology, corporate worship, and models of discipleship for 200 years. They will not easily be vanquished.

And they will not be vanquished without the scholars. Indeed, on a personal note, I have spent the best part of 35 years doing my best to help Christians and their leaders live out a biblical vision for Monday to Saturday life in general and work in particular. And I am acutely aware of the questions I was not able to answer, the eschatological conundrums I could not resolve, the textual interpretations that I could not make confidently, certainly in part because I didn't have the scholarship. So I know we will not make long-term sustained progress in missional discipleship without the robust theological foundations and acute biblical insights that come from the work of scholars, and that then form the hearts and minds, the imaginations and aspirations, the priorities and praxis of church leaders, and then of their communities.

And that is why this book is so vital.

The timing of its writing, coinciding with the celebrations of the 500th anniversary of the publication of Luther's 95 Theses, should be both an energizing encouragement for the potential of its ideas and a sobering reminder of how easily significant insights can be lost. Yes, in the Reformation, the word of God was given back to the people, but the ministry was also meant to be given back to the people. It wasn't. The 'sola system' – sola Scriptura, sola gratia, sola fides, solus Christus, soli Deo Gloria – may remain part of Protestant consciousness, but the biblical doctrine of the priesthood of all believers and its implications for the role of the laity in daily life and work do not. 'Omnes sacerdotes' (all priests) never became a slogan tripping off the tongue of seminary lecturers and students. Ultimately flawed theology has led us to a global church that is not dynamically committed to the comprehensive biblical vision for whole-life discipleship that we see from Genesis to Revelation. Ideas, after all, lead to action, beliefs to behaviour, ethos to praxis. Ideas matter.

The challenge to the scholars in the arena of work is a particularly difficult one, precisely because like Luther, the task is to find a way to set aside the received interpretation of texts and look afresh, wondering not only whether others have been affected by the sacred–secular divide but also whether we have been. This is certainly not to denigrate the brilliance or faithfulness of the scholars who have gone before but just to recognize, in humility, that even the greatest of scholars may have read and interpreted key texts, or aspects of them, through the sacred–secular divided lenses of their and our own era.

So I am hugely grateful to Trey Dimsdale and Keith Loftin for taking the initiative to commission such a rich book on such a vital topic from such a formidable and diverse group of scholars across a range of disciplines. As it turns out, I did indeed find an answer to an eschatological conundrum, substantial help in the interpretation of the text of Thessalonians, and joy and wonder in fresh perspectives from Genesis 1 and 2. But there are new insights and encouragements in every essay. Beyond that, there is an overall sense of new vistas opening up, of there being more to discover, as ever, about the beauty of Christ's character, the scope of his purposes, and the joy of walking with him in the high calling of our daily work.

May the Lord gladden your mind, stir your heart, and refresh your
    spirit as you read these essays.
May he enrich and establish the work of your hands,
    bless the places you work and the people you work with,
        and draw them close to his son.
            To his glory may it be.

Mark Greene

Executive Director
The London Institute for Contemporary Christianity
August 2017

I

Work in Christian Perspective: An Introduction

R. KEITH LOFTIN AND TREY DIMSDALE

'What is man, that you are mindful of him?' (Psalm 8.4). In reflecting on humankind, the psalmist marvels at our special status as creatures who are collectively and individually the subject of the creator's thoughts. The One who fixed in their place the moon and stars has a personal knowledge of and concern for the human race. In contemplating this reality, it is striking that the psalmist focuses on the convergence of humankind's identity and purpose in *work*. 'You grant mankind honour and majesty,' the psalmist writes, 'you appoint them to rule over your creation; you have placed everything under their authority' (Psalm 8.5b–6). By recalling to mind the cultural mandate of Genesis 1.28, the psalmist here connects our work to the *imago Dei*.

Traditional questions of theological anthropology – What is humankind? Are we more than our physical bodies? What constitutes our proper flourishing? (to name a few)[1] – are familiar to Christian theologues. Any adequate treatment of these questions must take its bearings from the doctrine of the *imago Dei*: that the human race is created in the image of the triune God. Various aspects of this doctrine (rightly) have received sustained attention, but swathes of the field remain untilled.

The relational aspect of humankind, for instance, has been explored in numerous contexts. Yet those relationships arising within the context of commercial and economic intercourse have gone largely overlooked by theologians and pastors. Our day-to-day engagement in work gives rise to relationship(s) in complex ways. This complexity invites scholarly engagement, not only in order to understand more fully our identity, the essence of the 'good life', and our mutual obligations, but also to facilitate the role of the church and pastor in helping the faithful to navigate a complex and often unpredictable world.

Closely related to this are questions of our work itself: How does the *imago Dei* connect to our work? What is the place of our work in God's ordering of creation? In redemption? How is work connected to spiritual giftedness? To the nature and purposes of the church? To the new creation? Although work presents us with important issues in Christian ethics and practical theology, questions such as these prompt us to recognize that the significance of work is not exhausted at the level of 'Christian living'. Indeed, we are prompted to think through a *theology* of work. This demands theological reflection on its own, but these reflections will yield a more holistic system of theology. This volume aims to aid in that task.

It is true, certainly, that the meaning and significance of work have been a concern of the Church throughout its long history. There is thus a sense in which thinking through a theology of work is a recovery operation. Contemporary theologians and churchmen have available to them insights into the place of work in Christian theology from across church history: from Tertullian to Gregory the Great, Maximus the Confessor to Martin Luther, and John Wesley to Abraham Kuyper. These voices agree that our work has theological significance, and we stand to gain much from tuning our minds to the recovery of this tradition.

Given work's prevalence in the narrative of Scripture, its emphasis across church history, and not least its prominent place in our daily life, one is somewhat surprised to note the dearth of attention given to work in the contemporary professional theological literature. Notable exceptions do exist,[2] but work has received sparse attention from contemporary theologians. A survey of standard systematic theology texts, for example, reveals little beyond occasional references to work, with these typically confined to 'Christian living' matters. Whether because work as a matter of theology has never impelled the Church to schism; because the familiar ruts of the various theological traditions have tended to steer contemporary theologians away from the issue of work; or perhaps for other reasons entirely, it is difficult to say with confidence why this is the case.

The assumption that there is a connection between the lack of engagement by theologians and the widespread misunderstanding of (and even lack of interest in) work among contemporary churchgoers is tough to avoid, although this does not by itself tell the whole story. Likewise, decidedly 'other worldly' eschatological stances – which, in view of their shared belief that the present earth will be utterly destroyed, posit a sharp discontinuity between earthly life and life everlasting – tend to discourage the development of a theology of work, although this too has limited explanatory scope.

One explanation, though, relevant to theologian and churchgoer alike, is the abiding but pernicious assumption of a sacred–secular divide. This is the notion that our lives are properly separated into distinct spheres, with our 'secular' interests, pursuits, and values (including, for example, the ordinary humdrum of day-to-day life) belonging in a lower, spiritually less significant sphere, whereas the overtly 'spiritual' parts of our lives (personal evangelism, Bible study, and church attendance, for example) belong in an upper, sacred sphere. Such thinking implies, among other things, that God cares little about our secular lives, being primarily concerned, rather, with our sacred lives. This has plain implications for contemplating work in theological perspective.

When presented in such blatant terms, we doubt many Christians would say that our lives are properly divided into sacred versus secular spheres. As Christians, after all, we all give our assent to the idea of Christ's Lordship over the *entirety* of our lives – or at least we know we're supposed to. The trouble is that many post-Enlightenment Christians seem to have absorbed such divided thinking, to some greater or lesser extent, unreflectively. Typical Monday–Friday jobs, for example, often are sharply distinguished from 'ministry' jobs. Both are regarded as being valuable, but in different senses: the latter are recognized as being *intrinsically* valuable, whereas the former are regarded as merely *instrumentally* valuable (in that they pay the mortgage and grocery bills).[3] Given the biblical link between (for instance) the *imago Dei* and work, this valuation must be rejected. Far from prescribing a compartmentalized view of life, with each stroke Scripture paints a portrait of how life is meant to be lived: holistically, before God. Upon reading the Mosaic law, for instance, one is hardly left with the impression that God cares only for Israel's formal worship or the 'spiritual' parts of their lives, showing no interest in the 'secular' sphere. Far from it: one may easily infer from his law that God wishes for Israel to recognize that *all* of life is sacred.

In terms of its effect on the theological task, the assumption of a sacred–secular divide detrimentally impacts the process from one's hermeneutic to the stratification of doctrinal *loci*. This effect is particularly evident in preventing the proper unification of meaning and pleasure in one's theologizing.[4] Not only is this unification essential for right thinking about human flourishing (not least to avoid descending into nihilism), as Miroslav Volf argues, its achievement reflects God's purposes in creation – specifically in creation as a *gift* of God:

> [I]f God created the material world inhabited by sentient beings (Genesis 1.1), if God became flesh in the person of Jesus of Nazareth (John 1.14), if the bodies of those bound to God in faith and love are the temples of the Spirit (1 Corinthians 6.19), all central claims Christians make, the opposition between attachment to God and the enjoyment of the ordinary things of life must be false. More: not only is there no necessary opposition between them, but the two can be aligned: *attachment to God amplifies and deepens enjoyment of the world.*[5]

Aristotle's sensible observation that a small mistake at the beginning returns great errors later in a discussion is apropos,[6] for assuming a sacred–secular divide precludes a biblical unification of meaning and pleasure.

Theologians are not unaware of the sacred–secular divide, and yet it must be admitted that none are immune from the slow creep of such thinking. As Mark Greene notes:

> There is hardly an evangelical in the country who does not now acknowledge the deleterious impact of the sacred–secular divide on the church ... but this is a case that has been won before ... by William Temple in the 30s, by Dorothy Sayers in the 40s, by C. S. Lewis and the World Council of Churches in the 50s, by Stott and Graham and Padilla and Escobar in 1974 in Lausanne, by Newbigin in the 80s, by Eugene Peterson in the 90s ... . This is a case that has been won before but the church has not substantially changed ...[7]

So long as the sacred–secular divide persists, it will continue to complicate Christians' attempts to understand the psalmist's focus on work as a key locus of humankind's identity and purpose. To be sure this is one among various factors, but the assumption of a sacred–secular divide is a principal obstacle to the development of a robust theology of work.

Despite the prevalence of the sacred–secular divide mentality within the Christian world, there are glimmers of hope from various traditions that point to the emergence of a renewed appreciation of both the spiritual and temporal value of work. This renewal is occurring across Christian traditions and around the world. Scores of organizations are presently working with church, seminary, and business leaders to shift their thinking towards a more holistic, integrated understanding of the Christian life and the scope of discipleship.

In the last decade or so several of the largest and most influential organizations within the faith and work space have dedicated considerable resources to producing media and other resources for church and educational use that present a robust vision of 'whole-life stewardship'. These include the Acton Institute's *For the Life of the World*[8] and the London Institute for Contemporary Christianity's *Fruitfulness on the Frontline*,[9] both produced in 2014, as well as *Reframe*, produced by the Marketplace Institute at Regent College from 2011 onward.[10] In addition to these resources, there has appeared a spate of popular level books, too numerous to list, addressing the meaning and value of work.

While there has been limited academic engagement with the theology of work, the Theology of Work Project, led by Will Messenger, has produced Bible commentaries and other resources that focus on themes related to work and vocation.[11] While not affiliated with a particular academic institution, the Project has organized the collaboration of scholars from various Christian traditions to participate in its work. Several Christian colleges and seminaries have also begun the process of investing in bringing these ideas to students, with the most notable being Fuller Theological Seminary, Asbury Theological Seminary, and Gordon-Conwell Theological Seminary, each of which offer degree programmes focused on the integration of faith with themes of work, vocation, and economics. Wheaton College's Opus: The Art of Work and LeTourneau University's Center for Faith and Work are notable among Christian college programmes aimed at helping faculty and students understand their fields through a uniquely Christian lens and how study and engagement in those fields is of temporal and spiritual significance.

It is rare to find any particular historical moment during which there is as much shared interest in a topic as there is today among Christians from across traditions. Even ten years ago it would have been all but unthinkable to pull together such a diverse and distinguished group of contributors as are found in the present volume, not to mention the denominational diversity that they represent. The Catholic world has seen a surge of interest in these themes, especially when the work of St Josemaría Escrivà (the controversial Spanish priest who founded the Roman Catholic organization Opus Dei) was endorsed by Pope St John Paul II as reminding the faithful that 'daily life reveals an unexpected greatness'.[12] Anglicans need look no further than the Diocese of London's 'Capital Vision 2020' campaign that seeks to 'equip and commission 100,000 ambassadors representing Jesus Christ in everyday life'.[13] In addition to the many city-focused initiatives, such as the Vere Institute in Boston and the Denver Institute for Faith and Work, Protestant evangelicals benefit from the efforts of organizations such as the Made to Flourish Network and the Oikonomia Network, which seek to engage pastors and seminary professors respectively. The successful work of these types of organizations and movements justify optimism that the academic world is ripe for serious, sustained engagement with the issues relevant to the theology of work.

In bringing together experts in biblical and theological studies, as well as from other disciplines related to the theology of work, the present volume presents a robust and nuanced paradigm for academic engagement with the theology of work. Beginning with biblical theology, in Chapters 2 and 3, John Bergsma and Eugene Merrill present the Old Testament foundations for a theology of work. Beginning with the creation narratives, Bergsma argues that God has assigned to humanity a priestly role in relation to creation, which role and relationship have become frustrated since the rebellion of Genesis 3. This calls for a reintegration of the human vocation, that the original unity of our work and worship may be restored. Building on this theme, in Chapter 3 Merrill explores the depiction of labour in the Old Testament. Focusing particularly on the book of Jeremiah, Merrill shows that Jeremiah (and other prophets, as well) presents work itself – not just the products of work – as noble and pleasing to the Lord.

Chapters 4 and 5 turn to the New Testament data concerning work. In Chapter 4 John Taylor considers the significance of work found in 1 and 2 Thessalonians, showing that Paul depicts work as an act of love. Importantly, their work is 'consistent with and derives from the eschatological nature of their life in Christ', and is indeed part of faithful Christian life. Darrell Bock, in Chapter 5, presents Jesus's teaching on the Christian values prominent within the context of work and relating to one another in working.

Having established in these four chapters the biblical theological foundations for the paradigm, Chapters 6 through 10 address the touch points of work and key *loci* of systematic theology. Miroslav Volf argues in Chapter 6 that 'a theology of charisms supplies a stable foundation on which we can erect a theology of work that is both faithful to the divine revelation and relevant to the modern world of work'. This requires that our work be work in the Spirit and consequently work done as cooperation with God. This means that humans are more than work-machines, as Jay Wesley Richards explains in Chapter 7. Humans are beings both material and immaterial, a duality that must be preserved if the biblical view of work is to be maintained in the face of alternatives such as Marxism and transhumanism.

Work itself (beyond the workplace) is a crucible in which believers are tested and can grow in Christlikeness. In Chapter 8, Scott Rae considers work in connection with Christian sanctification, showing that the connection between work and spirituality creates a space not only for developing in virtue but also for cultivating intimacy with God. Greg Forster, in Chapter 9, argues that a realization of work's theological significance has implications for ecclesiology. Observing that 'the destabilizing social environment of advanced modernity raises unique questions about what it means to be the church and to do what God calls us to do', Forster considers questions of the church's identity as well as its mission with regard to human flourishing. This naturally raises the question of whether the work we do here and now bears eschatological significance. In fact, as Darrell Cosden argues in Chapter 10, the Christian's 'historic hope is the promise that in Christ the creation itself, including what God and humanity have made, will be transformed and set free to be what God intended'.

The remaining four chapters carry the paradigm beyond biblical and systematic theology and into practical theology to consider certain important implications of a theology of work. Noting that economists have traditionally focused on labour rather than work, Jürgen von Hagen argues in Chapter 11 that changes in the productive structures of certain modern economies forces economists to take seriously the intrinsic motivations for work, especially those found in a Christian theology of work. In Chapter 12, Chris Armstrong takes up the pastoral problem of answering concerns tied to the question, How can one find God's purpose and presence in one's work within the 'secular' world? In dialogue with notable voices in church history, Armstrong appeals in his replies to a theology of work. Samuel Gregg, in Chapter 13, recalls to mind that the biblical concern for human flourishing must imply Christian concern for political economy. Gregg argues that market relations 'promote lasting and healthy relationships between individuals and groups that, in many respects, constitute a form of service', especially if developed against the backdrop of a theology of work. In the fourteenth and final chapter, Michael Matheson Miller takes up the vexed question of the relationship between poverty and work, arguing 'that a biblical vision of work, which sees labour as positive and essential for human flourishing, orients our thinking about poverty towards creating the conditions for justice and inclusion for the poor in a way that the dominant model of humanitarianism does not'.

Notes

1 Some of these issues are explored in *Christian Physicalism? Philosophical Theological Criticisms*, ed. R. Keith Loftin and Joshua R. Farris (Lanham, MD: Lexington Books, 2018).

2 Notable exceptions include Darrell Cosden, *A Theology of Work: Work and the New Creation* (Eugene, OR: Wipf & Stock, 2006) and Miroslav Volf, *Work in the Spirit: Toward a Theology of Work* (New York: Oxford University Press, 1991), and from the field of New Testament studies: Bruce W. Longenecker and Kelly D. Liebengood (eds), *Engaging Economics: New Testament Scenarios and Early Christian Reception* (Grand Rapids, MI: Eerdmans, 2009).

3 Acceptance of a sacred–secular divide has implications far beyond work, of course – indeed, it impacts how one perceives all of life, including the task of theology.

4 Miroslav Volf, *Flourishing: Why We Need Religion in a Globalized World* (New Haven, CT: Yale University Press, 2015), p, 201.

5 Volf, *Flourishing*, pp. 202–3; emphasis original.

6 Aristotle, *On the Heavens*, trans. J. L. Stocks, in *The Basic Works of Aristotle*, ed. Richard McKeon and C. D. C. Reeve (New York: Random House, 2001), I.5.271b8–13.

7 Mark Greene, in a 14 September 2014 address to Langham Scholars at Ridley Hall, Cambridge, titled 'Mission & the Missing Gene given to Langham Scholars'.

8 www.letterstotheexiles.com/.

9 www.licc.org.uk/resources/discover-fruitfulness-on-the-frontline/.

10 https://marketplace.regent-college.edu/Reframe.

11 www.theologyofwork.org/.

12 http://w2.vatican.va/content/john-paul-ii/en/speeches/2002/october/documents/hf_jp-ii_spe_20021007_opus-dei.html.

13 www.london.anglican.org/mission/capital-vision-2020/equip-and-commission-100000-ambassadors-representing-jesus-christ-in-daily-life/.

PART I

Biblical Theology

2

The Creation Narratives and the Original Unity of Work and Worship in the Human Vocation

JOHN BERGSMA

It is common in observant religious communities, both Jewish and Christian, to look upon the Bible primarily as a book that teaches the way to gain life in the world to come – and certainly it is that. However, the role of human labour in this present life plays a surprisingly important role in the Scriptures, and is not at all segregated from the issue of eternal salvation or the life of the world to come. Rather, in the biblical perspective, the sanctification of human labour is part of the process of salvation.

In the world view presented in the creation narratives of Genesis, for example, human labour is an expression of the divine likeness (*imago Dei*) in humanity, and there is an original unity of work (labour) and worship (liturgy) in the ideal state of peace (*šālôm*)[1] in which humanity was created. The biblical narrative presents this unity as disrupted by the rebellion of our first parents against the express will of God, and the rest of salvation history in the Old and New Testaments can be understood as an effort to restore the original unity of human work and worship; that is, *to reintegrate the human vocation*. This reintegration is a necessary aspect of the process of sanctification – growth in holiness – that both participates in, and leads to, the attainment of eternal life with God.

This essay will develop the biblical theme of the original unity of work and worship by first presenting the 'theology of work' of other ancient Near Eastern cultures as a foil to the one found in the creation narratives of Genesis 1—2, which will be carefully explored. Then the theme of human work will be traced through the rest of Genesis to the end of Leviticus, in which we find a provisional reintegration of work and worship in the establishment of the tabernacle in the midst of the people, and the restoration of Israel to a status of corporate priesthood. This restoration is short-lived, however, due to Israel's repeated infidelity to the covenant in her subsequent history. We conclude with a brief glance at how the New Testament presents Jesus as the new Adam who regains for himself and for those united to him the original royal priesthood of humanity, with its profound unity of work and worship.

Human Work in Ancient Near Eastern Cultures

The uniqueness of the biblical account of human labour becomes clearer when we contrast it with the perspectives of the other ancient Near Eastern cosmogonic myths against which Genesis polemicizes. For example, in the standard Babylonian account of the creation of man – reflected in the *Enuma Elish*, the *Atrahasis Epic*, and other texts – the gods complain to the mother goddess Mami of the burden of raising their own food, so she creates humanity from the clay of the earth and the blood of a slain god, as a race of slaves to do the work of the gods on their behalf.[2] In this world view, labour is a burden unworthy of the divine, and thus a kind of necessary evil shuffled off on to the collective backs of human beings, who constitute a slave race.

Unlike those of Mesopotamia, Egyptian mythological and cosmological texts pay little attention to the creation of humankind, and those texts that do address this issue do not present a consistent perspective.[3] Nonetheless, one can find in Egyptian traditions the concept of humankind being made in the image of a god, being formed from clay, and receiving the breath of life in their nostrils from a goddess.[4] Some texts speak of the heavens and earth as being created for the benefit of humanity.[5] However, there is little or no explanation in ancient Egyptian culture for the *purpose* of our creation, or the role of our labour in the cosmic system. On this issue we can only speculate, but Keel has shown in his iconographic studies that in Egyptian cosmology, every element of the natural environment – the earth, the sky, the rain, the crops – was a divinity.[6] Thus, when Egyptian peasants emerged from their dwellings in the morning to gaze at the world around them, they knew themselves to be the only non-divine element in their environment. Therefore, human beings, in pursuing the labour necessary to maintain their life – tilling the land, raising livestock, building shelters, etc. – were always the non-divine trespassers in a completely divinized world. Even if the Egyptian worshipper regarded the divine realm as ultimately benevolent (which is uncertain),[7] Egyptian religion tended to foster the view that human labourers were the ontologically lowest entity in their environment.

Human Work in Genesis 1.1—2.4a

In contrast to the world view of these cosmologies, the Hebrew Bible presents the one creator as a God who himself works, thus setting an example for humankind who bear his image.

Although the narrative of first six days of creation (Gen. 1.1—2.1) never uses the word 'work' (*'ăbôḏâ*) or 'labour' (*mělā'kâ*) for the divine activity, we see that the sacred author does regard the Lord as having performed 'labour' retrospectively, in his description of the seventh day:

> 2 And on the seventh day God finished his labour (*mělā'kâ*) which he had done, and he rested on the seventh day from all his labour (*mělā'kâ*) which he had done. 3 So God blessed the seventh day and hallowed it, because on it God rested from all his labour (*mělā'kâ*) which he had done in creating. (Gen. 2.2–3 RSV *alt*.)[8]

Three times in this concluding postscript reference is made to the 'his labour which he [God] had done' (*měla'ktô 'ăšer 'āśâ*), with variation the third time ('his labour which God had done in creating' (*měla'ktô 'ăšer-bārā' 'ělōhîm la'ăśôt*). The noun *mělā'kâ* covers a wide variety of human labour in the Hebrew Bible, both secular (Lev. 13.48, 51; Jer. 18.3; Ps. 107.23; 1 Chron. 27.26) and sacred (Ex. 36.2; 1 Kings 5.30; 1 Chron. 26.29; 2 Chron. 29.34). Unlike the Mesopotamian gods, the Lord God of Israel does not shrink from 'labour'. Rather, the divine labour of six days followed by the day of rest establishes the rhythm of human labour, such that the weekly productivity of human beings punctuated by the Sabbath is not an expression of their slave status *but of their likeness to God*.

Human beings are, after all, created in God's image (*ṣelem*) and likeness (*děmût*) (Gen. 1.26, 28). They are, therefore, entirely unique in all creation, for no other created being bears this designation.

Much ink has been spilled over the exact meaning of the phrase *běṣalmēnû kidmûtēnû*, 'in our image, as our likeness' (Gen. 1.26). Some have suggested a comparison with the images (statues) of themselves which ancient kings set up on the borders of their realms, with the implication that Genesis regards humankind as a visible, concrete representative of the authority of the divine king.[9] Others note a similarity to the ancient Near Eastern practice of placing an image (*ṣelem*) of a god in the inner sanctuary of his or her temple, with the implication that Genesis portrays humankind as an icon of the divinity within a sacred sanctuary consisting of the cosmos itself.[10] Yet again, it has been noted that the same two terms describe the relationship of Seth to his father Adam in Genesis 5.3, implying that 'image' and 'likeness' may be a hendiadys expressing a filial relationship.[11] It is unnecessary to choose between all of these options, unless we imagine the ancient author was too primitive to use his terms evocatively, taking advantage of their polyvalence. But studies of the structure and other rhetorical features of Genesis 1 suggest the work of a literary artist and not a primitive. Therefore, we are justified in pondering the rich connotations of 'image' and 'likeness'. In one of the most comprehensive studies of the phrase 'image and likeness' to date, Catherine McDowell compares the text of Genesis with Mesopotamian and Egyptian texts concerning divine images (cultic statues), and comes to the conclusion that the term is polyvalent and connotes 'kinship, kingship, and cult': *kinship*, inasmuch as Genesis 1.26 parallels Genesis 5.3 indicating a relationship of divine sonship; *kingship* or royalty, inasmuch as the commands to 'subdue' (*kābaš*; v. 28) and 'rule' (*rādâ*, vv. 26, 28) are royal terms indicating humanity as God's representative in law and justice; and *cult* inasmuch as cultic *ṣelāmîm*, 'images', were installed in temple precincts around the ancient Near East, suggesting Adam was like a living divine *ṣelem* installed in the sacred temple of Eden.[12] McDowell is persuasive; building on her work, one may also suggest that the cultic sense of Adam as divine *ṣelem* bleeds into the priestly view of Adam developed in Genesis 2.4b–25, where Adam is the priestly representative of God in the sanctuary. McDowell herself points out that the later Israelite high priest was clothed in a way similar to the garb of ancient Near Eastern cult statues, suggesting that the high priest was understood in one sense as an image of God similar to Adam.[13]

In polemical contrast to the creation myths of surrounding cultures, Genesis 1.1—2.4a demythologizes the universe and the environment. Contra Egyptian cosmology – and Mesopotamian as well, for that matter – nothing in the cosmos is a divinity, not even those things usually regarded as primary deities: the sea, the sky, or the sun. This last, which was so popular as the head of the pantheon in ancient Egypt (i.e. Amon-Re) and elsewhere, is merely a 'light' (*mā'ôr*) to rule the day and a 'sign' (*'ôt*) for *mô'ĕdîm* (Gen. 1.14) – traditionally translated 'seasons', but more literally 'meetings'; that is, 'times for meeting for worship', *liturgical seasons*. So then, the sun and the other heavenly bodies mark the time so that humanity may know when to worship the creator God; we may speak of heavenly bodies as having a *liturgical telos*. They and all the other elements of the cosmos do not rule over humankind, nor are human beings subservient to them. Quite to the contrary, human beings in the divine image are commissioned to rule over all other living things: 'let them have dominion (*rādâ*) over the fish of the sea, and over the birds of the air, and over the cattle, and over all the earth, and over every creeping thing that creeps upon the earth' (Gen. 1.26). The word used for 'dominion' here (*rādâ*) can designate a kind of forceful imperial rule, notably of Solomon

(1 Kings 4.24; Ps. 72.8; 110.2). In Genesis 1.28, humankind is similarly commanded to 'subdue' (*kābaš*) the earth, employing another term used for imperial subjugation (2 Sam. 8.11; 1 Chron. 22.18). Thus, human labour, by which we give expression to our 'image and likeness' of God, is a kind of *royal mastery* over the rest of creation, or at least all other living things (cf. Ps. 8). The connotations of kingship cannot be denied here: humankind is created as a 'son' and therefore vice-regent in imitation of the Lord God, the divine father-king. Human work is a royal work, not slavery to the gods or to a divinized environment.

Human Work in Genesis 2.4b–25

As we shift from the overview of creation in Genesis 1.1—2.4a to the more detailed account of the creation of man in Genesis 2.4b–25, we observe a complementary perspective on the role and significance of human labour.

First, we recognize that, from a formal literary perspective, the entire account Genesis 2.4b–3.24 is an integrated narrative marked by, among other things, an *inclusio* concerning 'working the soil': we move from a situation in which there 'was no man to work the soil' (Gen. 2.5) to the first humans being driven out 'to work the soil' (Gen. 3.23). It can strike the modern reader as a little incongruous to realize that this text, which has been so maximally freighted with theological significance in the tradition, can be read on a purely formal level as an aetiology of something as mundane as farming – one of the most fundamental, if not *the* fundamental, form(s) of human labour.

Second, we recognize that the labour of working the soil does not originate with human disobedience to God; it is not part of the curse of the broken covenant with the Lord. Rather, work is part of the original human vocation:

> The LORD God took the man and put (*nûaḥ*) him in the garden of Eden to till (*'ābad*) it and keep (*šāmar*) it. (Gen. 2.15)

The word used for 'putting' the man in the garden is unusual: the second *hiphil* (causative stem) of *nûaḥ*, the verb meaning 'to rest'; thus, 'to cause [something] to rest [somewhere]'. This second *hiphil* of *nûaḥ* can have a range of idiomatic meanings. It can function merely as a synonym of *śîm*, 'to put, set', but McDowell notes it can also take on a rather specialized meaning with respect to cultic objects in the sanctuary: 'to install, to establish in a sacred location' (Ex. 16.33–34; Num. 17.4, 7; 1 Kings 8.9; 2 Kings 17.29; 2 Chron. 4.8; Isa. 46.7; Zech. 5.11). She suggests it may form a link with the concept of the man as the 'image' of God, who is 'installed' in the sanctuary-garden just as cultic images were installed within temples throughout the ancient Near East.[14] It is likely that the sacred author's use of *nûaḥ* here is indeed specialized and significant, especially in light of the sanctuary symbolism in Eden (see below), and in light of what is said later of the person of Noah, whose name (*nōaḥ*) is derived from this same root, and who is promised to bring relief specifically from the toil and labour resulting from the cursing of the soil (Gen. 5.29). A typological relationship between Adam and Noah is being anticipated.

The phrase describing the man's duties, to 'till it and keep it' (*lĕ'obdāh ûlĕšomrāh*; Gen. 2.15), probably refers in the first place to the agricultural or at least horticultural efforts of Adam in the garden, but the phrase is also a hendiadys with richer connotations. From the earliest Jewish and Christian works of exegesis[15] to contemporary critical scholarship, it has been observed that these terms indicate a priestly status for Adam,[16] with more than one exegetical route to this conclusion.[17]

Literally, the meaning of *lĕ'obdāh ûlĕšomrāh* is 'to work [it] and to guard [it]', and this verbal pair 'work (*'ābad*) and guard (*šāmar*)' – as Gordon Wenham pointed out some years ago[18] – occurs elsewhere in the Pentateuch only in three passages of Numbers that describe the tasks of the priests and Levites in the sanctuary (Num. 3.7–8; 8.26; 18.7). Speaking of the clerical tribe of the Levites in Numbers 3.7, the Lord commands literally:

> They shall *guard* (*šāmar*) his [Aaron the high priest's] *guardianship* (*mišmeret*) and the *guardianship* of the whole congregation before the tent of meeting, and they shall *work* (*'ābad*) the *work* (*'ăbôdâ*) of the Tabernacle.[19]

Likewise, the Lord commands Aaron and his sons:

> Num. 18.5 You shall *guard* (*šāmar*) the *guardianship* (*mišmeret*) of the holy place and the *guardianship* (*mišmeret*) of the altar ... 18.7 You and your sons with you shall *guard* (*šāmar*) the priesthood concerning everything pertaining to the altar and that which is inside the veil, and you shall *work* (*'ābad*) *the work* (*'ăbôdâ*).[20]

It is difficult to accept as purely coincidental that the juxtaposition of the verbal roots 'work' and 'guard' occur together in the Pentateuch only in Genesis 2.15 and these texts in Numbers concerning the tasks of the Levites and priests in the tabernacle. Genesis 2.15 must be either assuming or asserting that Adam held a priestly role,[21] which fits into a pattern of correlation between the garden of Eden and the tabernacle/temple that is widely recognized and becoming almost a commonplace in biblical theology.[22] Following Wenham, we may note the following similarities between Eden and Israel's subsequent sanctuaries:[23]

- God's presence is said to 'walk about' (*hiṯhallēḵ*)[24] in the garden (Gen. 3.8) as it does in the tabernacle (Lev. 26.12; Deut. 23.15; 2 Sam. 7.6–7).
- The cherubim are present in Eden as guardians of the divine presence (Gen. 3.24) as they are in the tabernacle and temple (Ex. 25.18–22; 26.31; 1 Kings 6.23–29).
- The garden had only one entrance facing east (Gen. 3.24), as did the tabernacle and temple (Ex. 27.13; 38.13; Num. 3.25–26; Ezek. 47.1).
- At the centre of the garden was the mysterious tree of life, which was probably represented in the holy place of the tabernacle and temple by the menorah, crafted like a stylized tree of life (Ex. 25.31–35; 37.17–20).[25]
- A river flowed from Eden and split into four cardinal directions to water the world (Gen. 2.10–11). This 'river of life' motif is connected to many ancient Near Eastern temples and the Jerusalem temple as well (Ps. 46.5; Ezek. 47; Joel 3.18; Zech. 14.8; John 7.37–39).[26] In fact, Jerusalem's water source was named the 'Gihon' after one of the rivers flowing from Eden (1 Kings 1.33, 38, 45). In the case of the tabernacle, the great bronze basin of water in the courtyard probably stood in for this primordial sanctuary river (Ex. 30.18).
- The narrative calls attention to the proximity of high quality gold and precious stones to Eden (Gen. 2.12), two materials used in abundance in the tabernacle and temple, in their vessels, decorations, and priestly vestments (Ex. 25–31, 35–39; 1 Kings 6–7). Of particular significance are onyx (*šōham*) stones (Gen. 2.12), which are associated closely with some the holiest elements of the tabernacle worship (Ex. 25.7; 28.9, 20; 35.9, 27; 39.6, 13).

When the garden of Eden is recognized as a primordial sanctuary, it becomes clear that Adam's role within must be as the primordial priest. Seen in context with all the other tabernacle/temple motifs in the passage, it is more convincing that the hendiadys 'work and guard' in verse 15 constitutes an intentional allusion to the later duties of the priests and Levites in the sanctuary. McDowell recognizes this allusion, but also points out that ancient Near Eastern kings were considered to be sacred gardeners, as it were, with the responsibility to tend the gardens and orchards associated with the palace and temple(s).[27] After citing several ancient Near Eastern sources as well as the royal gardener imagery of Ecclesiastes 2.4b–6, she concludes: 'Thus the use of *abd* and *šmr* to describe Adam's work in the garden of Eden suggests that he functioned not only as an administrator of the kingdom but also, on some level, as a *royal priest* of Yahweh's "sanctuary" in Eden.'[28]

It is not that 'work and guard' refers only to sacral duty and excludes the 'mundane' tasks of cultivating the soil and caring for the plants, but that these tasks were also part of a larger royal priestly ministry that was bestowed on Adam. Therefore, in the biblical portrayal of the creation of humankind, the human being is primarily *homo liturgicus*,[29] whose work is simultaneously worship, and for whom there is no division between profane labour and the celebration of liturgy. This *royal priestly unity of life*, where all human activity is directed towards the adoration of God, is presented as the original intention of the creator, and thus a perennial ideal for which the people of God should strive.

Human Work in Genesis After the Fall

After the covenant-breaking act of Adam and Eve,[30] this original unity of work and worship is broken. The first couple are driven out of the sanctuary-garden into other regions of the earth, where Adam's *'ăbôdâ* of the soil will no longer meet with success because of the 'cursing of the ground' (Gen. 3.17). He has lost his vice-regal dominion over the environment. The fact that the soil Adam works is now 'cursed' makes clear that he no longer will experience his environment as a blessed sanctuary, and as a corollary, his work will no longer necessarily be a priestly act of worship that experiences the divine blessing of fruitfulness. Adam is driven out of the garden to 'work the soil' from which he was taken, but no longer to 'guard' the garden-sanctuary, a task that is taken over by the cherubim (Gen. 3.24). So Adam's task is reduced from 'working and guarding' (Gen. 2.15), the hendiadys that summarizes priestly duty, to merely 'working the soil' (Gen. 3.23), the common labour of the farmer. Adam's mission has, in a sense, been desacralized because of his failure to keep (*šāmar*) the divine command he received,[31] leading David Fagerberg to remark, 'The fall is the forfeiture of our liturgical career.'[32]

This theme continues into Genesis 4, where Adam's legacy seems primarily carried by Cain, his firstborn son, who continues his father's profession of 'working the soil' (Gen. 4.2). However, when Cain attempts to connect his labour with an act of priesthood by bringing 'an offering of the fruit of the ground', the LORD refuses to accept it (Gen. 4.3). This indicates that the work of man is no longer necessarily connected to a priestly status, at least in the case of Cain.[33] The alienation is only worsened by Cain's resentful slaying of his brother; now the soil itself refuses to respond to Cain's 'work' (Gen. 4.12), an intensification of the curse associated with Adam (Gen. 3.17–19). Humankind's work is no longer a blessed act of worship but a cursed and futile drudgery.

Restoring the priesthood of humankind and the priestly nature of their labour becomes a theme in the subsequent narrative of sacred history.

Significantly, after Cain there is no mention of working the soil until the saviour figure Noah is born, about whom it is said:

> And [Lamech] called his name Noah, saying, 'This one will give us rest from our effort (*ma'ăśeh*) and the toil (*'iṣṣābôn*) of our hands from the soil (*hā'ădāmâ*) which the LORD has cursed.' (Gen. 5.29)

Noah is thus clearly identified as the antidote for the Adam–Cain curse on human labour in the soil (*hā'ădāmâ*) from which Adam was originally taken (Gen. 3.23). Noah is, indeed, a new Adam figure, who experiences the flood as an act of re-creation by which the earth is plunged once more under the waters (cf. Gen. 1.2), after which the habitable dry land reappears (Gen. 8.13; cf. Gen. 1.9–10). After the flood, Noah exercises priesthood by the offering of sacrifice (8.20), and his priestly offering finds welcome acceptance by God (8.21–22).[34] Beginning in Genesis 9.20, Noah is identified as a 'man of the soil' (*'îš hā'ădāmâ*), linking him conceptually with Adam and Cain. Unlike them, however, he is successful, cultivating a vineyard that produces wine (9.20–21). This could have been a positive development, suggesting a mitigation of the curse and the reintegration of human work into a priestly relationship with God. But any such hope is immediately cut off, however, because Noah misuses the wine, becoming drunken and naked (Gen. 9.21): violations of his priestly role, for priests were never to be drunk (Lev. 10.9) or naked (Ex. 20.26; 28.42). In Genesis 9.20–28, we witness a recapitulation of the fall in the garden marked by the repetition of motifs of consumption of fruit (Gen. 3.6 // 9.21), nakedness (Gen. 3.7 // 9.21–23), shame (Gen. 2.25; 3.10 // 9.22, 24), and curse (3.14, 17 // 9.25) – Noah's foolish consumption of the fruit of the vine reintroduces conflict between his sons and curse on his descendants (Gen. 9.24–27). Noah will not be the definitive saviour who will reintegrate the human vocation by restoring the Adamic priesthood.

Human Labour in the Remainder of the Pentateuch

Human labour again becomes a prominent biblical theme in the book of Exodus, in which Abraham's descendants find themselves subjected to hard labour by Pharaoh (Ex. 1.11–14). There is a striking contrast in the book of Exodus in the context and usage of the term *'ăbôdâ* ('work'), which in the initial chapters of the book is used exclusively of Israel's bondage to Pharaoh and his task masters (Ex. 1.14; 2.23; 5.9, 11; 6.6, 9). The Passover legislation (Ex. 12.25–26; 13.5) forms a transition, where for the first time *'ăbôdâ* describes a liturgical act, the performance of the

Passover ritual. Finally, from Exodus 27 on, *'ăbôdâ* refers exclusively to the building of the tabernacle and the ministry that takes place inside it (27.19; 30.16; 35.21, 24; 36.1, 3, 5; 38.21; 39.32, 40, 42). One can say, then, that one of the themes of Exodus is the transformation of the work or *'ăbôdâ* of Israel from profane slavery to Pharaoh into the labour of worship to the LORD in his tabernacle sanctuary,[35] which is a kind of renewed, portable Eden. The exodus thus has the result of sanctifying the labour of Israel, restoring Israel to a priestly status and reintegrating work/worship and labour/liturgy.

There are at least two specific texts that function strategically in the development of this theme.

One is Exodus 4.22–23: 'And you shall say to Pharaoh, "Thus says the LORD, Israel is my firstborn son, and I say to you, 'Let my son go that he may serve (*'ābad*) me.'"'[36] By identifying Israel as the 'firstborn' son of God, the sacred author establishes a connection with Adam, the original 'firstborn' son. As noted above, Genesis 5.3 links the concepts of 'image' and 'likeness' to the status of sonship, and Adam's creation in God's 'image' and 'likeness' in Genesis 1.26 may be taken as indicating Adam's divine sonship (cf. Luke 3.38). The premise of Exodus then becomes that God takes Israel as a corporate 'new Adam', restoring to them 'all the glory of Adam', to use the phrase of the Qumran community (1QS 4.23; 1QHa 4.27). But, as we have seen, one of the roles of Adam was priesthood (Gen. 2.15). This priestly status that God intends for Israel is indicated in Exodus 4.23a: 'Let my son go that he serve (*'ābad*) me.' To this point, Israel has been serving Pharaoh, in the sense of manual slave labour. But in the canonical context of Exodus, we see that it is not physical labour that God desires for Israel; rather, their 'service' (*'ăbôdâ*) is going to be building the tabernacle and performing the sacrificial liturgy with it. The original request Moses makes for Israel's release is, after all, not for a complete departure from Egypt, but for a temporary journey into the wilderness to offer sacrifice (Ex. 3.23). Thus, the goal of the exodus was never primarily socio-economic, but rather liturgical. God wished to restore to Israel corporately the priesthood of Adam with its attendant responsibility to work (*'ābad*) for the Lord, to perform the sacred labour of worship (*'ăbôdâ*).

A second strategic text is Exodus 19.5–6:

5 Now therefore, if you will obey my voice and keep my covenant, you shall be my own possession among all peoples; for all the earth is mine, 6 and you shall be to me a kingship of priests (*mamleket kōhănîm*) and a holy nation. These are the words which you shall speak to the children of Israel. (RSV *alt.*[37])

Upon reaching Sinai, the Lord speaks through Moses to the people of Israel to promise them that obedience to the covenant will gain them the status of *mamleḵeṯ kōhănîm*, often translated 'kingdom of priests' but also possible to translate as 'a royal priesthood' (cf. LXX; 1 Peter 2.9).[38] This interpretation results from understanding *mamleḵeṯ* here as a 'kingship'; that is, a collective body exercising kingly rule. Thus, the *mamleḵeṯ kōhănîm* is a 'kingship of priests'; that is, a 'community of kings who are priests', or traditionally, 'a royal priesthood'.

This fits into the pattern of the Sinai covenant understood as the Lord accepting Israel as a corporate new Adam, because the responsibilities of kingship and priesthood were combined in the first man and model of the race, the one who was to 'subdue' and 'rule' (Gen. 1.26–28) as well as 'work and guard' (Gen. 2.15).

Thus, these two strategic texts (Ex. 4.22–23 and 19.5–6), together with the change in the pattern of usage of *ăḇōḏâ* in the course of the Exodus narrative, all contribute to emphasize a central theme of Exodus: the restoration to Israel of a priestly status, whereby their labour will no longer be the profane slavery to Pharaoh, but will be the divine service given to the Lord. The original unity of work and worship in the garden is restored to Israel along with the construction of the tabernacle as a 'portable Eden'.

The climactic point of the development of this theme comes in Exodus 39—40, which records the completion of the building of the tabernacle by Israel under Moses' direction in language whose similarity to the completion of creation in Genesis 2.1–3 has often been noted (cf. Ex. 39.32–43; 40.16, 33).[39] Then the Lord takes up his residence in the midst of the people (Ex. 40.34–38) as he once walked with Adam and Eve in the garden (Gen. 3.8).

The book of Leviticus follows naturally from this event, as it instructs the people of Israel in the ways of the Lord, so that the service of the Lord can take place in their midst. The theme of Leviticus may be taken as 'be holy, for I am holy' (11.44–45; 19.2; 20.7, 26). This *imitatio Dei* in the matter of holiness is similar conceptually to the idea of being made in the 'image and likeness' of God (Gen. 1.26, 28), and may be a development of it. But we note that Leviticus does not restrict itself only to stipulations of sacrifices (Lev. 1—7) or the ministerial priesthood (Lev. 8—10), but in the so-called Cleanliness Code (Lev. 11—15) and Holiness Code (Lev. 17—25), it includes regulations for nearly every aspect of the daily life of Israelites. Particularly poignant is Leviticus 19, a chapter that juxtaposes moral regulations (vv. 17–18) with economic ordinances (vv. 9–10, 13) and cultic prescriptions (vv. 5–8). These different laws are not segregated from one another, precisely because in Israel there is a certain unity of life: since God now dwells in their midst with the holy tabernacle, every aspect of their activity constitutes part of the divine worship that they offer as royal priestly people. The whole congregation of Israel is called to 'consecrate' (*hitqaddēš*) themselves (Lev. 20.7), a verb often associated with priestly ordination when applied to human beings (Ex. 28.3, 41; 29.1, 27, 33, 44; 30.30; 40.13, etc.).

Nonetheless, the reintegration of Israel's priestly vocation in Leviticus is imperfect. Due to their self-profanation with the golden calf, the firstborn sons of Israel of can no longer represent each Israelite family in the work of the sanctuary (cf. Ex. 32.1–29). Now this duty is taken over by the Levites (Ex. 32.25–29; Num. 3.11–51), who form a mediatorial body that 'buffers' the contact between God and Israel (Num. 1.53).[40] To worship, Israel must approach God through the Levites and the sons of Aaron, who alone may 'work the work' of the tabernacle. The only 'work' mentioned in Leviticus is the work of slaves (Lev. 25.39) and the 'laborious work' (*mĕle'ket 'ăbōdâ*) from which the lay Israelites must abstain on holy days (Lev. 23.7, 8, 21, 25, 35, 36). In contrast, except for the cultic calendar (Num. 28—29), the meaning of *'ābad* and *'ăbōdâ* in Numbers is always the sacred work of the sanctuary performed by the Levites and sons of Aaron (esp. in Num. 3—4, 7—8). Under the Mosaic covenant, Israel has a corporate priestly role, but only corporately: the non-Levitical Israelites do not regain the priesthood of Adam individually.

A Brief Look at Work in the New Testament

In Israel's subsequent history, the nation is largely unsuccessful even in fulfilling a corporate priestly role. The reigns of David and Solomon are high points of their history, in which David gains for himself a covenant from the Lord (2 Sam. 7.8–17), including a restoration of divine sonship (2 Sam. 7.14; Ps. 2.7) for himself and his heirs, involving the restoration of the dual roles kingship and priesthood (Ps. 110; 2 Sam. 6.14; 8.18).[41] Isaiah foresaw this Davidic economy being extended to others as well (Isa. 55.1–3) and future restoration and expansion of the priesthood to all the people (Isa. 61.6; 66.21), but the reintegration of work and worship for the people of God is not realized historically in the rest of the Old Testament.

Others in this volume will explore the theology of work in the New Testament. Here we briefly note that the New Testament presents Jesus as the embodiment of a new Israel (Matt. 2.15) who reunites in himself both the royal[42] and the priestly[43] roles. Particularly in John, Jesus is the one whose only and every work is the work of the Father (John 4.34; 5.17; 9.4; 10.37, etc.) and who – in language reminiscent of the completion of creation (Gen. 2.1–3) and the tabernacle (Ex. 39.32; 40.33) – 'finishes' the work of the Father (John 4.34; 5.36; 17.4). Every work of the Christ is sanctified, nothing is profane. Since his work is sacred, like that of the priests, he and his disciples may work on the Sabbath as the priesthood does (Matt. 12.1–8). Those who believe in him enter into this same divine labour: 'he who believes in me will also do the works that I do; and greater works than these will he do' (John 14.12). The doctrine of unity with the Son and the Father (John 17.22–23) implies that what is true of Christ becomes true of the believer.

The implications for human labour are made explicit by other apostolic authors. Paul famously urges Christians 'to present your bodies as a living sacrifice, holy and acceptable to God, which is your spiritual worship' (Rom. 12.1). 'Your bodies' here is metonymy for the entire lives and lifestyles of Christians. The apostle uses cultic language (*paristēmi, thysia, euarestos, latreia*)[44] to stress that the Christian has been restored to a priestly status, a concept also present in 1 Peter: 'But you are a chosen race, a royal priesthood, a holy nation, God's own people' (1 Peter 2.9), called 'to offer spiritual sacrifices acceptable to God through Jesus Christ' (1 Peter 2.5). Here the apostle alludes to the promise offered to Israel of the restoration of the Adamic status in Exodus 19.5–6, and asserts that it has been fulfilled in the present for 'those who believe' (1 Peter 2.7). The same theme is multiply attested in Revelation (1.6; 5.10; 20.6). The implication of the restoration of this priestly role for Christian labour is perhaps expressed in Colossians 3.23:

> Whatever you do, work (*ergazomai*) from the soul, as to the Lord and not to men, knowing that from the Lord you will receive the reward of the inheritance; you are serving (*douleuō*) the Lord Christ.[45]

Although priestly motifs are not explicit here, we see that every work of the Christian – in this case even menial work for those who are household slaves (Col. 3.22) – is sacred, an act of service to God in Jesus Christ, and therefore an act of worship.

Conclusions

The creation and Eden narratives of Genesis 1.1—2.4a and 2.4b—3.24 present a radically different view of humankind's place within the cosmos – and the value of human labour – from the views prevalent in other ancient Near Eastern cultures. Genesis 1.1—2.4a emphasizes the *royalty* of the human condition: the language of 'image and likeness of God' implies that *'ādām* is a divine son (cf. Gen. 5.3) and therefore also vice-regent of the divine king. God himself works (Gen. 2.3) and so does his vice-regent, his labour being to rule and fructify the earth (Gen. 1.29). Humanity is a slave neither to the gods nor to the environment, but a ruler who images the creator. Genesis 2.4b—3.24 places greater emphasis on the priestly dimension of the role of *'ādām*. The garden of Eden is presented as the primordial sanctuary, and *'ādām* as the primordial priest. The man's role is to 'work and guard' the garden (Gen. 2.15), a polyvalent phrase that encompasses physical labour as well as priestly service. There is no division of secular and sacred service for the first man: there is a unity of work and worship, as all his tasks in the garden constitute part of his priestly liturgy, as it were. This priestly perspective is not in competition with the royal dimension more obvious in Genesis 1.1—2.4a, since in light of ancient Near Eastern parallels, *'ādām* is being portrayed as a royal priest. The covenant-breaking in Genesis 3.6 disenfranchises humankind from the royal priesthood, renders our labour profane, and bifurcates work from worship. The Old Testament records covenantal initiatives (the Mosaic and Davidic) from God intended to restore this royal priesthood to the people of God and reintegrate the human vocation. But these initiatives are ultimately frustrated by covenant infidelity. In the Christian canon, the restoration of the royal priestly status occurs ultimately in Christ, the royal high priest whose covenantal self-sacrifice makes it possible for all the labour of those who believe in him to become, once more, a royal priestly service to God. A twentieth-century spiritual writer articulated the practical implications for Christians in these words:

> You cannot forget that any worthy, noble and honest work at the human level can – and should – be raised to the supernatural level, becoming a divine task.[46] Live and work for God, with a spirit of love and service, with a *priestly soul* ... . Then all your actions will take on a genuine supernatural meaning.[47]

Notes

1 The Hebrew term *šālôm* is usually translated 'peace', but is a richer concept and reality than what is denoted by the English word. The concept *šālôm* is not simply peace, but wholeness and integration, a state in which all is as it should be. 'Intactness' and 'well-being, state of health' are translational possibilities (L. Koehler and W. Baumgartner, 2001, *The Hebrew and Aramaic Lexicon of the Old Testament* (Leiden: Brill), pp. 1507–8 and also D. Clines, 2011, *The Dictionary of Classical Hebrew* vol. 8 (Sheffield: Sheffield Phoenix), pp. 365–6). Even though the term *šālôm* does not occur in Genesis 1—2, Eden nonetheless was the place of definitive peace, as demonstrated by use of the term in passages of Ezekiel that recall Eden and the creation (e.g. Ezek. 34.25; 37.26).

2 See *Enuma Elish* 6:33–36; *Atrahasis* 1:190–197; and 'Creation of Man by the Mother Goddess', in *Ancient Near Eastern Texts Relating to the Old Testament*, 3rd edition, ed. James B. Pritchard (Princeton: Princeton University Press, 1969), pp. 99–100.

3 See Siegfried Morenz, *Egyptian Religion*, trans. Ann E. Keep (Ithaca, NY: Cornell University Press, 1973), pp. 183–5. There are only a few texts/artefacts that speak directly to the question of the creation of man, which is variously attributed to Khnum or Aton/Amun. Almost nothing is said or indicated about the purpose of human existence or work.

4 See James K. Hoffmeier, 'Some Thoughts on Genesis 1 & 2 and Egyptian Cosmology', *Journal of the Ancient Near Eastern Society* 15 (1983), pp. 39–49; and Cyrus H. Gordon, 'Khnum and El', in *Scripta Hierosolymitana: Egyptological Studies*, vol. 28, ed. Sarah Israelit-Groll (Jerusalem: Magnes Press, 1982), pp. 203–14. Gordon describes iconography of the god Khnum fashioning mankind on his potter's wheel, and his consort animating the resultant figure(s) with the life-spirit (*ankh*). However, there is no clear indication of Khnum's purpose in creating humanity.

5 Hoffmeier, 'Some Thoughts', p. 48.

6 See the icon of the cosmos from a New Kingdom papyrus rendered in Othmar Keel, *The Symbolism of the Biblical World: Ancient Near Eastern Iconography and the Book of Psalms*, trans. Timothy J. Hallett (Winona Lake, IN: Eisenbrauns, 1997), pp. 31–46, esp. fig. 32 on p. 36.

7 Morenz, *Egyptian Religion*, pp. 26–7, points out that the Egyptians regarded the relationship of humankind to the divinities as variously hostile or benevolent.

8 I have changed the RSV's translation of *mĕlā'ḵâ* as 'work' to 'labour' in order to consistently distinguish in English from *'ăḇōḏâ*, which I will render 'work'.

9 E.g. H. W. Wolff, *Anthropology of the Old Testament*, trans. M. Kohl (Philadelphia: Fortress Press, 1974), p. 160.

10 So recently Catherine L. McDowell, *The Image of God in the Garden of Eden: The Creation of Humankind in Genesis 2:5–3:24 in Light of* mīs pî pīt pî *and* wpt-r *Rituals of Mesopotamia and Ancient Egypt*, Siphrut 15 (Winona Lake, IN: Eisenbrauns, 2015), pp. 43–116.

11 So Meredith G. Kline, *Kingdom Prologue: Genesis Foundations for a Covenantal Worldview* (Overland Park, KS: Two Age, 2000), pp. 45–6.

12 McDowell, *Image of God*.

13 McDowell, *Image of God*, pp. 210–11.

14 McDowell, *Image of God*, pp. 43–115.

15 Gregory Beale points out that both the Midrash Genesis Rabbah 16.5 and the Letter of Barnabas 4.11 take Genesis 2.15 as priestly or cultic terminology (Beale, *The Temple and the Church's Mission: A Biblical Theology of the Dwelling Place of God*, New Studies in Biblical Theology 15 (Downers Grove: InterVarsity Press, 2004), pp. 67–8, n. 91).

16 See, for example, the following works and the literature cited therein, in chronological order: Robin Scroggs, *The Last Adam: A Study in Pauline Anthropology* (Philadelphia: Fortress Press, 1966), pp. 43–4; Gordon J. Wenham, 'Sanctuary Symbolism in the Garden of Eden Story', in *I Studied Inscriptions from Before the Flood: Ancient Near Easter, Literary and Linguistic Approaches to Genesis 1–11*, Sources for Biblical and Theological Study 4, ed. Richard S. Hess and David Toshio Tsumura (Winona Lake, IN: Eisenbrauns, 1994 [1986]), pp. 400–4 (here 400–2); Wenham, *Genesis 1–15*, Word Biblical Commentary 1 (Dallas: Word, 1987), p. 67;

John H. Sailhamer, *The Pentateuch as Narrative: A Biblical-Theological Commentary* (Grand Rapids: Zondervan, 1992), pp. 100–1; Meredith G. Kline, *Kingdom Prologue* [1994], pp. 42–3, 54; Gary A. Anderson, *The Genesis of Perfection: Adam and Eve in Jewish and Christian Imagination* (Louisville, KY: Westminster John Knox Press, 2001), pp. 122–4; Crispin H. T. Fletcher-Louis, *All the Glory of Adam: Liturgical Anthropology in the Dead Sea Scrolls*, Studies on the texts of the Deserts of Judah 42 (Leiden: Brill, 2002), pp. 23, 63, 76; John H. Walton, 'Eden, Garden of', in *Dictionary of the Old Testament: Pentateuch*, ed. T. Desmond Alexander and David W. Baker (Downers Grove: InterVarsity Press, 2003), pp. 202–7 (here 205–6); Beale, *Temple and the Church's Mission*, pp. 68, 70, 78 n. 118, 81–121; Jeffrey Morrow, 'Creation as Temple Building and Work as Liturgy in Genesis 1–3', *Journal of the Orthodox Center for the Advancement of Biblical Studies* 2 (2009), pp. 1–13, available at www.ocabs.org/journal/index.php/jocabs/article/view/43/18; Morrow, 'Work as Worship in the Garden and the Workshop: Genesis 1–3, the Feast of St Joseph the Worker, and Liturgical Hermeneutics', *Logos: A Journal of Catholic Thought and Culture* 15, no. 4 (2012), pp. 159–78; and Steven C. Smith, *The House of the Lord: Temple Theology in the Old and New Testament* (Steubenville, OH: Franciscan University Press, forthcoming), pp. 64–78.

17 For example, Genesis Rabbah 16.5 develops an exegetical argument from the use of *'ābad* and *šāmar* in Exodus 3.12 and Numbers 28.2 respectively, ignoring the coincidence of the terms in Numbers 3.7–8; 8.26; 18.7. On the other hand, both Sailhamer and Walton present different grammatical-contextual arguments why *lĕ'obdāh ûlĕšomrāh* cannot refer simply to agriculture but must refer to cultic activity (see Sailhamer, *Pentateuch as Narrative*, pp. 100–1 and Walton, 'Eden', pp. 205–6).

18 Wenham, 'Sanctuary Symbolism', p. 401.

19 This woodenly literal translation is my own. Unfortunately, there is no felicitous English idiom that captures the structure and sense of the Hebrew verb + cognate (inner) accusative constructions *šāmar ha-mišmeret* and *'ābad hā-'ăbôdâ*. The force of the verse in idiomatic English is probably similar to this: 'They shall attend carefully to all the cultic duties that pertain to the person of the High Priest or the entire congregation of Israel generally, and they shall perform all labour necessary for the celebration of the tabernacle liturgy.'

20 Idiomatically: 'You shall attend carefully to all the duties relating to the holy place and the altar … You and your sons with you shall attend carefully to the duties of the priesthood with respect to the altar and that which is inside the veil, and you shall celebrate the whole liturgy.'

21 Note that this makes sense in light of the correlation that McDowell observes between the High Priest and Adam as 'image and likeness' (*Image of God*, pp. 210–11). Fletcher-Louis also writes that, 'The office of high priest was thought to recapitulate the identity of the pre-lapsarian Adam. This goes back at least as far as Ezekiel 28:12ff. where the prince of Tyre wears precious stones which are simultaneously those worn by the *Urmensch* in the garden of Eden and those of the Aaronic ephod according to Exodus 28' ('The Worship of Divine Humanity as God's Image and the Worship of Jesus', in *The Jewish Roots of Christological Monotheism: Papers from the St Andrews Conference on the Historical Origins of the Worship of Jesus*, Journal for the Study of Judaism Supplement 63, ed. Carey C. Newman, James R. Davila, and Gladys S. Lewis (Leiden: Brill, 1999), pp. 112–28 (here 126)).

22 Wenham, *Genesis 1–15*, p. 64; Silviu Bunta, 'The Likeness of the Image: Adamic Motifs and *ṣlm* Anthropology in Rabbinic Traditions about Jacob's Image

Enthroned in Heaven', *Journal for the Study of Judaism* 37 (2006), pp. 55–84 (here 64); Fletcher-Louis, 'The Worship of Divine Humanity', pp. 123–6; Martha Himmelfarb, 'The Temple and the Garden of Eden in Ezekiel, the Book of Watchers, and the Wisdom of ben Sira', in *Sacred Places and Profane Spaces: Essays in the Geographics of Judaism, Christianity, and Islam*, Contributions to the Study of Religion 30, ed. Jamie Scott and Paul Simpson-Housley (New York: Greenwood Press, 1991), pp. 63–78 (here 65–6); Lawrence E. Stager, 'Jerusalem and the Garden of Eden', in *Eretz-Israel: Archaeological, Historical and Geographical Studies 26: Frank Moore Cross Volume*, ed. Baruch A. Levine, Philip J. King, Joseph Naveh, and Ephraim Stern (Jerusalem: Israel Exploration Society with Hebrew Union College-Jewish Institute of Religion, 1999), pp. 183–94; Jon D. Levenson, *Sinai and Zion: An Entry into the Jewish Bible* (New York: HarperCollins, 1985), pp. 128–9; Carol Meyers, *The Tabernacle Menorah* (Missoula, MT: Scholars Press, 1976), p. 150; Fletcher-Louis, *All the Glory of Adam*, pp. 18–19; Warren Austin Gage, *The Gospel of Genesis: Studies in Protology and Eschatology* (Winona Lake, IN: Carpenter Books, 1984 [1982]), p. 50 n. 3; Dexter E. Callender, Jr, *Adam in Myth and History: Ancient Israelite Perspectives on the Primal Human*, Harvard Semitic Monographs 48 (Winona Lake, IN: Eisenbrauns, 2000), pp. 89, 100–3, 132, 210; Jon D. Levenson, *Theology of the Program of Restoration of Ezekiel 40–48*, Harvard Semitic Monographs 10 (Cambridge, MA: Scholars Press, 1976), pp. 21–36; Beale, *Temple and the Church's Mission*, pp. 75–6, 76 n. 110; Levenson, *Creation and the Persistence of Evil: The Jewish Drama of Divine Omnipotence* (San Francisco: Harper & Row, 1988), p. 93; Sandra L. Richter, *The Epic of Eden: A Christian Entry in to the Old Testament* (Downers Grove: InterVarsity Press, 2008), pp. 119–27.

23 Wenham, 'Sanctuary Symbolism', pp. 401–3.

24 I.e. the *hithpa'el* or iterative-reflexive stem of *hālak*, 'to walk'.

25 Carol Meyers, *Tabernacle Menorah*.

26 See Keel, *Symbolism of the Biblical World*, pp. 118, 140, 174; Beale, *Temple and the Church's Mission*, pp. 53–6.

27 McDowell, *Image of God*, pp. 140–1.

28 McDowell, *Image of God*, p. 141; emphasis mine.

29 I borrow this phrase from Scott W. Hahn, 'Worship in the Word: Toward a Liturgical Hermeneutic', *Letter & Spirit* 1 (2005), p. 106.

30 Whether there was an 'Adamic' covenant is disputed, but its existence is affirmed here. See Scott W. Hahn, *Kinship by Covenant: A Canonical Approach to the Fulfillment of God's Saving Promises*, Anchor Yale Bible Reference Library (New Haven, CT: Yale University Press, 2009), p. 388 n. 20; and discussion in John S. Bergsma and Scott Hahn, 'Covenant', in *The Oxford Encyclopedia of Biblical Theology*, ed. Kathleen Dell et al. (Oxford: Oxford University Press, 2015), pp. 151–66 (here 155); and bibliography in Bergsma, 'Covenant', in *Oxford Bibliographies Online* (2016), available at http://dx.doi.org/10.1093/obo/9780195393361-0225.

31 The term *šāmar* is the most common verb used to indicate fidelity to divine commandments in the Hebrew Bible. G. Sauer comments: 'This last notion [i.e. of 'keeping' the divine command] dominates the entire semantic field in the religious realm. It appears in almost all portions of the OT with widely varying expressions, grammatical constructions, and addressees' (G. Sauer, 'שמר', *Theological Lexicon of the Old Testament*, ed. E. Jenni and C. Westermann (Peabody, MA: Hendrickson Publishers), pp. 1380–4 (here 1382)).

32 David W. Fagerberg, 'Liturgical Asceticism: Enlarging our Grammar of Liturgy', *Pro Ecclesia* 13 (2004), p. 208.

33 We leave aside, for present purposes, the example of Abel, which would take us on a digression in another direction. Abel does not 'work the soil', and appears to be a type of the one who trusts in God's grace and therefore finds acceptance with God. But to develop this would take us too far afield.

34 Ancient interpreters saw Noah as a priest. The medieval *Glossa Ordinaria* – the study notes used to assist *lectio divina* (meditation on Scripture) in the monasteries – relates the Jewish tradition of Noah's priesthood: 'Aiunt Hebraei ... omnes primogenitos, a Noe ad Aaron, sacerdote fuisse' ('The Hebrews claim that ... every firstborn, from Noah to Aaron, was a priest', *Patrologia Latina* 198.1094–5).

35 Interestingly, the LXX recognizes the different senses of *'ābad* and *'ăbôdâ* in Exodus–Numbers, usually rendering work for Pharaoh as *ergon*, 'work' (Ex. 1.14) or *douleia*, 'slavery' (Ex. 6.6), but work for God as *latreias*, 'worship' (Ex. 4.23; 12.25–26) or *leitourgia*, 'liturgy' (Ex. 38.21 (37.19 LXX); Num. 4.24).

36 The LXX renders: *Exaposteilon ton laon mou, hina moi latreusē*, 'Send away my people, so that they may worship me.'

37 I have altered the RSV's translation of *mamleḵet* as 'kingdom' to 'kingship', for reasons explained below.

38 Exodus 19.6 LXX has *basileion hierateuma*, 'royal priesthood', for *mamleḵet kōhănîm*. First Peter 2.9 follows this tradition. For a modern defence of this translational option, see John A. Davies, *A Royal Priesthood: Literary and Intertextual Perspectives on an Image of Israel in Exodus 19:6*, Journal for the Study of the Old Testament Supplement 395 (London/New York: T. & T. Clark, 2004), esp. pp. 61–102.

39 Wenham, *Genesis 1–15*, p. 35; Menahem Haran, 'The Priestly Image of the Tabernacle', *Hebrew Union College Annual* 36 (1965), pp. 191–222; Peter J. Kearney, 'Creation and Liturgy: The P Redaction of Ex 25–40', *Zeitschrift für die alttestamentliche Wissenschaft* 89 (1977), pp. 375–8 and 385–6; Umberto Cassuto, *A Commentary on the Book of Exodus*, trans. Israel Abrahams (Jerusalem: Magnes Press, 1967 [1951]), pp. 476–7, 483. For more bibliography, see Morrow, 'Creation as Temple-Building', p. 4, n.15.

40 On the replacement of the firstborn by the Levites as cultic functionaries in the Pentateuch, see *M. Zevachim* 14:4; Jacob Milgrom, *Numbers*, JPS Torah Commentary 4 (Philadelphia: Jewish Publication Society, 1990), pp. 431–2; Baruch Levine, *Numbers 1–20*, Anchor Bible 4 (New York: Doubleday, 1993), p. 177; Hahn, *Kinship by Covenant*, pp. 146–7, and literature cited in 415–17.

41 Both David (1 Sam. 21.1–6; 2 Sam. 6.12–19; 8.18; Ps. 110) and Solomon (1 Kings 8.1–66) can be observed functioning as priests, in addition to their role as king.

42 Cf. Matt. 2.2; Mark 15.2; Luke 1.32–33; John 1.49.

43 Cf. Matt. 12.1–8; Mark 2.23–28; Luke 24.50–53 // Sir. 50.20–21; John 19.23 // Jos. *Ant.* 3.159–61; Heb. 1—10.

44 On the cultic background of the language in Romans 12.1, see James D. G. Dunn, *Romans 9–16*, Word Biblical Commentary 38B (Dallas: Word, 1988), pp. 708–11. Paul's phrase *parastēsai ... thysian* is probably his rendering of the Hebrew idiom *hiqrîb zebah*, 'to present (bring forward) a sacrifice', although the LXX does use *paristēmi* also to describe the priests presenting themselves before the LORD (Deut. 17.12; 18.5, 7; 21.5). See Reicke's comments in *Theological Dictionary of the New Testament*, ed. G. Kittel and G. Friedrich (Grand Rapids, MI: Eerdmans, 1974–6), vol. 5, p. 841. Paul's *euarestos*, 'well-pleasing, acceptable' probably

renders the Hebrew *nîḥōaḥ* 'pleasing' or *rāṣôn*, 'acceptable', both used in sacrificial contexts in MT, although the LXX employs other terms (e.g. *dekton*).

45 This is my own literal translation of the Greek.

46 St Josemaría Escrivà, *The Forge* (New York: Scepter, 1988), p. 249 (§687). St Josemaría Escrivà (1902–75) was a Spanish priest, spiritual director, and writer best known as the founder of Opus Dei ('The Work of God'), a pastoral organization within the Roman Catholic Church dedicated specifically to supporting lay people in attaining holiness through the sanctification of the professional work and daily life (www.opusdei.org). Known as 'the saint of the ordinary', Escrivà was canonized by St John Paul II in 2002. Strikingly, Genesis 2.4b–15 is the First Reading for the eucharistic celebrations on his feast day (26 June).

47 Escrivà, *Forge*, p. 131 (§369); emphasis mine.

3

Work as a Blessed Gift in the Prophets and Writings: A Thematic Study with Special Emphasis on Jeremiah 29

EUGENE H. MERRILL

The term 'work' conjures in the mind of most postmodern people a multitude of cognitive and sensory reactions. Some regard it as a necessary evil, something one must do in order to 'get by' in the world. Others view it with disdain, as a day-by-day drudgery that calls for tasks far beneath what they perceive their education, skills, and talents make them worthy of doing. Others tolerate or even enjoy work because it affords stimulating companionship, a sense of collegiality, a pleasant environment, or the pleasure in seeing tasks undertaken and completed in a fulfilling way. But work as a blessing? The majority of men and women either hate what they do for work or put up with it as essential to survival. Monday morning's commute to the workplace seems to lead nowhere except to the beginning of another 40 hours of insignificance.

The Bible, however, presents a totally different view of gainful (or even ungainful) employment in the workaday world. Its pages from beginning to end suggest that work is a veritable gift from God, which, done well, meets with hearty approbation. Far from being a source of dread and helpless resignation, work from the biblical perspective is an honourable, noble, and privileged thing. In fact, the second word of the Bible (בְּרָא, bārā' 'he created'; cf. Gen. 1.21, 27; 2.4, 23) describes God himself at work, as do other verbs in Genesis 1—2.[1] If the Almighty worked (and works), then surely it is an uplifting, responsible, and appropriate thing for those created as his image to do. The first words spoken about and to humankind also had to do with work, in both the broad and narrow senses.[2] Moreover, it is something expected, nay, commanded, by the Lord in both Testaments as an inescapable element of what it means to be a worthy kingdom citizen. The great apostle was no dainty when it came to work, noting to the Corinthians that he 'worked hard with his hands', referring, of course, to his avocation of tent-making (1 Cor. 4.12; cf. Acts 18.3). But what was true of him, he said, must be true of all in the fellowship of the saints. Likely quoting a proverb, he ascribed to labour a fundamental principle when he said to the Thessalonians, 'if a man will not work, he shall not eat' (2 Thess. 3.10; cf. 1 Thess. 4.11). These sentiments of Jesus and the apostles find their seed-bed in the Old Testament, the special focus of this study. More specific to this chapter is to view Jeremiah as a case study on which and from which subsequent prophets very likely drew in their respective treatments of the concept of work.

Far from being something to be feared and shunned – or even viewed as a curse – work was ordained by God before humankind fell into sin and selfishness as one of the good things inherent in his being the divine image.[3] The inspired narrative says that God planted (נָטַע) a garden eastward in Eden (Gen. 2.8) and he placed the man there expressly to do two things: 'to work it (עָבַד) and to take responsibility (שָׁמַר)[4] for it'. Both of these verbs encapsulate all that is meant to view biblical labour as an offering to God. One way to look at the juxtaposition of the two mandates is to see them as incorporating (1) the making, building, construction of something and (2) the ongoing maintenance of what has been done. The garden, as many scholars have noted, is a microcosm of the whole creation, a testing-ground, as it were, for humankind in its role of ruling over all things (Gen. 1.26–28). If the two could exploit the riches of this limited territory for the glory of God, then God would have established them and all their descendants until now as his vice-gerents. One is reminded of the words of Jesus to this effect after relating the parable of the talents: 'Well done, good, faithful servant; [because] you have been faithful over a few things, I will appoint you ruler over many' (Matt. 25.23).

Technical Terms for 'Work', 'Labour', etc. in the Hebrew Bible

The concept of work as labour (as opposed to 'works' as the process or object of artistic creativity such as music, painting, sculpture, and the like) is lexically defined in many ways in the Hebrew Bible:

1 By far the most common is by the verb *עבד (*'bd*) and its nominal cognates.[5] It is also the preferred lexeme of the rich vocabulary of the Old Testament by which work is celebrated as something positive and which, when done for the glory of God, is in itself an act of worship.

By semantic category, the term occurs in contexts of (1) 'ordinary' work (Ex. 34.21), (2) agriculture (Gen. 2.5), (3) servanthood (1 Sam. 4.9), (4) slavery (Ex. 14.5), and (5) cult, as in the work of priests, Levites, and even private citizens in worship and in serving at the tabernacle or temple (Ex. 13.5).

2 Near synonyms include the nominal מַס (*mas*), of unknown etymology, but with verbs such as שִׂים (*śîm*), 'set or place over', means to be the victim of forced labour, a concept certainly foreign to the nobility of work (cf. Ex. 1.11; Deut. 17.15). Akkadian attests *massu* with the same negative meaning. Another common term often parallel to עבד is פָּעַל/פֹּעַל*, 'make, do'/'achievement, deed, work'. When used with God as subject it generally conveys the nuance of creation or other accomplishment of a supernatural kind: Yahweh created a dwelling place (Zion) for himself (Ex. 15.17); causes a scattering (Deut. 32.27); keeps secure (Ps. 31.20). Though humans cannot create in the divine sense, they can make (Isa. 44.12), do (or not do; Ps. 11.3), or achieve (2 Sam. 23.30). The lexeme פֹּעַל, like עֶבֶד, is so broad and generic, however, it lends little or no substance to the semantic analysis attempted in this chapter.

3 Another term suggesting work as an unpleasantness little short of slavery is יְגִיעַ (*y⁰gîa'*), 'struggle, strive',[6] as in Jacob's complaint to Laban that his labour of 20 years to obtain a wife was virtual coercion (Gen. 31.42). He likens it to 'oppression' (עֹנִי). Among the prophets, Isaiah uses the term most freely. He expresses God's displeasure at the punishing labour he had wasted on an unreceptive people (Isa. 49.4). Moreover, he excoriates them for the way they have abused each other as forced labour. At the same time, he commiserates with those same people because of the way they have had to serve the nations while in exile, and he foresees the day when it will end (Isa. 62.8; cf. 65.23). Jeremiah speaks of the onerous labour done by Babylonian slaves who had built the walls and gates of the great city in vain (51.58; cf. Hab. 2.13).

The sages and poets lament this kind of labour. Job asks, 'Why do I labour (אִיגַע) in vain' (9.29)? Again, he asks of God, 'Why do you despise the work (יְגִיעַ) of your (own) hands?' (10.3). That is, Job sees even himself as one born to laborious struggle. Proverbs 23.4 advises that one should not put oneself through this kind of semi-slavery just to become rich. The substantive עָמָל and its cognate verb עָמַל (Qal only)[7] denote gain or profit from work (Ps. 103.2 – benefits of God's work); far more often they have the negative nuance of work that is arduous or painful (Ps. 90.10),[8] forced to be done in order to avenge a wrong or to force recompense for a personal mistreatment of one kind or the other (Obad. 15; Ps. 28.4; 94.2; 2 Chron. 32.25), or as a judgement of God on his people (Ps. 107.12).

4 The most extreme expression of the bitterness of forced labour is the relatively rare *עצב. The substantive עֶצֶב denotes pain or hurt, as in Psalm 127.2 of those who try to build a house (or family) apart from Yahweh. Their labour yields nothing but pain. Well-known examples

are Genesis 3.16, where the woman is told she would give birth with such pain and Adam would till the cursed soil with the same debilitating effort, this time with a derivative noun, עִצָּבוֹן, and in Genesis 5.29 where Laban names his son נֹחַ, 'rest', named thus in the hopes he would deliver humankind מֵעִצְּבוֹן יָדֵנוּ ('from the harsh labour of our hands'). The verb in Niphal means to be grieved or saddened (Gen. 45.5; 1 Sam. 20.3). The Hithpael is especially striking in that it speaks anthropologically of Yahweh who is grieved about the creation he has made, here, in particular, about humankind's utter depravity (Gen. 6.5).

Jeremiah and the Theme of Work

The Setting and Background of Jeremiah's Letter to the Exiles[9]

The most crushingly tragic date in the history of ancient Israel is arguably the conquest of the holy city Jerusalem and the utter destruction of its glorious temple by the armies of the Babylonian King Nebuchadnezzar in July 586 BC. The tragedy was not so much in material and physical terms as it was in a symbolical, indeed, theological sense, for the City of David – known also as Zion – was understood from the beginning of the monarchy 420 years earlier to be the seat of the Davidic line of kings that represented on earth the kingdom of the Lord God in heaven. And as for the temple, it housed the cloud of divine presence, a tangible sign of the enthronement of Yahweh himself who sat in regal splendour on the Ark of the Covenant as his throne in the Most Holy Place. Now all was lost, it seemed, perhaps never to be recreated. Yahweh was no longer 'at home', the Kingdom of Judah had become a Babylonian subject state, and the city of Jerusalem was emptied of the leadership of its citizenry, ruled now by Jewish surrogate governors under the watchful eye of imperial overseers.[10]

Jeremiah the Man and Prophet

In the prophet's own words, he introduces himself to the reader as belonging to the family of Hilkiah[11] the priest in Anathoth, a village on the northern slopes of the Mount of Olives (Jer. 1.1). The village-folk were not impressed by the local boy and, like many another prophet, he was not held in honour (Matt. 13.54–58). Like Jesus, his life was in jeopardy so he had to flee to escape his townsmen (Jer. 11.21). For this harsh and wicked treatment, the village was called to judgement by Jeremiah himself in his role of prophet (Jer. 11.23). Yet, in another strange turn of events, he was notified that he was heir to some property in Anathoth as the nearest of kin to the owner (Jer. 32.6–15). However, there was a lien on the property that had to be paid before the transaction could be completed. Jeremiah came up with the 17 silver shekels (about £1,150 in 2016 silver), took over the deed, and asked his friend and amanuensis Baruch to bury the deed in a jar. This prophetic visual aid served as an assurance that the Babylonian exile would end and he (and they) would return to repossess and reinhabit their properties.

But Jeremiah's persecution at the hands of his own kinsmen was only the beginning of his troubles. He suffered imprisonment (20.14–18; 26.8–15; 32.1–5; 37.11–21) and other abuse, and finally arrived at what was tantamount to suicide. Rhetorically, he questioned his mother as to why she bore him to suffer (15.10) and then went so far as to curse his birthday and even the unknown man who had brought the news of his birth to his father (20.14–15).[12] It is not for nothing that he has been known through the ages as 'the weeping prophet'.

Jeremiah's double calling – priest and prophet – is not common in the Old Testament, with Ezekiel being the best-known example of another such individual (Ezek. 1.3), these two being the only ones among the so-called 'canonical' prophets.[13] However, there are no examples of Jeremiah's functioning in a cultic context. He is referred to as 'the prophet' at least 40 times but never as 'priest'. As a prophet, he, like Isaiah, moved in the highest circles of the royal courts of Israel and Judah. He was not always very welcome there to say the least, but he was frequently called by Yahweh to go to the king, or the king himself would call on the prophet when he could be of benefit in times of crisis.[14]

Jeremiah's heart went with the exiles to their distant place in Babylon, so after the catastrophic destruction of Jerusalem and the temple that resulted in their being in exile, he sent at least one letter to them (Jer. 29) in order to: (1) encourage them to settle down, go to work, and be good citizens in their new setting (vv. 1–7); (2) enjoin them twice to pay no attention to false prophets and diviners (vv. 8–9, 21–32);[15] (3) predict the return of the exiles to the holy land (vv. 10–14); and (4) relate the defeat of King Zedekiah and his ungodly countrymen who had survived the captivity of 598 BC (vv. 15–20). On another occasion (and final to the prophet himself), a group of assassins led by Johanan, who had slain Ishmael, a man related to the Davidic dynasty, and who had in turn murdered the Babylonian appointee governor Gedaliah, fled to Egypt to avoid the repercussions certain to come from the Babylonian authorities (Jer. 41.1–3, 11–18). They took with them, much to their opposition and resistance, both Jeremiah and his devoted disciple Baruch, to Tahpenes[16] in Egypt where they both continued their ministry, presumably till the end of their lives (Jer. 43.7–9; 44.1; 46.14; Ezek. 30.18).

Jeremiah and the Concept of Work

The theological concept of work in general in the Old Testament has already been dealt with briefly; attention turns now to that theme in Jeremiah and, in particular, as it is expounded in his letter to the Babylonian exiles, his fellow Jews now in Babylon, who had been taken there in the various conquests of Nebuchadnezzar[17] (Jer. 29.4–32). Though his letter was directed to Babylon, the great city, its message was no doubt intended for all who had been carried away in the three major deportations, most in lands or cities that are only sparsely mentioned in the Bible and/or that can no longer be identified.[18]

Outline of the Letter

The writer and his credentials (v. 4a)
The recipients (v. 4b)
The injunctions (vv. 5–9)
  Build houses and plant gardens (v. 5)
  Marry and create families (v. 6)
  Settle in and become part of the host community (v. 7)
  Avoid false prophets (vv. 8–9)
The promise of return from exile (vv. 10–14)
Future acts of judgement (vv. 15–32)
  Against Zedekiah (vv. 15–20)
  Against false prophets (vv. 21–29)
  Against Shemaiah (vv. 30–32)

An Exegetical Reading of Jeremiah 29

The letter itself is preceded by the identification of the author and the recipients, time and circumstances, and the names of the couriers who were entrusted to deliver it to its intended destination (vv. 1–3). Jeremiah was of course well known because of the uproar he had occasioned by his very public and very controversial ministry in and about Jerusalem, especially in the royal palace itself. After all, he had been called to drive out, tear down, exterminate, and annihilate: messages not designed to gain their purveyor popularity.

The recipients were all the exiles without exception, from the political and religious leaders to the lowest echelons of society. The timing was hard on the heels of the second deportation of the Jewish populace by Nebuchadnezzar's forces in 597 BC. Jehoiachin was the hapless ruler of Judah at the time and he was among the captives (see 2 Kings 24.8–17), along with 10,000 of the general population ('captives'),[19] 7,000 soldiers, and 1,000 skilled craftsmen, virtually emptying the capital and its environs of population except for peasants of the poorest kind. The two carriers of the letter were obviously men to be trusted, one named Elasah and the other Gemariah. The former was quite likely a son of the famous scribe Shaphan who served King Josiah so faithfully (2 Kings 22.9, etc.) and the latter a son of the equally prominent figure, Hilkiah, the chief priest (2 Kings 22.4, etc.). They had already proved their dependability by having delivered letters for King Zedekiah to King Nebuchadnezzar (unmentioned elsewhere).

The letter proper (vv. 4–32) consists of instructions and advice of the prophet, five in number: (1) build houses and (2) plant gardens (v. 5); (3) get married, have children, ensure that your children marry, and have grandchildren (v. 6); (4) pray for the peace of your new city (v. 7); (5) avoid false prophets (vv. 8–9). His further topics and instructions, also numbering five, are: (1) the promise of a return home after 70 years (vv. 10–14); (2) warning to the exiles because of their heed to false prophets (vv. 15–20); (3) prediction of the demise of King Zedekiah (vv. 21–23); (4) the captivity of false prophets still in Judah (vv. 24–28); and (5) in an addendum to the letter, the singling out of the false prophet Shemaiah for a special coming judgement because of his opposition to Jeremiah (vv. 29–32).[20]

The prophet's special focus on building and planting (vv. 5–7) embodies a series of rapid-fire imperatives to show that these activities are not optional: 'build' וּבְנ (*b^enû*), 'live' שְׁבוּ (*šēbû*), 'plant' נִטְעוּ (*niṭû*), 'eat' וְאִכְל ('*iklû*), 'take' קְחוּ (*q^eḥû*), 'beget' הוֹלִידוּ (*hôlîdû*), 'give' תְּנוּ (*t^enû*), 'multiply' רְבוּ (*r^ebû*), 'seek' דִּרְשׁוּ (*diršû*), 'pray' הִתְפַּלְלוּ (*hitpallû*). The first four of these pertain to what is required to make a living and the remainder with how to live. The circumstances of the rag-tag exiles were not conducive to an optimistic view of the future. They had doubtless been unable to take but meagre furnishings and supplies with them the 1,200 miles of their sojourn and must have been fatigued, disoriented, and fearful when they finally arrived and for a long time afterwards. The people of their captors' land were different in dress, diet, language and, most important, religion. They had left a land of villages, hills, forests, fields, and streams, and now were dumped down as it were into the midst of a flat, endless desert, searing heat, scarcity of rainfall, and urban centres crowded with people scurrying here and there on businesses and enterprises unfamiliar to their new immigrants.

At the same time, it seems the Jews had a modicum of independence within the regions allocated to them. As noted above, there were Jewish settlements with a measure of self-government, including the right to worship Yahweh as they pleased and in holy places led by authorized priests and Levites. Thus, the instructions sent in Jeremiah's letter to them early in their deportation were not unreasonable – all they had to do was to rise up from their indolence, awaken to the fact they would be there for many decades, and put their shoulder to the wheel of initiative and press forward so they could live their lives in the new land as normally and as comfortably as possible.

The reason Jeremiah issued his instructions in the imperative is then clear: his kinsmen, to survive and preserve their identity as a God-called people, must get about their community-building as expeditiously as possible. Get busy building houses, the prophet said, lest you find yourselves in public housing administered by Babylonian overlords. Plant your gardens so you can avoid living like beggars at harvest time. Then eat what you have grown with thanksgiving to God for enabling you not only to just scrape by but to prosper.

In due time, said the prophet, begin family-building and generational continuity by the arrangement of marriages among yourselves and the establishment of households that form the nuclei of networks of the uniquely Jewish community. At the same time, develop such good relations with your Babylonian 'hosts' that genuine friendships can be formed to your mutual benefit. In other words, don't become cocooned in such a manner that your role as 'a light to the nations' (Isa. 49.6; 51.4) will be obscured, but at the same time, do not sacrifice what is central to your identity as the chosen race of Abraham to the point you become as pagan as they. That is to say, be good citizens of Babylon and do your utmost to gain favour with the majority population and participate with them in the affairs of civil society and statecraft.

How successful they were is not recorded in the Old Testament except most indirectly, as argued above. The very fact that many were financially secure enough to engage in big business with the House of Murashu provides sufficient extra-biblical evidence that some, at least, heeded the prophet's call to 'rise up and get to work'. And the reluctance of many more to leave Babylon once they were free to do so cements this conclusion.

At the very beginning of Jeremiah's ministry – in fact, as part of the so-called 'call narrative' (Jer. 1.4–10) – he was told to do six things, four negative and two positive:

'Drive out' (*n^etôš*)	'Build' (*b^enôt*)
'Tear down' (*n^etôṣ*)	'Plant' (*n^eṭôa'*)
'Exterminate' (*he'ăbîd*)	
'Annihilate' (*hǎrôs*)	

The two positives are central to the continuation of this study. In Jeremiah the verbs *bānāh* and *nāṭa'* occur in all forms eight and fourteen times respectively, usually in a metaphorical sense with reference to building or planting a people, community, institution, and the like. Here in Jeremiah's letter this is clearly not the case because literal houses (*bātîm*) and literal gardens (*gannôt*) are in view inasmuch as the result of such labour makes it possible to have food to eat (vv. 5, 28). The more metaphorical usage intended in Jeremiah's call is found in reference to building a people (24.6; 31.4) and planting them as a garden (31.27). Most striking is the prophet's reversal of the curse of the call narrative in several passages in the same words: 'I will build them and not annihilate them, plant them and not uproot them, and I will plant them and not drive them out' (24.6); 'just as I ordained them to drive [them] out and to tear [them] down and to annihilate [them] and to exterminate [them] and to injure[21] [them], so I will build them and plant them' (31.28); 'I will build you and not annihilate you and I will plant you and not drive you out' (42.10). These texts are, of course, eschatological and speak of a day when Israel will once more be returned to their land (Jer. 24.7b; 31.31–34; 42.10b–12).

At first glance, it seems that Jeremiah is acting the traitor of his people that he has been branded to be by some because of his insistence that the exile of his people will be long and that they should not resist their captors, but rather accommodate to them by settling among them and conforming to their customs and traditions.[22] Quite to the contrary, it is most evident that Jeremiah's communication to the exiles was prompted by several motives: (1) Since Yahweh had irrevocably determined that the exile would indeed extend over 70 years, there was no need or value in lying idle with vain hope of imminent release (Jer. 25.11–12; 29.10). (2) Since 'idle minds are the Devil's workshop', Jeremiah recognized this principle and therefore urged his countrymen to be busy about things both mental and physical. (3) To imagine that the exiles were in concentration camps or ghettoes is to misread the texts that demonstrate clearly that the Jews and other captives enjoyed rather benign and even prosperous conditions.[23] Further confirmation, as noted above, comes from Akkadian texts that speak of Murashu, a wealthy Babylonian businessman and financier who lists prosperous Jews among his clients.[24] (4) Jeremiah clearly is undergirding his emphasis on building and planting on a plethora of teaching on the nobility of work and self-reliance. Paul would state it most succinctly more than six centuries later: 'If any will not work, let him not eat' (2 Thess. 3.10).

Jewish Population in Babylonia

Jeremiah had personally escaped the trauma of deportation, but his heart had gone with his less fortunate compatriots. He was obviously concerned about their well-being from every vantage-point. How would they fare in a strange land at the hands of strange overlords who sometimes mistreated those whom they had taken away?[25] Yet he knew their captivity was an inevitable result of their covenant unfaithfulness; in fact, it was his own prediction of their plight that informed him and them as to how and why things turned out as they did (Jer. 4.5–8; 6.16–21; 25.1–11; 29.10). They must now remain the 70 years prophesied and make the best of their situation, one, he prayed, that would yield a repentance towards Yahweh that would enable them once more to be a 'light to the nations' (Isa. 49.5–7).

Estimates of the total number of captives taken in each deportation vary considerably. The total at 598 BC appears to be 18,000, consisting of 10,000 men, women, and children; 7,000 warriors (גִּבּוֹרֵי הַחַיִל); and 1,000 smiths and craftsmen. This compares with the totals of returnees recorded by both Ezra and Nehemiah – 42,360, not counting slaves and liturgical choirs (Ezra 2.64; Neh. 7.66). There is no way to determine the number of the peasants who were not taken captive.

The difference between the number deported and the larger number of those who returned can be explained in many ways: (1) Seventy years had passed and the population had grown considerably while in the comfortable surroundings of Babylonia. (2) Many Jews had already been deported in the 605 and 598 conquests, an undesignated number in 605, and the reminder of the people who were either forcibly or voluntarily removed, except for the 'poorest of the land', in 586. These could have amounted to several thousand. (3) The numbers mentioned in Ezra 2 returned under several Jewish leaders at different times, including Zerubbabel (538), Nehemiah (444), Ezra himself (458), and others who cannot clearly be identified (Ezra 2.2). Esther also provides some enlightenment in mentioning the Jews of Persia in the days of Xerxes (486–465), who, said Haman, were 'scattered and dispersed among the peoples of all the provinces of the kingdom' (Esth. 3.8), already identified by him as Jews (v. 4).

The Old Testament Prophets and the Concept of Work

Some of the prophets before and after Jeremiah (Isaiah, Ezekiel, Daniel, and the 12 'minor' prophets) joined their illustrious brother in emphasizing the theme of work as a proper and even blessed thing.[26] They will have a voice here as a member of the 'fellowship of the Prophets', as it were, and will speak to the practical and theological aspects of work as a blessed gift of God. In line with established principles of biblical theology, the theme will be traced longitudinally, in chronological sequence.

The Prophets of the Eighth Century

Amos, very likely the earliest of the 'canonical' prophets (c.760 BC), has nothing to say about the matter until the very end of his book, where he speaks in strictly eschatological terms of what Yahweh will do for and through his people at the end of the ages: the farmers in those days will find the soils so rich and idyllic that reapers will overtake planters and threshers will outpace the sowers (Amos 9.13). More to the point, he iterates that when Israel is back in the land they will rebuild (*ûbānû*) the destroyed cities, plant (*wᵉnāṭᵉ'û*) vineyards, and make (*wᵉ'āśû*) gardens, all signs of reinvigorated, intentional labour (v. 14). Yahweh then says he too will do some planting – he will plant (*ûneṭa'tîm*) Israel there in the land and they will never again be uprooted (v. 15). Hosea (c.750 BC) has nothing to add to the topic, nor do Obadiah, Jonah, and Micah.

The great prophet Isaiah (740 BC), however, writes plainly of the eschatological renewal of Israel, engaged as it will be in the latter days in the work of building houses and planting vineyards, using the very wording and pairing of Jeremiah 29.5: 'They [the returnees] shall build houses (*bᵉnû bātîm*) and settle (*wᵉšēbû*) in them; and they shall plant gardens (*wᵉniṭ'û*) and eat (*wᵉ'iklû*) their produce' (Isa. 65.21); and 'my chosen [ones] shall fully enjoy (*yᵉballû* Piel) the work (*ma'ăśēh*) of their hands' (v. 22d). The linkage of building, dwelling, planting, and eating is striking, mimicking as it does the command of Jeremiah to the exiles of his time. The enjoyment of work is also an important idea in support of its excellence, one hinted at in a number of texts.

The Prophets of the Seventh Century

Nahum (c.610 BC) does not address the topic of labour, preoccupied as he was with the judgement of God directed towards Nineveh. Habakkuk, in a most negative view of things, announces that the soon coming destruction of Judah will result in the decimation of the fig tree, the vineyard, the olive tree, the pasturelands, the flocks and the herds (Hab. 3.17). Yet, he says, 'I will triumph (*'e'lôzâ* in Yahweh, I will dance before my saving God' (Hab. 3.18). Zephaniah turns the cliché on its head when he joins the chorus of prophets anticipating the looming judgement: 'They [the people of Judah] will build (*ûbānû*) houses but will not inhabit them, they will plant (*wᵉnāṭᵉ'û*) vineyards, but will not drink of their wine' (Zeph. 1.13).

Ezekiel, also with a view to the future, proclaims of those who return to the land, 'They will settle unmolested there [in the land] and they will build (*ûbānû*) houses and plant (*wᵉnāṭᵉ'û*) vineyards ...' (Ezek. 28.26). It is clear that 'building and planting' has become a cliché for settling in, working, and becoming self-sufficient.

The Prophets of the Sixth Century

Haggai (520 BC), a prophet of the early post-exilic period, presents two contradictory messages about work, in particular about building. The returnees have built their own fine houses (1.4a) but have failed to build the temple of Yahweh (1.4b, 8). One should note that Yahweh says of what he wants them to do, 'I will be pleased with it אֶרְצֶה־בּוֹ ('erṣeh-bô) and I will be glorified in it אֶכָּבֵד ('ekkābēd).' The result of his scolding prompted the people then to go to work and build the sanctuary of Yahweh (1.14). They had also made attempts at planting, but with miserable results (1.6, 11). Finally, it is clear that Yahweh will do both the destruction and the reconstruction of Jerusalem and the nation (1.9; 2.7–9, 22). Zechariah (520 BC, 516 BC), contemporary with Haggai, shared his colleague's concern about the lack of progress in temple building and other aspects of settling down in Yehud, the new nomenclature for Judah introduced by the Persians. Cyrus the Great and other Persian monarchs had given the Jews a free hand in doing whatever they wished in terms of re-establishing their homeland provided, of course, that they recognized Persian sovereignty over the whole satrapy of Abar Nahari ('across the [Euphrates] River') of which Yehud was a part.[27] Haggai's and Zechariah's messages, then, had royal authority behind them as well as God's promise to enable the resettlement to go well and to full completion. However, and mystifyingly, Zechariah says nothing about the people building or planting for themselves as did Haggai. He refers to the temple only, and then only in eschatological terms (Zech. 1.16; 2.4; 8.3, 8; 12.6; 14.11). Equally puzzling is Malachi's (c.470 BC) omission of building, planting, or any other work either in this age or the next.

Old Testament Wisdom and Poetry and the Concept of Work

Ecclesiastes

Ecclesiastes appears to have conflicting views about work or working. He says early on, 'my heart rejoiced because of all my labour' (Eccl. 2.10; עָמָל 2×) but quickly goes on to lament, 'I looked on all the works that I had made and all the labour I had done; behold, it was vanity and a striving after wind, and there was no profit[28] under the sun' (2.11; cf. v. 17). In fact, he goes so far as to say he hated his work because it would only benefit his heirs (vv. 18, 21). But then he observes that 'there is nothing better than that a man should rejoice in his works for that is his profit (חֶלְקוֹ, lit. 'his portion').'[29] That is, work itself, and not just its product, is something worth doing and something in which one should rejoice (3.22). The author of Psalm 126 notes that 'They who sow tearfully shall reap joyfully' and 'he who goes out weeping, carrying seed for sowing, will without fail come back gain joyfully, bringing his sheaves with him' (vv. 5–6).[30] Moreover, the reward for this kind of work comes from God himself, not some human employer. The sage goes on to say that 'man should eat and drink and see something good, [even] in all his struggle'. The author also makes the point that cooperative labour is beneficial, for if one worker fails, the other can come with support to keep the project moving (4.9). Finally, Ecclesiastes realizes and emphasizes the fact that great riches are a blessing from God if one recognizes that they come from God as well as does the ability to work to acquire them (5.19).

Ecclesiastes's ambivalence about work is only apparent, for as in many other instances in wisdom literature, opposite extremes are often employed in order to establish (1) a 'happy medium' (thus Prov. 26.4–5) or (2) a sense of perspective. That is, work is good or bad depending on circumstances and outcomes. On the one hand, he says, human beings work and die and then are soon forgotten along with their work (Eccl. 1.3, 11; 2.16–17; 8.17; 9.1, 6). On the other hand, he muses that 'There is nothing better for a man than that he should eat and drink, and enjoy good in his labour' (2.24; cf. 3.13, 22; 5.18–19). Work, then, is neither good nor bad but both, depending on motive – how and why it is done.

Proverbs

The collector of the maxims of this book thought of work as profitable, as is clear from 12.14: 'A man can be satisfied by the fruit of his mouth (i.e. his words)/and the work (לוּמַג) of his hands (his works) can (also) benefit[31] him.' In the spirit of Jeremiah, the sage instructs that one should undertake and make ready his outside work first (i.e. prepare a food supply), and then attend to the building of his house (Prov. 24.27). He then illustrates his point from personal experience: 'I went by the field and vineyard of a sluggard,'[32] he said, 'a man devoid of common sense, and I noticed that all his land was infested with thorns, thistles covered its surface, and its stone wall had collapsed' (vv. 30–31). What he learned, he went on to say, was that a little (too much) sleep and idleness invites poverty as though a robber or brigand had stolen all one has (vv. 32–34). Proverbs 14.23 expresses the same sentiment but employs the rare term מוֹתָר (only here, in 21.5, and Eccl. 3.19), clearly a derivative of יָתַר, for labour's reward (see above on Eccl.). To the contrary, those who are slow to do their duty in work are as bad as a destroyer, a band of pillagers (מַשְׁחִית, Prov. 18.9; cf. 1 Sam. 13.17; 14.15; Isa. 54.16). That is, to do nothing can be as harmful as to do the wrong thing.

Somewhat in the same vein, the wise man warns that words without works are of no value: 'He who works his land will have abundance, but he who pursues idleness (רֵיקִים) is devoid of sense' (12.11). Even worse, the sluggard,[33] it seems, is so consumed by pleasure that he would rather die than work (Prov. 21.25). The sage also warns about 'working oneself to death' (אַל־תִּיגַע) only to get rich (Prov. 23.4), for what has been earned can also be lost to strangers and aliens if one is not prudent (5.10). Words are of no worth in the end, but only diligent labour. This is so self-evident, that 'even a child makes himself known to others by his good works' (מַעֲלָלִים) (20.11).

The prime example in the book of Proverbs of the ideal of good, hard, and honest work is that of the ideal wife of Proverbs 31.10–31. The passage abounds with a plethora of nouns and verbs describing what she does to provide for her family and herself. 'She works (עָשָׂה) with her own hands with delight (v. 13b)'; 'she provides (Hi. בוֹא) for her food supplies from afar (v. 14b)'; she plants (נָטַע) vineyards (v. 16); she makes clothing for her family and as a business (vv. 19, 21, 24); she manufactures (עָשָׂה) carpets (v. 22a) and clothing of the finest kind (v. 22b); and she makes deliveries (נָתַן) of her products (v. 24b). Her industriousness is summed up in the accolade that 'she does not eat the bread of idleness (עַצְלוּת)' (v. 27b). Her earthly reward for such selfless diligence is summed up in verse 31: 'Give to her the results (lit. 'fruit') of her labours ('hands'), and may her works (מַעֲשֶׂיהָ) give her praise in the gates' (my translation). That is, her work speaks for itself and needs no further self-expression.

Psalms

The Psalter is rich in teaching about work and its necessity; indeed, its pleasure and profitability. The model for human endeavour is God's work, a theme pervasive throughout the Psalms, and occasionally expressed by the verb עָשָׂה. The heavens are the works of his hands (Ps. 8.3; 102.25) and he is renowned to his people for his works of old (143.5). More common is פָּעַל, also referring to God's ancient deeds in general (64.9; 77.12; 90.16; 92.4) and as creator (95.7; 111.3). The same verbs also occur, of course, with human activity, some of it good and some of it bad. David confessed that Yahweh rewards every man according to his work (Ps. 62.12) and he is the one who enables humankind to work (90.1). With that ability we go about our daily work to provide for ourselves and our dependants (104.23). Unfortunately, some of that labour is expended on the creation of idols (Ps. 115.4; 135.15) and other practices inimical to the worship of Yahweh (58.2). David's prayer is that God will deliver him from such deeds (101.3; 141.4). Failure on the part of God's people to adhere to covenant obligations results sometimes in punishing labour (107.12).[34]

More apropos of our main topic, it will be helpful to see what the Psalter has to say about building and planting, the two main categories of work emphasized in the Old Testament with respect to God's plans and expectations for his people. Planting (נָטַע), surprisingly then in light of the last sentence, occurs in the Psalms only once and that in an eschatological text reminiscent of Isaiah. Here the poet speaks of the preparation of inhabited cities (וַיְכוֹנְנוּ עִיר מוֹשָׁב) and the planting of vineyards (Ps. 107.36b–37a; cf. Isa. 65.21).

The term בָּנָה, the only verb in Psalms used for building, is found in either a figurative sense or in eschatological passages concerning the building of the kingdom in time to come. Thus David prays that God will build up the spiritual walls of Jerusalem (Ps. 51.18; 69.35; 102.16; 147.2) and Psalm 89.4 echoes the petition with the answer 'Your seed I will establish (כּוּן) forever, and build up (בָּנָה) your throne generation after generation.' In one instance, David avers of those who pay no regard to God's works (פְּעֻלָּה), that he will break them down and not (re)build (בָּנָה) them (Ps. 28.5). Only one passage describing human building is attested to in Psalms, and that in partnership with Yahweh: 'If Yahweh does not build (בָּנָה) a house, they who labour at building (עָמְלוּ בוֹנָיו)[35] it will do so in vain' (Ps. 127.1; my translation).

Conclusion

This chapter has wrestled with the concept of labour in the Old Testament Prophets and Writings in the full orb of its presentation. In general, the various *termini technici* employed in the Hebrew Bible display a wide range of meaning from 'ordinary' labour to onerous, even crushing slavery induced by human overlordship or divine judgement. Specifically, Jeremiah's letter to the Jewish exiles in Babylonia lays down a number of principles to guide all of God's people in all situations in making the best of them. One must settle in, plant for provision of needs, and build as though one belongs where he or she is. In God's time, as the prophet makes clear, they will return to the homeland to enjoy the blessing of God in fulfilment of his irrefragable covenant promises. These observations lead to three points of summary: (1) Work is a *gift* of God to humankind, one first illustrated by his own work of creation, sustenance, and salvation, and then secondarily as mandated by him to those created as his image. (2) Work is a *blessing* from God, when done constructively and with an eye to God's sovereign plans and purposes, as opposed to drudgery, mere obligation, or punishment. (3) All work can and should be *creative, productive, pleasurable,* and *purposeful*. The messages of the prophets, poets, and sages are one in these respects and they should enable us who claim to be 'bond-slaves of Jesus Christ' to work with the highest ideals in mind.

Notes

1 Other 'work-words' are מְרַחֶפֶת ('was hovering over', v. 2); בָּדַל ('he divided', v. 4; cf. v. 7); עָשָׂה ('he made', v. 7; cf. vv. 16, 25, 31; 2:2, 3, 4, 9); נָתַן ('set, place, give', vv. 17, 29); יָצַר ('he formed', 2.7, 19); נָפַח 'he breathed', 2.7); נָטַע, 'he planted', 2.8); לָקַח ('he took', 2.15, 21); חִנַ ('he settled [him]', 2.15); בּוֹא ('he brought', 2.19, 22); נָפַל ('he made to fall [asleep]', 2.21); בָּנָה ('he built', 2.22).

2 In the former case, God's first words to the original parents were to 'fill' the earth (מִלְאוּ) and 'subdue' it (כִּבְשֻׁ). Next was the command to 'have dominion (רְדוּ) over all things' (Gen. 1.28).

3 'In/as the image' (בְּצֶלֶם) as used here is taken to be not 'in the image' but 'as the image'. See Eugene H. Merrill, *Everlasting Dominion: A Theology of the Old Testament* (Nashville: Broadman & Holman, 2006), pp. 169–73. It is true, of course, that the blessedness of work was somewhat ameliorated after the fall by a curse on the ground (אֲדָמָה) but not on Adam (אָדָם). However, it was because of him (בַּעֲבוּרֶךָ), and there was the additional coda that work would thenceforth become toil (עִצָּבוֹן).

4 HALOT attests meanings as broad as 'watch, keep, heed to, save, retain, keep in mind, keep in order, keep covenant, revere' (Ludwig Koehler and Walter Baumgartner (eds), *The Hebrew and Aramaic Lexicon of the Old Testament*, vol. 2 (Leiden: Brill, 2001), p. 1582).

5 Of 290 attestations in BHS, 272 are in Qal and the remaining 18 are distributed among Niphal, Pual, Hiphil, and Hophal. Moreover, Pual is not matched by Piel but functions as the passive of Qal. The root is common Semitic, especially NW and South, occurring also in Ugaritic ('bd), Syriac (ăbôdâ), Phoenician ('bd), Arabic ('abada), and Ethiopic ('abäṭä). The closest corresponding semantic term in E Semitic (Akkadian) is epēšu. In Hammurabi Law 13, a command is given, nidītka epuš '(Re)build your ruined (house)', a phrase very much like this in Jeremiah. G. R. Driver and John C. Miles (eds), *The Babylonian Laws* (Oxford: Clarendon, 1968), H:8–9, 38. Related nominals to the Hebrew verb are עֶבֶד ('ebed), 'servant/slave', עֲבוֹדָה ('ābôdâ), 'labour' (usually forced), and עַבְדוּת ('abdût), 'slavery'.

6 HALOT, vol. 2, p. 386.

7 Of 10 occurrences of the verb in MT, 7 are in either Eccl. or Prov.; of about 50 occurrences of the noun, fully half are in wisdom settings.

8 Attributed to Moses, who himself died at the age of 120 (Deut. 34.7), the relevant lines read concerning longevity in years: 'Eagerness for them (רָהְבָּם) [results in] meaningless labour (עָמָל וָאָוֶן).'

9 See Eugene H. Merrill, *Kingdom of Priests: A History of Old Testament Israel*, 2nd edition (Grand Rapids, MI: Baker, 2008), pp. 471–80.

10 For the doleful state of affairs in Judah and Jerusalem during the period of the Exile, see Peter R. Ackroyd, *Exile and Restoration* (Philadelphia: Westminster, 1968), pp. 20–31.

11 Very likely this is Hilkiah the priest who played a rather minor role in the reign of King Hezekiah of Judah (729–686 BC; 2 Kings 18.18–37). A later scion of the same name was chief priest in the time of King Josiah (640–609; 2 Kings 22.4—23.25). The Chronicler provides a full genealogy for Hilkiah from Levi through Aaron to Jehozadak, great-grandson of Hilkiah, and the priest at the time of the fall of 586. That Hilkiah was the same as he who served in the time of Hezekiah 125 years earlier. Whether בֶּן חִלְקִיָּהוּ means literal 'son of Hilkiah' or of the Hilkiah clan cannot be determined.

12 For parallels to this in Job, see there 3.1–19; 10.18–22.

13 Others in the OT record were Moses, a descendant of Levi and brother of Aaron, the first of the line of Levitical priests in a formal way (Ex. 6.16–20; 24.5–8; Lev. 8.14–29). His role as prophet is clearly established in a number of places (Deut. 18.15–18; 34.10).

14 Examples are Yahweh's command to Jeremiah to preach against Jehoiakim (26.1–7); Zedekiah's appeal to Jeremiah to intercede for him before Yahweh to see if Yahweh might deliver him from Nebuchadnezzar (21.1–8); Yahweh's commission to the prophet to go to Zedekiah to warn him to repent and return to him (22.1–9, 11); still another word that the time for repentance had passed (32.1–5); once more a word to Zedekiah that Jerusalem would be soon destroyed (34.1–22); Jeremiah's appeal to Zedekiah for release from the dungeon (37.16–21); and finally, Zedekiah's release of the prophet once more and his permission to live near the palace itself (38.14–28). After the destructions and deportations, the remnant population asked for Jeremiah's intercession for survival (42.1–6); and the conspirators among the Jews also had encounters with Jeremiah, condemning him for having lied to them (43.1–7); and another word to captive Zedekiah in faraway Babylon to give him assurance that in God's own time the Jews would return to the homeland (51.59–64).

15 The root of this term (קֹסֵם<*קסם>קֹסְמִים) refers to a subcategory of prophetism especially adept at using divinatory objects: in one OT example, arrows (Ezek. 21.21–23, 29).

16 Heb תַּחְפַּנְחֵס, likely the same as Tell Dafnē, some 20 miles south-west of Tanis in the eastern delta (cf. Jer. 2.16).

17 The first of these was in the reign of Jehoakim in 605 (2 Kings 24.1; 2 Chron. 36.6; cf. Jer. 25.1; Dan. 1.1–7); the second in the reign of Jehoiachin in 598 (2 Kings 24.10–17; 2 Chron. 36.9–10; Jer. 24.1, 6–7; Ezek. 1.1–3); and the third in the reign of Zedekiah in 586 (2 Kings 25.11; 2 Chron. 36.17–21; Jer. 39.1–10).

18 Some of these are Tel Melach (tēl melaḥ), Tel Harsha (tēl ḥāršā'), Cherub (kĕrûb), Addan ('addān), and Immer ('immēr), all in Ezra 2.59; Ahava ('ahăwā), in Ezra 8.15; Casiphia (kāsipyā'), Ezra 8.17; Susa (šûšan), Esth. 1.2; passim; Neh. 1.1; Dan. 8.2; Halah (ḥălaḥ), 2 Kings 17.6; 'the other Jews in the king's provinces' (Esth. 9.16); and 'cities of the Medes' (2 Kings 17.6). Susa is, of course, the well-known capital of ancient Elam in SW Persia but apart from that one can only speculate as to the locations of the others.

19 With LXX, Syriac, and Targum read גּוֹלָה for Q גּוּלָה. This is generic for a population with no reference to gender (Ludwig Koehler and Walter Baumgartner (eds), *Lexicon in Veteris Testamenti libros*, 2nd edition (Leiden: Brill, 1958), p. 175).

20 For studies on the letter, its purpose, content, and effect, see, among others, J. A. Thompson, *The Book of Jeremiah*, New International Commentary on the Old Testament (Grand Rapids: Eerdmans, 1980), pp. 651–6; F. B. Huey, *Jeremiah, Lamentations*, New American Commentary 16 (Nashville: Broadman & Holman, 1993), pp. 249–60.

21 The verb רָעַע does not occur in the call narrative.

22 See Eugene H. Merrill, 'Jeremiah in the Crossfire: The Politics of Divided Loyalties', lecture given at the University of Haifa, Israel, 30 May 2012. Available from ehainesmerrill@aol.com.

23 As for the overall situation described in the OT, it is a matter difficult to ascertain, but the beneficence shown in certain instances may shed some light on the whole nature of exile whether under Babylonia or Persia. For example, Jeremiah

himself was rescued from his Jewish captors by Babylonian officers who then promised him a good life in Babylon (40.4); Ezekiel, who was among the exiles of 598 BC, testified to the existence of elders in the Jewish enclaves of Chebar in Babylonia, which presupposes some kind of rudimentary exercise of religion and self-government in the very centre of the Empire (Ezek. 8.1, 11, 12; 14.1; 20.1, 3). He also carried out public meetings of the elders in and around is own private house (3.24; 8.1). Nehemiah, in the reign of the Persian King Artaxerxes II (464–424 BC), was the king's butler and the recipient of many favours, including permission to return to Jerusalem twice to assess the situation there (Neh. 1.11; 2.8; 13.6). Daniel and his three Jewish friends prospered under both Babylonian and Persian regimes (Dan. 1.3–7; 2.46–49; 6.28). The book of Esther attests to an initially benign situation for the Jews in Persia in the period of Xerxes (486–465) if the high position of Mordecai is any indicator (Esth. 2.5–7; 7.3–4; 8.15–17; 10:2–3). Not to be overlooked is the gracious treatment accorded King Jehoiachin by Evil-Merodach, successor to Nebuchadnezzar in 562 BC, who released him from prison and put him on a generous pension until he died (2 Kings 25.7–8). Finally, the very reluctance of the exiles to return to Yehud following the decree of Cyrus in 539 attests to their comfortable circumstances in their places of exile, a point reinforced by the paucity of people necessary to fully occupy Jerusalem (Neh. 7.4; 11.1).

24 For the Babylonian cuneiform tablets that contain the so-called 'House of Murashu' tablets, see Albert T. Clay, *Business Documents of Murashu Sons of Nippur* (Philadelphia: University Museum, 1912); Michael David Coogan, *West Semitic Personal Names in the Murashu Documents* (Missoula, MT: Scholars Press, 1976); D. Winton Thomas, *Documents from Old Testament Times* (Eugene, OR: Wipf & Stock, 2005), pp. 95–6.

25 Evidence of this is seen in the OT itself, especially in the book of Daniel (cf. 3.1–23; 6.10–23). See also Ackroyd, *Exile and Restoration*, pp. 36–8.

26 Space limitations have precluded close examination of Torah texts and the Former Prophets (Joshua–2 Kings) on the matter except as occasional cross-reference.

27 See 2 Chron. 36.22–23; Ezra 1.1–4; 4.17–24; 6.1–12; 7.1–26; Neh. 2.1–8.

28 Heb יִתְרוֹן, which occurs only in Eccl. (1.3; 2.11, 13; 3.9; 5.8, 15; 7.12; 10.10, 11) expresses the idea of labour with nothing to show for it, nothing left over (as profit).

29 This way of expressing the idea of profit for work is unique in the OT to Eccl. (2.10, 21; 3.22; 5.16; 9.6, 9; 11.2).

30 Of all the interpretations proffered for this passage, the best in context seems to favour the view that this is principal language: those who work hard and faithfully, even to the point of overwhelming labour, can expect their investment of labour to bring a harvest of both joy and satisfaction.

31 MT יָשׁוּב should be read (with *K*) יָשׁוּב 'return;' *Q* reads יָשִׁיב, 'bring back, return' (Hiphil שׁוּב).

32 The term here (אִישׁ־עָצֵל) suggests a person whose habit is to be slothful or lazy.

33 The descriptor עָצֵל, 'lazy, sluggish (<*עצל), occurs only in Proverbs (6.6, 9; 10.26; 13.4; 15.19; 19.24; 20.4; 21.25; 22.13; 24.30; 26.13). The latter text describes the sluggard as one who makes excuses not to work, loves to lie in bed, is too lazy even to feed himself, and thinks himself wiser than seven sages. Clearly, work is not an option for him.

34 Speaking to Israel following the exodus, Yahweh says he had 'crushed their spirit with hard labour (עָמָל) and brought them down with no one to help them'.

35 This vocable is found only here in Psalms and in this construction with בּוֹנָיו ('they labour in its building') bears the nuance of great difficulty in its construction and, in the end, its futility.

4

Labour of Love: The Theology of Work in First and Second Thessalonians

JOHN TAYLOR

Introduction

Given the importance of work to human life, finding a biblical approach to work is of vital importance. But Miroslav Volf argues in his 1995 book *Work in the Spirit* that it is a mistake to try to formulate a theology of work by starting with the biblical data which discusses work. The Bible, and especially the New Testament, simply does not contain enough material directly on work successfully to undergird a theology of work.[1] It is true that a fully orbed systematic theology of work cannot only be based on the explicit biblical data concerning work, but must set work in the wider context of biblical Christian theology. We should be grateful for the careful and theologically rich way in which Volf has addressed the topic, but we should not underestimate the extent, value, and significance of the biblical data, which is not, of course, limited to that discovered by a concordance search or a word study.[2] It is rare that biblical scholars concern themselves with elucidating a biblical view of work, but there is far more relevant material than is sometimes recognized, and we are helped by the increased volume of research being produced on the social, archaeological, and economic setting of biblical literature. Our limited goal in this chapter is to look at the evidence of two of Paul's letters which are most concerned with work: 1 and 2 Thessalonians. These letters, particularly the first, focus on work more than any other letters in the Pauline corpus, and in a far-from-incidental manner. There is evidence that Paul intended to make work one of the key threads in his argument.

Until recently, there has been something of a consensus that the problem of work – or the lack of it – in the church at Thessalonica was due to eschatological enthusiasm, a misguided expectation of the immediate return of Christ, which led to people abandoning their proper work, there being no need to prepare for the future.[3] Both Thessalonian letters do display a lively expectation of the return of the Messiah.

The traditional scenario, however, is implausible for several reasons. First, it is highly doubtful, at least in regard to 1 Thessalonians, that there was a serious problem with an overly enthusiastic eschatology in Thessalonica. It is true that they were alive to the possibility that Jesus would return in their own lifetime. But Paul does not correct this as a mistaken belief. Instead, the first letter to the Thessalonians seems to reveal a loss, for some at least, of eschatological hope, especially in regard to the situation of those believers who have died. Hope is the last element in the triad of faith, love, and hope in 1.3, and therefore likely the one with most significance for the recipients of the letter, much as in 1 Corinthians 13.13, where love as the last element in the triad is the most significant in the argument there. The Thessalonians began with faith, love, *and* hope (1 Thess. 1.3), but they are commended later only for their continuing faith and love (3.6). Though they are exhorted repeatedly to grow further in both faith (3.10; 5.8) and love (3.12; 4.10; 5.8), the loss of hope is even more significant. Paul does not want them to be distressed like outsiders who have no hope (4.13). They are rather to comfort one another in view of the coming resurrection (4.18). They are told to put on hope, the hope of salvation as a helmet, because they were appointed not for wrath but for salvation through Christ, at his return (5.9–11). There is also the distinct possibility that an eschatological carelessness has crept in. Calls to holiness in the letter are based on the expectation of the *parousia* and the judgement that awaits (3.13; 4.6; 5.23). Paul insists: 'Let us not sleep, like others do, but let us watch and be sober' (5.6). The warning in 2 Thessalonians not to believe reports that the Lord had already returned is based on the possibility of a false teaching coming in, through pseudonymous letter, or false prophecy, claiming that the Lord had already returned (2 Thess. 2.1–2). Paul makes the point that other apocalyptic events had to take place first (2.3–8). But he also tells them (2.2) not to be shaken (σαλευθῆναι) or alarmed (θροεῖσθαι). Both these terms indicate not excitement but distress and alarm, and so even here Paul is not addressing eschatological enthusiasm.[4]

Second, the traditional scenario envisages people *leaving* work; therefore, they would be those who were already working, who had to work for their living. They would not be the rich, who had property and passive income, nor clients, who did not have to work but were provided for in daily distributions by rich patrons, nor slaves, who had no choice but to work. Most people in the cities of the early empire lived in vulnerable and tenuous economic conditions. Labourers were usually paid daily. It was difficult to store food. In these conditions, any ordinary people who gave up work, expecting to survive until the Lord returned, would be quickly disabused of their presumptions. A workless period of eschatological enthusiasm would be unlikely to last long; certainly not for the months it took for Paul to write his second letter to the church, addressing the same practice of idleness. Paul in a later letter singles out the Macedonian churches, which would include the Thessalonians, as experiencing real poverty (2 Cor. 8.2), especially by comparison to Corinth, where we are informed that at least some people in the gathering are wise humanly speaking, powerful or well-born, implying wealth. Few people in the Thessalonian church would have food reserves sufficient to enable survival for months without doing any work, or the financial reserves repeatedly to buy food other people produced.

Third, Paul nowhere makes any particular connection between imminentist belief and the problem of idleness.[5] Rather, his argument against idleness is largely made on moral and missional grounds, as we shall see below. If anything, it is more likely that eschatological carelessness contributes to the problem of idleness in Thessalonica than does eschatological enthusiasm. It is possible that the older imminentist scenario was overinfluenced by the spectacle of nineteenth-century millenarian movements where people abandoned work and possessions in anticipation of the Lord's return on a particular date.

Fourth, there are other possible explanations for the problem Paul is addressing, which shall be discussed below. A better overall approach, though, is to place the warnings against idleness within the broader discussion of work that inhabits the Thessalonian letters. The approach here is briefly to examine in turn the main passages, which concern work to find out whether there are common threads that allow the reader to start to develop a coherent theology of work. It will be argued that Paul's main thrust is to picture work as an act of love. In so doing he is adopting the kind of approach he also takes in Romans 12, 1 Corinthians 12—14, and Galatians 5, which places love at the centre of ethical reflection – love which has the key place in the world-in-waiting, both in Christ and through the Spirit.

1 Thessalonians 1.1–3

The main body of the first letter to the Thessalonians is bracketed by the triad of faith, love, and hope (1.3; 5.8). At the beginning of the letter, Paul recalls and celebrates the Thessalonians' early experience in Christ in terms of this triad. At the close of the body of the letter, Paul defines the response he expects from his readers in terms of the same triad: putting on the breastplate of faith and love, as well as the helmet of the hope of salvation (5.8). It has been suggested that the triad provides an outline for the entire letter,[6] but even if this is unlikely, faith, love, and hope are prominent throughout.[7] The same triad is also found elsewhere in a number of passages, most of them in the Pauline corpus,[8] and many commentators see the triad as a summary of the essence of Christian life or existence.[9] For Collins, 'eschatological existence ... is an existence in faith, love and hope'.[10] Such a claim could be made more strongly on the basis of 1 Corinthians 13.13, but it is likely that the Thessalonians also would have read Paul in this way. Concerning the origin of the triad, all the non-Pauline references 'are clearly later than Paul', making it 'possible that Paul himself is its creator',[11] despite the common suggestion that it reflects pre-Pauline tradition.[12] Given that this is likely to be the earliest of Paul's letters that we have access to, we may be seeing the triad in its first formulation, much as we see the early and unelaborated use of the Pauline greeting formula, 'Grace to you and peace' (in 1.1).

But it is the other triad in verse 3 which has received comparatively little attention, even though the work, labour, and endurance of the Thessalonian believers are the actual objects of Paul's thankful remembrance. We may ask why Paul is interested in these aspects of the Thessalonians' experience. Why is it these things that Paul celebrates? If faith, love, and hope are constitutive of eschatological existence in Christ, then work, labour, and endurance seem for Paul to be intrinsic to Christian experience. But unlike his use of the language of faith, love, and hope, which he repeats in varying forms in other letters, Paul nowhere else repeats the triad of work, labour, and endurance; it has particular relevance for the Thessalonians. In other words, verse 3 is far from a generic pre-formulation mildly adjusted for the Thessalonians, even though the unwarranted tendency to dwell on the possibility of 'faith, love, and hope' being a pre-Pauline expression has led to the disregarding of the true significance of this verse. The point is that work, labour, and endurance are just as much Paul's focus in this document as the more lofty-sounding faith, love, and hope, and this is confirmed later in the letter, where Paul repeatedly returns to the topic of work in various ways.

How are the two triads related to one another? How do work, labour, and endurance relate to faith, love, and hope? Most commentators, and rightly so in my opinion, see the genitive relationships (τοῦ ἔργου τῆς πίστεως καὶ τοῦ κόπου τῆς ἀγάπης καὶ τῆς ὑπομονῆς τῆς ἐλπίδος) as indicating source or origin: work, labour, and endurance derive from faith, love, and hope.[13] But to what does the triad of work, labour, and endurance, with its modifiers, refer? Commentators vary at this point, especially on the first two elements. Most discussion concerns the first element, the 'work of faith' (τοῦ ἔργου τῆς πίστεως), because of abiding interest in the relationship of faith to works, particularly in Romans, Galatians, and Philippians. Here (and in the similar expression in 2 Thess. 1.11) nothing in the context suggests that Paul is addressing the issue of the law and faith, or comparing 'works of the law' with faith in Christ as, say, in Galatians 2.16. The use of the singular ἔργον makes it unlikely that simply 'deeds' of any kind are in view.

Malherbe thinks that the triad points to the Thessalonians' strenuous preaching of the gospel, in light of 1.5–10, where the 'preaching and reception of the word' is discussed, and especially verse 8, where the word of the Lord and faith of the Thessalonian believers are described as going out into the surrounding region.[14] Paul in this letter (2.9; 5.12–13) and elsewhere (1 Cor. 3.13, 15; 16.16; 2 Cor. 11.23; Eph. 4.12; Col. 1.29) emphasizes the nature of Christian ministry and proclamation as work and labour, and the expression in 1.3 would certainly include that. But in view of the frequent references to working for a living in the letter, more than gospel ministry is included here, and it is unlikely in any case that Paul would distinguish starkly between his work as a tentmaker and his work as an apostle. The kind of sacred versus secular or 'bi-vocational' division which is presently common does not make an appearance in Paul.

Fee takes 'work of faith' as 'probably Christian service', work directed towards Christ, and 'labour of love' as 'probably manual labour', work done in love for others.[15] Green takes 'work of faith' as equivalent to 'good works' towards all, whereas 'labour of love' signifies strenuous action on behalf of other believers.[16] Wanamaker sees 'work of faith' as the 'Christian lifestyle that distinguished [the Thessalonians] from the pagans', while their labour of love was possibly their acts of love towards other believers living in Macedonia.[17] But these explanations neglect the fact that the difference, if any, between the 'work of faith' and the 'labour of love' is not so much in the outcome but the source. And the stylized nature of the overlaying of the two triads, along with the juxtaposition of work and labour (ἔργον and κόπος), suggests that the expressions 'work of faith', 'labour of love', and 'endurance of hope' are not to be strongly contrasted but treated as near-synonymous, with the contribution of κόπος emphasizing the nature of work as toil, and ὑπομονή its duration.

Κόπος can mean 'trouble', as well as labour or toil, and the use of ὑπομονή, 'endurance', following may suggest that sense as appropriate. But although the Thessalonians have undoubtedly had their troubles (1.6; 2.14–15), Paul uses θλίψις for their sufferings under persecution, as well as his own (3.3, 7), and we must ask whether Paul would be so eager to express thanks for trouble visited upon them, in a list which otherwise thanks God for their own actions of work and perseverance. Elsewhere, including several instances in Paul, ἔργον and κόπος, or their cognates, are brought together in synonymous fashion in discussion of work (Wis. 3.11; Sir. 6.19; 1 Cor. 4.12; 15.58; 16.16; Eph. 4.28). And in 1 Thessalonians 2.9 (and 2 Thess. 3.8; 2 Cor. 11.27), κόπος and the similar term μόχθος are brought together as a pair to emphasize the laborious nature of the work Paul was doing to support himself.[18] In the thanksgiving section in

2 Thessalonians, Paul boasts of the 'endurance and faith in the midst of all your persecutions and afflictions which you are undergoing' (2 Thess. 1.4). We do find works, labour, and endurance listed together in Revelation 2.2, and 'works and love and faith and service and endurance' in Revelation 2.19, though in those verses ἔργον is in the plural. There seems to be a common field of terms appropriate for describing the work performed in faithful endurance, the hopeful waiting of God's people who are looking for final salvation.[19]

Thus the thanks given for the triad ἔργον, κόπος, and ὑπομονή implies that Paul is reflecting on a difficult period endured by the church. Malherbe claims that the sufferings described in 1 Thessalonians (1.6; 2.2; 3.3–5) leading up to Timothy's mission, whether for Paul or the church, were not the result of persecution or outward trouble, but are inner struggles, whether because of 'Paul's own "internal distress", the knowledge of which may upset the young believers',[20] or, for the Thessalonians, 'the distress and anguish of heart experienced by persons who broke with their past as they received the gospel'.[21] We may acknowledge the likelihood that social dislocation and distress might add to the pressure on the young church. But the account in Acts 17 describes persecution in the early days of the church in Thessalonica, and this letter was not written all that long after the church was begun. Marcus Bockmuehl has highlighted the sixth-century account of Malalas of Antioch, who describes a persecution taking place in Judaea in the year 48/49, which, although a late testimony, may help also to reinforce the historical accuracy of the Thessalonian persecution, mentioned alongside the Judaean persecution in 2.14–15.[22] Further evidence of the reality of persecution taking place in Thessalonica comes from 2 Thessalonians 1.4: 'Therefore, among God's churches we boast about your perseverance and faith in all the persecutions and trials you are enduring.'

I suggest, then, that Paul's thanksgiving, functioning as so often to introduce themes which will appear later in the letter, is written to a church that has suffered and is in need of encouragement that the path it began was no mistake, despite the early departure of the apostle. Their life as believers has consisted of work, labour, and endurance, and Paul encourages them that this is consistent with and derives from the eschatological nature of their life in Christ, a life of faith, love, and hope as they wait for the Son of God from heaven. There is no contradiction between the faith, love, and hope which constitute and define their existence in Christ, and their experience of work, labour, and endurance. On the contrary: work, labour, and endurance are the necessary outcome and demonstration of their faith, love, and hope in the Lord Jesus Christ. And in a letter filled with reminders of what the Thessalonian church had experienced and learned from their conversion onwards, it is of particular interest in interpreting later portions of the letter that not only does Paul remind them of the work that derives from faith, and the endurance that derives from hope in the Lord Jesus, but also of the labour and toil that derives from love.

1 Thessalonians 2.8–9

Discussion of 1 Thessalonians 2.1–12 has focused on genre. By describing his virtuous behaviour in Thessalonica, was Paul defending himself against already-voiced accusations? He may be responding to charges of being a false prophet,[23] or of being a money-grubbing glory-seeking sophist, such as in the similar defence he mounts for working to support himself in 2 Corinthians 11.7–15. He may have been making an ethos appeal (of the kind described in Acts 20.33–35, where he recounts his working practices in Ephesus), perhaps to contrast himself with disreputable travelling sophists, without having any particular accusations made against him.[24] Or he may have been reminding them of his way of life, as a model to imitate, as he mentions explicitly in the similar passage in the second letter (2 Thess. 3.7–9; cf. 1 Thess. 1.6; 1 Cor. 4.16; 11.1). The confidence that the Thessalonians retain in Paul, as reported by Timothy (1 Thess. 3.6), and the tone of the letter, suggests that he was not under sustained attack, but he does feel the need to explain his absence, and to remind the church of the way of life which he practised among them, and so perhaps some combination of the above is to be preferred. Paul's overall paraenetic purpose in 2.1–12 is to affirm the validity of his readers' faith in the gospel by establishing the integrity of the messenger. Paul is emphasizing his integrity as an apostle whose word was received and believed.

Much of the letter is filled with reminders of what the Thessalonians ought to have kept in mind. In 2.6 he says that his lifestyle among them was not a cover for greed. In 2.9 he reminds them of the labour and toil of Paul and his companions. They worked for their own living while in Thessalonica, so as not to be a burden to anyone. The participle ἐργαζόμενοι is a temporal modifier of the aorist ἐκηρύξαμεν, so that Paul's 'labour and toil' was not simply his hard work in supporting himself, but in particular *preaching the gospel* while working night and day not to be a burden to anyone. Paul wants the Thessalonians to remember his preaching in the context in which it was given. Communication of the gospel is mentioned four times in the passage (vv. 2, 4, 8, 9). The issue is the financial and ethical credibility of Paul and his companions as apostles of Christ, in the preaching of the gospel of God.

Just how does his preaching while working to support himself establish his integrity, and how might that reveal aspects of his theology of work?

First, self-support is opposed to flattery, greed, and seeking financial rewards through gaining honour (2.5–6). In a world trammelled by self-seeking teachers of philosophy,[25] and clients sponging off patrons, in which love of money was pervasive (1 Tim. 3.3; 6.10; Heb. 13.5), work was for Paul the arena to live out and demonstrate his genuineness. Second, Paul saw no contradiction between his self-supporting labour, and the preaching of the gospel. The phrase 'working night and day' may be some-what hyperbolic, but the genitive nouns indicate the kind of time when Paul was working, not the length of time.[26] The language of 2.9 means that his preaching was contemporaneous with his work; it was the arena for his proclamation of the good news. His customers, suppliers, market neighbours, and even perhaps fellow guild members would have provided a steady stream of potential converts – some at least of the recipients of the letter were the 'you' whom Paul evangelized while working.

Third, Paul explains that the motive of his self-support was to avoid being a financial burden to anyone. The term used here, ἐπιβαρέω, is one of a group of terms which Paul uses on the several occasions when he insists that he will not become a burden to others.[27] Elsewhere it can also be used in regard to financial burdens.[28] The prefixed ἐπι- seems to be an intensifier, indicating *overburdening* someone. The passage here accepts that there was an obligation on the Thessalonians, or some of them, to provide for Paul if necessary, though we are not told explicitly why such an obligation would exist.[29] It may have been simply a function of the common practice of providing hospitality, even to strangers, though that obligation did not usually require the provision of hospitality for extended periods.[30] The obligation could derive from Jesus's instructions, as under-stood by Paul, that 'those who proclaim the gospel should get their living by the gospel' (1 Cor. 9.14), which is the basis of the 'right not to work' that Paul identifies in 1 Corinthians 9.9–18, a right which he claims not to use (cf. also Acts 20.34–35), though he did accept support from believers *outside* the cities where he was working (2 Cor. 11.7–9; Phil. 4.16–18).

The obligation to provide hospitality could be a significant burden, especially to those who were poor.[31] Paul sometimes stayed with wealth-ier believers, as with Gaius in Corinth (Rom. 16.23), but here he shows awareness of the cost that housing a guest could impose. Further, Paul explains his decision to work for his living as motivated by love. The γάρ in 1 Thessalonians 2.9 is illustrative. The work of Paul and his companions exemplified or demonstrated the truth of the claim made in verse 8, where he says, 'Having in this manner [i.e. the affection of a nursing mother for her children, v. 7] such an affection for you, we were pleased to share with you not only the gospel of God but also our own selves, because you were beloved to us.' 'Beloved' here translates ἀγαπητοί. Work, especially work as self-support, was for Paul an act of love. As unlikely as it may sound to modern ears, he was a church leader who wanted his people to give less. His working for money did not derive from selfishness – quite the opposite. It ensured that he was not a burden on others. It was the practice of love.

1 Thessalonians 4.9–12

Paul recognizes the Thessalonians' love in 1.3 and again in 3.6. In 3.12 he prays for their love to increase, both for each other and for all. In 4.9 he exalts their love in lofty terms, using the figure of speech known as paralipsis. He says that their love is something which need not be written about, directly before writing about it.[32] 'You yourselves are taught by God to love one another, for indeed you are doing so towards all the brothers in the whole of Macedonia.' In 4.10 he urges them to abound all the more in that love for one another and for all. Thus, he is saying to them: 'You do love; love more.' In the same sentence he urges them to follow what he had previously commanded them – that is, to aspire to live quietly, look after their own affairs, and to work with their own hands. Once again, then, contextually Paul is associating love with work. Grammatically the connection between love and work here is not absolute; the καί ('and') at the start of 4.11 followed by the infinitive verb may indicate simply a second characteristic which Paul is urging upon his readers. But the way the sentence starts with the thematic subject of love, the alliterative use of φιλαδελφία and φιλοτιμεῖσθαι, and the goal of walking properly before outsiders (4.12) tie this long sentence together. As in 3.12, they are to love one another and those outside, and here, they are to do so through the way they work.

In the light of what Paul already said in chapter 2, the exhortation to work as an act of love, for one another and for all, should be seen as an instruction to the church to work so as to be self-supporting, in the manner that Paul was, so as not to be a burden on others. This is confirmed by the last clause in verse 12: 'that you should have no need of anyone' (taking μηδενός as masculine, not neuter). Love for all meant maintaining the credible witness of their lifestyle. Believers through self-supporting work will live in a seemly manner before outsiders. There is evidence of public disdain for those who begged,[33] or those clients who relied on rich patrons for their food, visiting them every morning for a formal greeting, and to receive handouts of food or money.[34]

The three ambitions or aspirations of verse 11 have presented challenges to interpreters. The commands to live quietly and tend to one's own affairs have frequently been interpreted as the requirement to withdraw from political life, not in the sense of abandoning civic life altogether, but to maintain a low profile, especially where persecution is a reality.[35] But the verb ἡσυκάζω, which usually means to stay quiet, can sometimes signify resting, as in Luke 23.56, which says that the women who had come to prepare the body of Jesus 'rested on the Sabbath, according to the commandment'.[36] It is intriguing to speculate whether Paul is telling his readers both to rest and to work. In the light of the warning against disorderliness or idleness in 5.14, and the similar warning in 2 Thessalonians 3.6, along with the strictures there against being busybodies, it seems there were some who were causing trouble in the city, having the spare time to do so, either because they were supported by wealthy patrons or perhaps because the church was supporting them. Paul told them to look after their own affairs. Πράσσειν τὰ ἴδια is likely to mean to take care of one's own financial affairs or occupation.[37]

Paul also insisted that they work with their hands. There is evidence of disdain among the elite of Graeco-Roman society, including some philosophers, for manual labour. Aristotle, envisaging an ideal city, considered manual labour to be necessary for the maintenance of the state, but a hindrance to virtue. Only those who did not work with their hands had the leisure to study and attain virtue, and so only these should be citizens involved in government:

> The citizens must not live a mechanic or a mercantile life for such a life is ignoble and inimical to virtue, nor yet must those who are to be citizens in the best state be tillers of the soil, for leisure is needed both for the development of virtue and for active participation in politics.[38]

Cicero says:

> The callings of hired labourers, and of all who are paid for their mere work and not for skill, are ungenteel and vulgar; for their wages are given for menial service ... Those who buy to sell again as soon as they can are to be accounted as vulgar ... Least of all can we speak well of the trades that minister to sensual pleasures; 'Fishmongers, butchers, cooks, poulterers, and fishermen', as Terence says. Add, if you please, to this list perfumers, ballet-dancers, and the whole tribe of dice-players ... Commerce, if on a small scale, is to be regarded as vulgar; but if large and rich, importing much from all quarters, and making extensive sales without fraud, it is not so very discreditable ... . nothing is better than agriculture, nothing more productive, nothing more pleasant, nothing more worthy of a man of liberal mind.[39]

Plutarch comments:

> When we are pleased with the work, we slight and set little by the work-
> man or artist himself, as for instance, in perfumes and purple dyes, we
> are taken with the things themselves well enough, but do not think dyers
> and perfumers otherwise than low and sordid people. It was not said
> amiss by Antisthenes, when people told him that one Ismenias was an
> excellent piper. 'It may be so,' said he, 'but he is but a wretched human
> being, otherwise he would not have been an excellent piper.'[40]

This is often contrasted with a less delicate Jewish attitude to manual
work. Some rabbis at least approved of artisan occupations, as in the
Mishnah we read, from a fourth-generation Tannaim (c. AD 140–65):

> Rabbi Meir said: Let a man always teach his son a cleanly and a light
> trade; and let him pray to Him whose are wealth and riches; for there
> is no trade which has not both poverty and riches, and neither does
> poverty come from the trade nor yet riches, but everything according to
> one's deserving.

Philo exalts labour, which, although it exists because of sin in the world
(*Leg. Alleg.*, 1.25), is not only necessary for survival (*De opificio mundi*,
1.167), but is the occasion of moral improvement:

> But labour is the enemy of laziness, as it is in reality the first and greatest
> of good things, and wages an irreconcilable war against pleasure; for,
> if we must declare the truth, God has made labour the foundation of
> all good and of all virtue to man, and without labour you will not find
> a single good thing in existence among the race of men. (*De sacrificiis*,
> 1.35)

But this apparent Jewish/Gentile distinction is by no means universal.
The Hellenistic Jewish writer Ben Sirach, though he like the Greeks and
Romans acknowledged the need for manual occupations (at least those
which were not inherently bad), thought manual workers too concerned
with their occupations to have the understanding of the law and of the
world necessary to be able to govern: 'Without them [i.e. manual workers]
no city can be inhabited, and wherever they live, they will not go hungry.
Yet they are not sought out for the council of the people' (Sir. 38.32).
Wisdom only comes with a life of leisure: 'How can one become wise who
handles the plough?' (Sir. 38.25).

On the other side, the Greek orator Dio Chrysostom saw manual work
as fitting for free men who wished to escape poverty:

Now so much for the life of the farmer, the hunter, and the shepherd. Perhaps I have spent more time on this theme than I should have done, but I desired to show in some way or other that poverty is no hopeless impediment to a life and existence befitting free men who are willing to work with their hands, but leads them on to deeds and actions that are far better and more useful and more in accordance with nature than those to which riches are wont to attract most men.[41]

The majority of the people the church was connected to were not the wealthy, but poor or middle-income working people. For Paul, manual work was enabling not demeaning.

We are not told why some were not working. As we have seen, it is unlikely to be eschatological enthusiasm. Bruce Winter suggests that suffering due to famine may have lain behind some of the issues in the Thessalonian letters.[42] Hunger pushed believers into seeking a patron to feed them, whether a wealthy church member or a non-believer, and the client could repay this provision by offering political support in the polis. There is some uncertainty that personal patronage, on the scale Winter envisages, was as significant a factor in a largely Greek city like Thessalonica, as it was in Rome, or Roman colonies like Corinth or Philippi. There certainly was a developed system of patronage in the first-century Roman world. Personal patronage involving the daily distribution of money was largely a phenomenon of the educated Romans.[43] Wealthy and influential people would act as patrons to their clients, or followers, dispensing favours and financial benefactions in return for loyalty and service. But Roman influence in Thessalonica was strong, even though it was a free city. Thessalonica was the capital of the Roman province of Macedonia, where Roman governors and other officials lived. The head of the city council 'served as the high priest in the cult of Augustus'.[44]

The gospel was counter to the hierarchical distinctions prevalent in the culture. In Paul's vision, this hierarchical and stratified community is transformed into a community of love, living with mutual obligation and care. It is possible that the practice of giving and care for the poor, including regular common meals, such as is seen in Acts 2—6, 1 Corinthians 10—11, and 2 Corinthians 8—9, made it possible for believers who were in need to find help in their church community. Perhaps it also allowed them to become continually dependent on that help. Paul expected believers to work hard to provide for themselves rather than to seek the indulgence of wealthy patrons, or even the patronage of the church, in a way that brought the church into disrepute. The point was not to meet outsiders' expectations in every possible way, but was to act in a manner appropriate to the gospel and its credibility, and consistent with their God-taught love for one another.

1 Thessalonians 5.12–14

The double use of 'brothers' (ἀδελφοί, 5.12, 14) along with the two first-person-plural requests with synonymous verbs ('Now we ask you', ἐρωτῶμεν δὲ ὑμᾶς; 'Now we urge you', παρακαλοῦμεν δὲ ὑμᾶς) signals not only a change of subject matter but the transition to the final set of exhortations in the letter. The two requests (5.12–13, 14) are united also by the repetition of νουθετέω ('admonish'), and by the contrast made between hard-working leaders and some people who are idle. Verse 11, beginning with διό παρακαλεῖτε ἀλλήλους, concludes the section on the resurrection of believers at the *parousia* which started in 5.1, much as the ὥστε παρακαλεῖτε ἀλλήλους in 4.18 concludes the section on preparedness for the *parousia* which started in 4.13. The effect of this context, along with the concluding prayer in 5.23 which mentions the *parousia*, is that the exhortations of 5.12–22 have an eschatological focus. That is, in view of the return of Christ, this is how the Thessalonians are to live. Thus, again we can see that the working habits of the church are meant to be motivated by the second coming of Christ; quite the opposite of the view of some that enthusiastic eschatological expectation led to idleness.

A single Greek article governing three participles is used in 5.12 to let the readers know that 'those who labour among you, are over you in the Lord, and admonish you' are, at least largely, the same group. All three participles are present tense, the imperfective aspect indicating the ongoing nature of the activities. The significance of work is again addressed: the church is urged to acknowledge their spiritual leaders because of their labour (κοπιάω) and work (ἔργον). Indeed, the church is to 'regard them very highly in love' (ἡγεῖσθαι αὐτοὺς ὑπερεκπερισσοῦ ἐν ἀγάπη) because of their work.[45] Paul is not condemning church leaders to a life of mere busyness or constant activity. Rather, as some in the community are avoiding work, as is briefly indicated in 5.14, he is setting forth those who work hard as examples to the community. These are the leaders who are worthy of honour.[46] And by calling for this honour Paul reiterates his emphasis on the right view – the right value – of work and labour, in light of the return of Christ.

Honour is given to leaders who admonish the church (5.12), but the whole church is called to join in admonishment for those who are idle, while encouraging the fainthearted. As is well known, ἄτακτος (5.14) can be translated as 'unruly', particularly in regard to soldiers who did not maintain order in battle,[47] or disordered,[48] but the context, with its commendation of leaders' work, and indeed the interest in work displayed in the entire letter, selects the meaning 'idle'.[49] Far from being eschatologically overeager, some have become careless about the return of

Christ. Paul has just reminded them 'So then, let us not sleep, like others do, but let us watch and be sober' (5.6). Perhaps some wanted to continue the life of a client, or are taking advantage of the church's practice of generosity. Nevertheless, despite this apparent abuse, Paul instructs the church to continue doing good 'to one another and to all' (5.15).

2 Thessalonians 3.6–15

This letter, written about six months after the first, repeats several of the same points about work, in even stronger fashion.[50] Idle believers are not simply to be admonished, but to be avoided (2 Thess. 3.6). If they are not willing to work, they should not eat (3.10). This means at least that the offenders would be excluded from the church's gatherings, including gatherings for common meals. This also would mean exclusion from the Lord's Supper, assuming that the Thessalonian church had a similar practice to that evident in Corinth (1 Cor. 11.20–34). It is a safe assumption that the Thessalonian church had a regular common meal, given the evidence of 3.10,[51] and the discussion of meal practices in letters to several of the Pauline churches (Rom. 14.1—15.13; 1 Cor. 5.11; 10.16–21; 11.20–34; Gal. 2.11–14). Similar regulations for discipline are found at Qumran. The Community Rule prescribes punishment for lying about property ('If one of them has lied deliberately in matters of property, he shall be excluded from the pure meal of the congregation for one year and shall do penance with respect to one quarter of his food', 1QS 6.24–25). Likewise, for 'speaking in anger' against a priest: 'he shall do penance for one year and shall be excluded for his soul's sake from the pure meal of the congregation' (1QS 7.2–3). A similar kind of discipline is seen in 1 Corinthians 5.11, for immoral believers,[52] which also included a ban on association, and the church was commanded 'not even to eat with such a one'.

The avoidance would presumably be wider than the context of the assembly of the church. In 2 Thessalonians 3.14–15 the ban on association is extended to 'anyone who does not obey' the message of the letter. In both 1 Corinthians and 2 Thessalonians the intent of the punishment is restorative (1 Cor. 5.5; 2 Thess. 3.12, 15). For Paul to command this kind of action on account of someone's unwillingness to work shows how seriously he took the problem.

There also are clues in the text itself as to the theological approach Paul took to work. First, immediately before our passage, Paul has prayed for the Lord to direct the Thessalonians' hearts 'to the love of God and to the endurance of Christ' (2 Thess. 3.5). As we have seen already, notions of love and endurance have been key in Paul's discussion of work in 1 Thessalonians (e.g. 1 Thess. 1.3). It was love that led Paul to earn his own living while preaching in Thessalonica, love that laboured and endured, that would not be a burden to the community: 'With labour and toil working night and day so as not to burden any of you' (2 Thess. 3.8). This way of life was intended to set an example for all believers (2 Thess. 3.9). In other words, the Thessalonian believers were commanded to work, enduring long and hard toil, so as to be self-supporting, and this enduring labour was an act of love. To live this way required the heart's focus on the love of God and the endurance of Christ. Even if some in the church have been taking advantage of others' generosity, and have made themselves burdens to the community, Paul tells the church, 'Do not be weary in doing good.' The prohibitive subjunctive command raises the possibility that the believers had already grown weary of well-doing. Paul wanted them to renew their love for those with needs, at the same time as they disciplined idle brothers and sisters.

Second, the commands to dissociate from the idle and to work are made 'in the Lord Jesus Christ': 'Now we command you, brothers, in the name of our Lord Jesus Christ, that you keep away from any brother who is walking in idleness' (2 Thess. 3.6); 'And such people we command and urge in the Lord Jesus Christ, that working quietly they should eat their own bread' (2 Thess. 3.12). The point is that the instructions regarding work are not simply Paul's own admonishments. The attaching of the name of Jesus to the instructions not only gives them significance, but Christological weight. Everything the church does, including work, is to be done in and for the Lord Jesus Christ, as an act of faith. Paul prays that Jesus would lead the church into good work: 'For this reason we are always praying for you, that our God may make you worthy of the calling and may fulfil every desire for good and every work of faith by power' (2 Thess. 1.11). 'Now may our Lord Jesus Christ himself, and God our Father, who loved us and gave us eternal comfort and good hope by grace, comfort your hearts and establish them in every good work and word' (2 Thess. 2.16–17). The working lives of believers are not separate somehow from their religious experience, but are the place of faith and obedience to Jesus Christ, the place of response to the love of God the Father, and the place where prayer makes work a response to the grace of God.

Conclusion

We have seen that the problem of idleness in the Thessalonian church cannot simply be resolved by pointing to an extreme imminentist enthusiasm, largely because Paul himself does not point in that direction. Instead he sets his comments on idleness in the context of a broader discussion of work. The working lives of the believers are the proper place for the expression of love and faith. Work is meant to be an act of love. Paul celebrates the work, labour, and endurance of the Thessalonians as the proper products, and therefore evidence, of their faith, love, and hope in Jesus. Working to support themselves, and refusing to burden others, as Paul had set an example, is an act of love and faith, and an expression of eschatological hope. Thus, believers should, where possible, avoid dependence on a patron, particularly if avoiding labour themselves, and should refuse to abuse the generosity of the church. Rather, through humbly working with their own hands they should establish a credible witness to the surrounding community. Those who refuse to support themselves are acting counter to love and should be disciplined, even to the point of being unable to eat the church's common meal, with the hope of course of transformation and restoration.

Notes

1 Miroslav Volf, *Work in the Spirit: Toward a Theology of Work* (New York: Oxford University Press, 1991), p. 77.

2 For example, Volf only mentions two verses in Ecclesiastes (4.4, p. 121; 6.19, p. 159), a biblical book which reflects substantially on work, but he ignores, for example, Ecclesiastes 2, which focuses almost entirely on work, and which includes 2.24: 'There is nothing better for a man than to eat and drink, and cause his soul to see good in his labour', surely a reflection on human work in relation to God's creative work in Genesis 1. He also ignores most of the discussion of work in 1 Thessalonians.

3 See for example Ernest Best, *The First and Second Epistles to the Thessalonians* (London: A. & C. Black, 1972), pp. 175–8: 'Work is neglected for the future can be ignored' (p. 175). Frame has a psychologizing approach with the same frame of reference: 'Paul recognizes that the source of meddlesomeness and idleness is inward, the excitement created in the minds of some by the expectation that the day of the Lord is at hand' (James Everett Frame, *A Critical and Exegetical Commentary on the Epistles of St Paul to the Thessalonians* (Edinburgh: T. & T. Clark, 1912), pp. 161–2). Some have challenged this perspective, arguing that the idleness or disorder in Thessalonica was simply an ethical issue, and that when Paul brought eschatology and ethics together it was to show that the expectation of the *parousia* should in fact motivate holiness. See B. N. Kaye, 'Eschatology and Ethics in 1 and 2 Thessalonians', *Novum Testamentum* 17, no. 1 (1975), pp. 47–57.

4 For σαλεύω, see e.g. (LXX) Isa. 7.2; Zech. 12.2; 1 Macc. 6.44; and Acts 2.25; for θροέω, see Matt. 24.6 and Mark 13.7. Paul also describes the return of Christ in startling terms as both a day of judgement and vengeance for the persecutors of the church (1.7–9), and as a day of glory as the saints are gathered to meet him (1.10—2.1). That is, that day will be dramatic in its finality; there will be no secret return of Christ.

5 See, for example, Gene L. Green, *The Letters to the Thessalonians* (Grand

Rapids, MI: Eerdmans, 2002), p. 341; Abraham J. Malherbe, *The Letters to the Thessalonians: A New Translation with Introduction and Commentary* (New York: Doubleday, 2000), p. 253.

6 Robert W. Thurston, 'The Relationship between the Thessalonian Epistles', *Expository Times* 85, no. 2 (1973), pp. 52–6, suggests as an outline: faith, 1.1—3.11; love, 3.12—4.12; hope, 4.13—5.22. The division he advocates between 3.11 and 3.12, in the middle of a prayer, seems an attempt to force the threefold structure on to the letter.

7 ἀγάπη: 1.3; 3.6, 12; 5.8, 13. ἀγαπάω: 4.9. φιλαδεφία: 4.9. ἐλπίς: 1.3; 2.19; 4.13; 5.8.

8 Rom. 5.1–5; 1 Cor. 13.6–7, 13; Gal. 5.5–6; Col. 1.4–5; Heb. 6.10–12; 10.22–24; 1 Peter 1.3–9, possibly 1.21–22; Barnabas 1.4; 9:8; Polycarp, *Phil.* 3.2f.

9 Günther Bornkamm, *Paul*, trans. D. M. G. Stalker (New York: Harper & Row, 1971), p. 219; Willi Marxsen, *Der erste Brief an die Thessalonicher*, Zürcher Bibelkommentare. NT 11.1 (Zurich: Theologischer Verlag, 1979), p. 35; Colin R. Nicholl, *From Hope to Despair in Thessalonica: Situating 1 and 2 Thessalonians*, Society for New Testament Studies Monograph Series 126 (Cambridge: Cambridge University Press, 2004), p. 85; B. Rigaux, *Saint Paul: Les Épîtres aux Thessaloniciens*, Études Bibliques (Paris: J. Gabalda et Cie, 1956), p. 368; Thomas Söding, *Die Trias Glaube, Hoffnung, Liebe bei Paulus*, Stuttgarter Bibelstudien 150 (Stuttgart: Verlag Katholisches Bibelwerk, 1992), p. 216.

10 Raymond F. Collins, 'The Faith of the Thessalonians', *Louvain Studies* 7 (1978), pp. 249–69 (253, 267).

11 Best, *Thessalonians*, p. 67.

12 See Traugott Holtz, *Der erste Brief an die Thessalonicher*, Evangelisch–Katholischer Kommentar zum Neuen Testament (Zurich: Benziger, 1986); Franz Laub, *1. und 2. Thessalonicherbrief*, Die Neue Echter Bibel (Würzburg: Echter Verlag, 1985), p. 16; Leon Morris, *The First and Second Epistles to the Thessalonians* (London: Marshall, Morgan & Scott, 1959), p. 43; Karl Friedrich Ulrichs, *Christusglaube: Studien zum Syntagma* πίστις Χριστοῦ *und zum paulinischen Verständnis von Glaube und Rechtfertigung* (Tübingen: Mohr Siebeck, 2007), p. 71. It is not possible to say for certain that the triad began with Paul, but it is most probable, especially given Paul's demonstrated linguistic and theological creativity.

13 The other main possibility is that they are genitives of description: 'Faithful work, and loving labour, and hopeful endurance', but the meaning does not change significantly, and in view of the letter's later interest in the ongoing faith of the Thessalonian church, faith rather than faithfulness should be preferred here for πίστις.

14 Malherbe, *Thessalonians*, p. 108.

15 Gordon D. Fee, *The First and Second Letters to the Thessalonians* (Grand Rapids, MI: Eerdmans, 2009), p. 26.

16 Green, *Thessalonians*, p. 90.

17 Charles A. Wanamaker, *The Epistles to the Thessalonians*, The New International Greek Testament Commentary (Exeter: Paternoster Press, 1990), p. 75.

18 When κόπος and πόνος are brought together as a syntagm, the emphasis is on trouble and strife (Job 5.6; Ps. 10.7 [9.28, LXX], 90.10 [89.10, LXX]).

19 See 4 Macc. 17.4: τὴν ἐλπίδα τῆς ὑπομονῆς βεβαίαν ἔχουσα πρὸς τὸν θεόν ('bravely maintaining with God the hope of endurance'); Rom. 5.3–5; 8.24–25; 15.4–5; Gal. 5.5–6; James 1.3–4.

20 Malherbe, 'Conversion to Paul's Gospel', in Abraham J. Malherbe, Frederick W. Norris, and James W. Thompson (eds), *The Early Church in its Context: Essays*

in Honor of Everett Ferguson (Boston: Brill, 1998), p. 236; Malherbe, *Thessalonians*, p. 193. This view is found in St John Chrysostom, *Homilies on First Thessalonians*, 3.3.3, where he claims that 'the temptations of the teachers trouble their disciples', and 'they are not so much troubled at their own temptations, as at those of their teachers', and in von Dobschütz, though he saw θλίψις in Paul as always referring to tribulations, not so much internal anguish (Ernst von Dobschütz, *Die Thessalonicher-Briefe* (Göttingen: Vandenhoeck & Ruprecht, 1974), p. 134. See also Holtz, *Der erste Brief an die Thessalonicher*, p. 127). Best thinks that the sufferings of both Paul and the Thessalonians are in view, on the basis of the first-person plurals of 3.3–4 (*Thessalonians*, p. 135). Likewise Lightfoot interprets, 'in the midst of these afflictions which befall us and you alike' (J. B. Lightfoot, *Notes on Epistles of St Paul* (London: MacMillan, 1895), p. 42). Neil thinks that these troubles are 'in this case not Paul's troubles – the new converts needed someone to strengthen them' (William Neil, *The Epistle of Paul to the Thessalonians* (London: Hodder & Stoughton, 1950), p. 63).

21 Abraham J. Malherbe, *Paul and the Thessalonians: The Philosophic Tradition of Pastoral Care* (Philadelphia: Fortress Press, 1987), p. 48.

22 Bockmuehl is assiduous in not giving the account too much historical certitude, but he suggests that there is little reason for such a tale to be manufactured (Marcus Bockmuehl, '1 Thessalonians 2:14–16 and the Church in Jerusalem', *Tyndale Bulletin* 52, no. 1 (2001), p. 23).

23 William Horbury, '1 Thessalonians 2:3 as Rebutting Charges of False Prophecy', *Journal of Theological Studies* 33 (1982), pp. 492–508, and *Jews and Christians in Contact and Controversy* (Edinburgh: T. & T. Clark, 1998), pp. 14–16, and cf. Jeffrey A. D. Weima, 'An Apology for the Apologetic Function of 1 Thessalonians 2:1–12', *Journal for the Study of the New Testament* 68 (1997), pp. 73–99.

24 The language Paul uses is similar to that found in defending charges made against Graeco-Roman philosophers. For the idea that Paul is not defending against accusation but deliberately distancing himself from comparison to the Sophists, see Abraham J. Malherbe, '"Gentle as a Nurse": The Cynic Background to 1 Thess ii', *Novum Testamentum* 12 (1970), p. 205, who writes that Paul is presenting himself as an example: 'It is understandable that the genuine philosophic missionary would want to distinguish himself from other types without his having explicitly been accused of acting like a particular type'; and Bruce W. Winter, 'The Entries and Ethics of Orators and Paul (1 Thessalonians 2:1–12)', *Tyndale Bulletin* 44, no. 1 (1993), pp. 55–74.

25 See Bruce W. Winter, *Philo and Paul among the Sophists: Alexandrian and Corinthian Responses to a Julio–Claudian Movement*, 2nd edition (Grand Rapids, MI: Eerdmans, 2002), pp. 91–4, 166–9.

26 See Daniel B. Wallace, *Greek Grammar Beyond the Basics: An Exegetical Syntax of the New Testament* (Grand Rapids, MI: Zondervan, 1996), p. 124.

27 Ἐπιβαρέω: 1 Thess. 2.9; 2 Thess. 3.8 (though the range of the word is not limited to financial burdens: e.g. 2 Cor. 1.8; Josephus, *Ant.*, 15.55); its cognates βαρέω (2 Cor. 5.4; 1 Tim. 5.16) and καταβαρέω (2 Cor. 12.16); καταναρκάω (2 Cor. 11.9; 12:13, 14).

28 Josephus, *War*, 2.273; Appian, *Civil Wars*, 3.2.17, 4.5.31.

29 Verse 6 may hint at the possibility that apostles could demand financial support.

30 See Andrew E. Arterbury, *Entertaining Angels: Early Christian Hospitality in its Mediterranean Setting* (Sheffield: Sheffield Phoenix, 2005), pp. 94–7.

31 That is why later Christians legislated limits to the provision of hospitality for extended periods. See *Didache*, 11.3–6.

32 The περὶ δέ of 4.9 makes it possible that Paul is responding to a question the Thessalonians have communicated.

33 Dio Chrysostom (*Or.* 32.9) excoriates 'these Cynics, posting themselves at street-corners, in alley-ways, and at temple-gates, pass round the hat and play upon the credulity of lads and sailors and crowds of that sort, stringing together rough jokes and much tittle-tattle and that low badinage that smacks of the marketplace. Accordingly they achieve no good at all, but rather the worst possible harm, for they accustom thoughtless people to deride philosophers in general, just as one might accustom lads to scorn their teachers, and, when they ought to knock the insolence out of their hearers, these Cynics merely increase it.'

34 Juvenal, *Satires*, III.126–70.

35 Wanamaker, *The Epistles to the Thessalonians*, p. 163; Bruce W. Winter, *Seek the Welfare of the City: Christians as Benefactors and Citizens, First Century Christians in the Graeco-Roman World* (Grand Rapids, MI: Eerdmans, 1994), p. 48.

36 καὶ τὸ μὲν σάββατον ἡσύχασαν κατὰ τὴν ἐντολήν. See also Philo, Quod deus sit immutabilis 1.38; Quis rerum divinarum heres sit 1.13.

37 In Prov. 11.24, and Luke 18.28, τὰ ἴδια indicates finances or occupation. In Luke 19.28, πράσσω is used in the context of handling money.

38 Aristotle, *Politics*, 1328b.

39 Cicero, *On Duties*, 1.42 (44 BC). The exception of farming from the list of disreputable manual occupations exempts wealthy Romans whose incomes derived from agriculture from Cicero's criticism.

40 Plutarch, *Lives*, 'Pericles', 1.1.4–5.

41 Dio Chrysostom, 7.103.

42 Bruce W. Winter, '"If a Man Does Not Wish to Work..." A Cultural and Historical Setting for 2 Thessalonians 3:6–16', *Tyndale Bulletin* 40, no. 2 (1989), pp. 309–12.

43 Erlend D. MacGillivray, 'Re-evaluating Patronage and Reciprocity in Antiquity and New Testament Studies', *Journal of Greco–Roman Christianity and Judaism*, 6 (2009), p. 43, despite Peter Garnsey and Greg Woolf, 'Patronage of the Rural Poor in the Roman World', in *Patronage in Ancient Society*, ed. Andrew Wallace-Hadrill (London: Routledge, 1989).

44 Green, *Thessalonians*, p. 24.

45 Ascough notes, 'It is likely that the leaders at Thessalonica continued with both kinds of activity, manual labour alongside community members and the labour of community formation' (Richard S. Ascough, 'The Thessalonian Christian Community as a Professional Voluntary Association', *Journal of Biblical Literature* 119, no. 2 (2000), p. 318). Ascough's larger point, that the Thessalonian church was a voluntary association of workers in the same trade as Paul, is however a stretch too far. It is based on what Ascough himself notes is a presumption: 'Presumably Paul and the Thessalonians worked at the same trade, or at least trades within the same general area, thus facilitating contact between Paul and the Thessalonians. And it was while at work that Paul preached the gospel and presumably made his initial converts. Thus, the core of the Thessalonian community comprised handworkers who shared Paul's trade' (Ascough, 'Voluntary Association', p. 315). But while this is interesting speculation, there is nothing in the letters or the account in Acts 17 that lends it support.

46 See Green, *Thessalonians*, pp. 248–51.

47 Josephus, *Ant.*, 15.150, 152; *War*, 1.101, 1.382.

48 Philo, *De Agr.* 74; *De Abr.* 151.

49 Frederick Danker, Walter Bauer, William Arndt, and Wilbur Gingrich, *Greek-English Lexicon of the New Testament and Other Early Christian Literature*, 3rd edition (Chicago: University of Chicago Press, 2000), sv. ἄτακτος. The cognate verb ἀτακτέω, though it most often is used to describe disorder on the battlefield, is also used for those who refused to fight. Demosthenes (*Olynthiacs*, 3.11) complains of laws which grant impunity to those who will not line up alongside (οἱ δὲ τοὺς ἀτακτοῦντας ἀθῴους καθιστᾶσιν) their fellows to serve in the war (Demosthenes, *Olynthiacs I–III*, ed. H. Sharpley (Edinburgh: William Blackwood & Sons, 1900), p. 67). Likewise, Lysias (*Against Alcibiades*, 1.17–18) criticizes those who avoided military service (τοὺς οὕτως ἀτακτοῦντας) because of cowardice (οὐκ ἐτόλμα μεθ' ὑμῶν μάχεσθαι: 'he did not dare not fight alongside you'). Demetrius (*On Style*, 53) uses the adverbial comparative form ἀτακτοτέρως to mean 'negligently', suggesting that good style allows, even prefers, negligence in not always matching every μεν with a contrasting δέ. The cognates in 2 Thess. 3.6, 7, 11 refer to idleness or shirking of work, as is evident from the context (see the discussion below). There is enough evidence to allow that ἄτακτος and its cognates can refer to someone who refuses to undertake difficult tasks, or is negligent in the performance of duties.

50 Despite a minor academic tradition going back to Hugo Grotius, and including Charles Wanamaker (*Thessalonians*, pp. 37–45), we can assume that this work was written subsequent to the first. Among other reasons, especially the second letter's mention of a prior epistle (2 Thess. 2.15), the discussion of idleness, in expanded and more vehement form, suits a situation where the first letter failed to elicit a satisfactory response. The 'tradition which you received from us' (2 Thess. 3.6) may include the discussions of work in 1 Thessalonians. I am assuming the Pauline authorship of 2 Thessalonians. See the discussion in Fee, *Thessalonians*, pp. 237–40, and Paul Foster, 'Who Wrote 2 Thessalonians? A Fresh Look at an Old Problem', *Journal for the Study of the New Testament* 35, no. 2 (2012), pp. 150–75.

51 Jewett says that 'the creation of the regulation required a community that was eating its meals together, for whom the willingness or unwillingness to work was a factor of sufficient importance to require regulation, and in which the power to deprive members of food was in fact present' (Robert Jewett, 'Tenement Churches and Communal Meals in the Early Church: The Implications of a Form–Critical Analysis of 2 Thessalonians 3:10', *Biblical Research* 38 (1993), p. 38). While it would be pressing too hard to require that the community was eating all its meals together, certainly the text makes sense where common meals were frequent.

52 The punishment also covers greed, idolatry, abuse, drunkenness, and robbery.

5

Jesus and Character Values in Work

DARRELL L. BOCK

Christian Identity and Work

Our calling to work goes back to Genesis 1.26–28 where God tells human-kind to subdue the earth. It is a mandate God gave to both male and female, whom God made in his image. The text reads:

> Then God said, 'Let us make humankind in our image, after our likeness, so they may rule over the fish of the sea and the birds of the air, over the cattle, and over all the earth, and over all the creatures that move on the earth.' God created humankind in his own image, in the image of God he created them, male and female he created them. God blessed them and said to them, 'Be fruitful and multiply! Fill the earth and subdue it! Rule over the fish of the sea and the birds of the air and every creature that moves on the ground.'

In the call to subdue the earth, God called people into managing creation well, into work. Today that stewardship extends in all directions, involving an array of jobs. This work is still a basic structure of society and lives, yet we rarely discuss it in spiritual terms. Most people see a job as a means to other ends, whether it be caring for one's family or gaining resources to do what one really wants to do in and with life. But Genesis shows us that from the beginning God wanted us to see our lives as given to the service of managing the creation well and helping each other as a result. Our work is at the core of our lives, so the question becomes: 'How should we then live?' or 'How should we then work?'

In thinking about this question, I am not speaking so much of how we do our job in terms of job performance. The idea of doing our job responsibly is a given. We are paid to do that. The question I wish to pursue is how should we do our work relationally and how should we engage in our work.

For this I want to look at core values Jesus taught about how we relate to others in general and think about how they apply to the place where we spend the bulk of our adult lives: at work. I want to consider four areas that tie into how we work: service, love, compassion, and power. I then want to take a further look at what grounds these four ideas together.

Service

When it comes to the issue of service, Jesus clearly sets forth a choice with his remarks in Matthew 6.24. One cannot serve both God and Mammon. What was Jesus saying by this contrast?

To understand that saying, one needs to consider what Jesus said about money and possessions in Luke's Gospel. In Luke 12.13–21, Jesus tells the parable of the rich fool. This man came into the blessing of a large harvest but saw no issues of stewardship in that other than to provide for himself. In an amazing cluster of self-references, the man refers to himself twelve times in the space of three verses. Life is all about him. One of the dangers of serving wealth is that it can make us into demigods. This is why Ephesians 5.5 labels the greedy person an idolater. The pursuit of money for money's sake risks making us too self-focused.

In Luke 16.19–31, another parable involves the rich man and Lazarus. Here the problem is that the rich man never sees Lazarus as a person. He is seen as an impersonal means to an end. So when Lazarus sat poor and miserable at his gate, the rich man paid that beggar no attention even though he knew Lazarus's name. Once their circumstances were reversed, the rich man urges Abraham to send Lazarus as a lackey to relieve his pain. The rich man ends up being measured by the standard of life he applied. Abraham will do nothing for him, as he did nothing for the poor man in this life. So a danger of the privilege of wealth is that we may dehumanize others. Serving money often devalues itself into service of self. One of the subtle dangers of work is that this negative value can creep in. Our pursuit of security can devolve into a pursuit of self. Jesus not only challenges this as inadequate. It is critiqued as heading us to dishonouring the God we are called to serve.

The example of Jesus's character gives the positive take on this value. Whether one looks at Matthew 20.28 or Mark 10.45, what we are told is that Jesus as Son of Man came to seek and serve the lost. He did not come to be served but to serve. We will return to this key passage later under another theme, but the point here is that Jesus's lens for his own ministry was calibrated by a desire to serve. He had a rank that might have allowed others to serve him, but his desire to show the heart and intent of God meant he served. We are called to model what he does.

Jesus thinks about his neighbour as he acts on behalf of God. The interaction between how we relate to God and to our neighbour are never very far from each other in Scripture. It is seen in the fact that the Ten Commandments deal with issues tied to loyalty to God followed by issues about how we treat those around us. It is seen in how John the Baptist is said to be a forerunner to the Christ by not only turning Israel back to God, but also by turning fathers back to their children and the disobedient back to the just (Luke 1.16–17). These verses define repentance in such a way that relating well to God also expresses itself in relating well to others in the same breath. So when looking to John to explain what concrete repentance looks like, Luke 3.10–14 has John the Baptist noting how we treat others and use our power in our choices about relating to others. We are to give to those in need. We are not to defraud. We are not to abuse the social power we may have. At the root of this value is another value that is to drive our work. That value is love.

Love

The most basic of values Jesus taught was love. Love extended in all kinds of directions. In John 13.33–35, he calls on disciples to love one another. In fact, he says that the world will know that we are his own disciples by this love. But loving those who love you is not special. In Luke 6.27–36, Jesus urges those listening to him to love their enemies, noting that if you only love those who pay your love back, that is no different from how sinners love. Disciples are to do better than that. So Jesus extends the call to love not just to one's neighbour, as the Great Commandment urges us to do (Mark 12.31), but also to one's enemies (also Matt. 19.19; 22.39). It is in this kind of love that one demonstrates one understands the character of God and imitates it, as God provides for those who reject him (Luke 6.35–36). We are called to show mercy as God does in this passage. It is a significant text, and Luke's version of the Sermon on the Mount highlights this feature of Jesus's teaching over all the other exhortations in that sermon. So we see an ever-extending call: to love from disciples, to one's neighbour, to one's enemies.

If there was any doubt about this being the point, a famous parable lays that to rest. The parable of the good Samaritan is Jesus's response to a scribe's question about who is my neighbour (Luke 10.29–37). The question implies that there are people who are 'non-neighbours' and no obligation to love them applies. Jesus's response rejects the premise of the question by describing in detail the care and compassion a Samaritan, a 'non-neighbour' to many Jewish eyes, showed to a man who fell among robbers. Every act of compassion is detailed. In contrast to the priest and Levite, who crossed the road to avoid the situation, he stops, moved with pity. He went to the man, bandaged his wounds, poured oil and wine on them, brought him to his own animal, put him on it, took him to the inn and then left money with the innkeeper to make sure the man would be restored without any worries. Here is a value that looks outside of oneself to meet needs that simply pop up. It is a value that can work at work.

Jesus answers the scribe's question not in the direction he asks but by reframing the question. Instead of describing who the neighbour is or is not, he tells the scribe to be a neighbour while showing him neighbours can come in surprising packages. Perhaps the last person the scribe would have regarded as a neighbour would be a Samaritan, who now is elevated as an example to follow. People from different places can surprise us, and we should be willing to surprise them.

The thrust of what Jesus is teaching in these texts is that our attention should be directed not towards ourselves and our own needs but towards the needs of others. When we have regard for others our attention is directed towards them. Our concern is not to do as little as we can, but what can be done for another to try to make sure they land in a good place. Our concern is to seek the highest good of others.

The life of a disciple is to be exceptional in how he or she cares for others. The love is to be exceptional, as well. Mercy and concern are to reign. That means possessing a sensitivity that is developed by seeing need and moving towards it. A work environment is a perfect place to display that kind of exceptional presence of being a neighbour in the imitation of Christ.

Compassion

Compassion is one of the neglected features in presentations about what Jesus showed and taught. This virtue was something he showed more than something he discussed. It is something the evangelists loved to note about Jesus. Compassion shows a heart that looks beyond itself. We already noted the compassion of the good Samaritan as he helped the man who fell among the thieves. That is one of the few places Jesus taught about compassion, but he exhibited it consistently in his ministry.

In Matthew 9.36 Jesus has compassion on the people who exist without a guiding shepherd (also Mark 6.34). They are described as bewildered and helpless. These two terms point to a person beaten down by life. They are weary, dejected, and worn down. If this were a colloquialism, they were done, cooked when it came to life. Jesus comes to their rescue by providing guidance and encouragement. In this context, Jesus tells the disciples to pray for workers for the harvest. He is asking for people who will dive into the lives of folks who feel weary and give them hope through the gospel. Jesus's presence also is a cause for such hope.

Compassion expresses itself in service, according to Jesus in Matthew 14.14 and 20.34. It is compassion that leads Jesus to heal the sick. This kind of ministry underscored and powerfully illustrated his message that God cares for people. That care is evident in Jesus's initiative to help people in need. Today we sometimes separate the word of the gospel from actions that reinforce and give evidence of its underlying motives. Jesus has no such separation. In Luke 4.16–44, Jesus preaches about being anointed to give liberation to people and then demonstrates that care and liberation concretely in the service he gives in Capernaum. We see word and deed together, and the combination is critical. Word without deed is expressionless and empty. Deed without word carries no message. Both together allow people to ask why one shows such exceptional compassion when much of the world does not care. Together they stir people to ask the question, because our concrete care opens the door for a credible word of explanation with the reality of caring already established. This allows room for offering the challenge of the gospel, with it already established that one cares about the person being challenged. People will not care about a critique of their lives unless they think you care about them. Compassion and service concretely expressed allow for that kind of deep engagement with a chance that the exchange might be heard.

Mark 9.22 looks to another healing scene where Jesus has established he is compassionate. Here he gains an opportunity to meet the need of another. The healing of the leper (possibly out of compassion) in Mark 1.41 works similarly if that is the wording of this text.[1] Luke 7.13 has Jesus act out of compassion for a widowed woman of an only son. Taking the initiative to meet a need, he tells the woman not to weep in mourning as he prepares to give her back her deceased son.

Similar compassion motivated Jesus not to send a crowd away hungry in Matthew 15.32 (also Mark 8.2). Now these last two Matthean scenes involve miracles from Jesus, but that may miss the point. Jesus was using his power in the service of others and out of concern for them. The point is not just that Jesus provided miraculously for them, but also that he served them well.

Another trait of compassion is a willingness to forgive. This is portrayed as an attribute of God that we are to imitate because we appreciate being the recipients of God's mercy. The parable of Mathew 18.23–35 argues for this characteristic among disciples. It pictures the big debt God has forgiven us and urges us to forgive the little debts owed to us each day as an appropriate response to God forgiving us of far more.

These glimpses of Jesus's compassion in the Gospels shows a heart value of the Son of God. He sees and meets needs. He serves. His eyes are directed towards helping others. Ultimately service is motivated by a caring compassion that expresses itself concretely in demonstrable love.

This is how Jesus lived among us as his neighbours. We are to imitate him in the places God has us labouring.

Power

Jesus addressed the issue of power and rank very directly in his ministry. It is an important discussion because the issues of power, authority, and position are in play. Three important texts cover this theme.

The first is in Mark 10.35–45. Here the sons of Zebedee ask for seats of honour to be given to them. They are concerned about their rank. Jesus replies, noting the baptism (of death) that he is facing, and asks if they are ready to face something similar. They reply that they are. Jesus then says they will face such an end but that to grant them a rank in his kingdom is not his to give.

The query left the remaining ten disciples angry with James and John, so Jesus directs his response to the whole group. Jesus says the way to live and function in the world is not to be concerned with authority in ways where that authority is used with respect to others. Rather it is the servant and slave of all who is to be great among them. Two terms dominate this text: *diakonos* and *doulos*. These are terms for a minister and a slave, respectively. The minister is an agent or an intermediary for another group or person.[2] He serves people on behalf of a government or as a servant for God in a church or in the temple. He tends tables. Slave is an even stronger term. Here is a person whose whole life is one of service. This theme of serving versus being preoccupied with rank or status actually encapsulates what we have said already about service, love, and compassion. Greatness emerges when it is directed towards caring for others. It looks for how one can help.

Jesus then appeals to his own example. The Son of Man, a figure from Daniel 7.9–14, came not to be served but to serve. He is a human who rides the clouds and receives judgement authority. He is a powerful figure. Yet he does not seek to be served but to serve. His service is best summarized in one act: the giving of his life as a ransom for many. This is not only an allusion to the baptism he faces, but it also depicts how his service extends to the giving of his life for the sake of others. He loses his life so others may gain theirs.

In doing this, Jesus turns the handling of rank and power upside down. The person of greatness lifts others up, not oneself. He uses authority in ways that edify and support others. This giving means that rank is not a means by which we elevate our own status. It is the use of power in ways that open doors for others. So many of our debates about rank and power in myriad areas bypass Jesus's point that the issue of rank is not about self-aggrandizement or about gaining authority and privilege for oneself. Rather, it is about drawing on those resources so others can be helped. That this kind of principle would be important in the workplace, and exceptional, is transparent.

Luke 22.24–27 is the parallel to Mark 10.35–45. Once again, the text is introduced because the disciples are fighting over which one of them is the greatest. Jesus responds by speaking of the benefactors that occupy the Graeco-Roman world. They seek honour. When they give or serve the city, it is so they can receive honour back. In fact, such honour was expected to be given in return for the patron's acts. Jesus says they lord their power over others. Jesus's disciples are not to be like that. The great one is the one who serves. Jesus contrasts the one who sits at the table with the one who serves it and notes the greater one is the one who sits at the table. Then Jesus flips the world upside down by noting that he is one who serves. The implication is that his example is the path followers of Jesus who are learning from him should follow. After all, the word disciple means learner. Jesus's example shows the way.

The third key text involves an action by Jesus in John 13.1–17. Here Jesus washes his disciples' feet. This is a shocking act because in Judaism a Jewish person, should they become a slave, was told removing sandals was too demeaning a task to do in that role.[3] So Jesus is not only performing an act of service. Culturally, this was seen as a demeaning act of service. Jesus concludes his symbolic act with a full explanation of why he did it. John 13.14–17 reads, 'If I then, your Lord and Teacher, have washed your feet, you too ought to wash one another's feet. For I have given you an example – you should do just as I have done for you. I tell you the solemn truth, the slave is not greater than his master, nor is the one who is sent as a messenger greater than the one who sent him. If you understand these things, you will be blessed if you do them.' Jesus exhorts them to live by the example he has just shown them as their teacher. By doing so, he lifts up service and care for another to a prioritized value for a disciple. Jesus says this most emphatically here. If this is not too demeaning for me as your teacher, then it is not too demeaning for you.

Jesus's teaching with regard to rank and power turns everything upside down. The one who wishes to be great needs to be the least, the one who serves. Greatness is not seen by the title on the door, but by the service that opens the door. In a business world where competition, getting ahead, and having rank counts for so much, this perspective calls for a different set of values at work. Just as the Son of Man came not to be served but to serve, so is the calling of a disciple who wishes to follow the example of the teacher of God's ways.

Relating to God Impacts Relating to Others

We have considered core values Jesus presents in relating to others. These values are in play in all our relationships. That observation means they would fit into how we do our work as well. Work matters. How we do our work and how we view our work involves carrying out the divine mandate to manage the earth well in line with what God commanded in Genesis 1.26–28. How we work with others and do our work, including especially how we treat others, builds credibility for us in any other endeavours we undertake with them.

At the core of the four values we have surveyed is another very prominent idea that is often unaddressed. It is seen in how Jesus's coming is introduced by John the Baptist. Once this idea is probed we can see it stands as a foundation to the values Jesus teaches.

In Luke 1.16–17 the angel announces how John the Baptist will prepare people for the arrival of the Messiah. The text reads, 'He [John] will turn many of the people of Israel to the Lord their God. And he will go as forerunner before the Lord in the spirit and power of Elijah, to turn the hearts of the fathers back to their children and the disobedient to the wisdom of the just, to make ready for the Lord a people prepared for him.' The double use of the term 'turn' points to a call to change direction, to a change of mind about how we live. This usage is in keeping with the Hebrew verb 'to turn', which also is used to point to repentance. This makes sense because John the Baptist's message was to be built around a baptism of repentance for the forgiveness of sins, an act undertaken to prepare for the coming of the Lord as our passage notes.

Now normally when one thinks of repentance, one thinks of one's relationship to God. Luke 1.16 says as much. John 'will turn many of the people of Israel to the Lord their God'. However, this is not the only case of turning in the passage. In the next verse it is worth noting that the turning involves a different audience. Here fathers are turned back to their children and the disobedient are brought back to the wisdom of the just. This extension is an interesting one. It points to the fact that when one turns back to God, the impact is to be seen in how we relate to others. There is an 'ethical triangle' of three parts. I relate to God on the one hand and relate to others on the other. So God, myself, and others are tied together in how I am to react to coming to God. My approach to God is to impact how I approach others as well. My walk with God is not merely a private exercise between God and myself. It is a fascinating idea. It also is embedded more deeply in the Scripture than we tend to think.

In Luke 3.8–14, the topic again surfaces in a passage that is mostly unique to Luke's Gospel. Here again in view is the message of John the

Baptist in preparing people for Jesus's coming. John calls on the people to make fruit worthy of repentance in Luke 3.8. This exhortation we see also in Matthew 3.8. It is built around the Greek verb *poieō*, which means to do or make something. In Luke 3.10–14 we get an expansion of the scene in three questions coming from the audience. This is the part that is unique to Luke. In three cases three different groups ask, 'What shall we do?' The Greek verb is *poieō*. It links back to the exhortation.

What is fascinating is each answer John gives. One would think that repentance would involve how I interact with God. In all three cases that is not the direction of John's answer. Here is the full text:

> So the crowds were asking him, 'What then should we do?' John answered them, 'The person who has two tunics must share with the person who has none, and the person who has food must do likewise.' Tax collectors also came to be baptized, and they said to him, 'Teacher, what should we do?' He told them, 'Collect no more than you are required to.' Then some soldiers also asked him, 'And as for us – what should we do?' He told them, 'Take money from no one by violence or by false accusation, and be content with your pay.'

In each case, the reply treats how we interact not with God but with others. To the crowds, one is to be generous. Tax collectors are to be fair in their assessments. Soldiers are not to abuse their power. There is a generosity, fairness, and justice that is to guide and guard our relationships. Repentance before God entails all of this. How I relate to God is to impact how I relate to others. This is such an important idea that it is placed in a context where people are preparing for the arrival of God and his salvation through Jesus. This connection points to a core ethical idea of Scripture. God designed us to manage the creation well, and managing our relationships well is part of that.

If one thinks about this even further, its centrality and importance are transparent. If one thinks of the Ten Commandments, they are structured in two tablets, in two parts. One part has to do with how we relate to God. Worship God alone. Have no other idols. Give a day of rest dedicated to God. Do not take the Lord's name in vain. Tablet two is about how we relate to others. Honour your father and mother. Do not murder, commit adultery, steal, give false testimony, or covet. The exhortation of the core commandments is both vertical and horizontal in relationship. The ethics described here is not exclusionary. It is not just to other believers. It is directed to all our relationships. Obviously, our work fits into that scope.

Yet another angle shows the importance of this idea. Jesus speaks of the Great Commandment in Mark 12.28–31. Here is that teaching:

Now one of the experts in the law came and heard them debating. When he saw that Jesus answered them well, he asked him, 'Which commandment is the most important of all?' Jesus answered, 'The most important is: "Listen, Israel, the Lord our God, the Lord is one. Love the Lord your God with all your heart, with all your soul, with all your mind, and with all your strength." The second is: "Love your neighbour as yourself." There is no other commandment greater than these.'

Again, two dimensions drive the commandments. One is vertical, about our love for God. The other is horizontal, concerning how we treat others. Jesus links the two here, making it one exhortation. He also notes that no commandment is ranked higher than these, pointing to its importance.

Still there are other indications of how central this core idea of relating to God and others is. In the Disciples' Prayer, better known as the Lord's Prayer, Jesus actually is teaching disciples how to pray. One of the prayer requests is that we are to ask to have our sins forgiven as we are ready and willing to forgive others: 'Forgive us our sins as we forgive those who have sinned against us' (Luke 11.4). In the Sermon on the Plain, Jesus makes the point that when we are merciful and forgiving we show the character of the Father and live as children who imitate our God. This exhortation comes in a section where Jesus is exhorting us to love our enemies, proving the values we are considering are to be applied broadly, not just to an inner group (Luke 6.27–36, esp. 35–36). In an even more powerful picture, Jesus tells a parable about forgiving where a man forgiven a debt of over 175,000 years of wages fails to forgive a man with a few months' debt and is judged for not being forgiving. The exhortation is that Jesus's followers are to be so forgiving (Matt. 18.23–35). We are to learn from the greatness of God's grace to be forgiving in spirit as God has done with us.

So we see a core ethic here. It should drive us to service, love, compassion, and avoiding all abuse of power.

Conclusion: How We Work Matters, as Do Character and Service

Work matters. It was the topic of God's first command to humanity. God calls us to be fruitful and subdue the earth. We are to manage the creation well. That includes not only valuing our work for its contributing to a well-managed world, but also giving care to how we do our work – and how we interact with others in the midst of that work. This is so important that the Ten Commandments point to how we relate to God and others. It is so central that Jesus encased it in the Great Commandment.

Within that larger ethical call and presentation of core Christian values we see additional calls to service, love, and compassion. We are to act out of a reversal of rank that looks to serve. This attitude is a result of having turned to God with an appreciation that our experience of grace is to mark how we treat others. Character matters to God. God wants us to mirror who he is and what he is like. Our regard for others, not self, is to drive our relationships. These are values to live by. They reflect being a child of God and a disciple who models the very character of God. They are values to be on display as we work. These values point to our core identity and how God's involvement in our life changes how we live. For when we show how our work matters by who we are as we work, we mirror God's character and testify to him. Work matters because God matters and so does the character he works to put in us.

Notes

1 A textual issue appears here as some manuscripts read that Jesus acted out of anger, not compassion. The anger would have been at life being lived in a fallen, hard-nosed world.

2 Walter Bauer, *A Greek-English Lexicon of the New Testament and Other Early Christian Literature*, rev. and ed. Frederick W. Danker, 3rd edition (Chicago: University of Chicago Press, 2000), p. 230.

3 Here are the texts from later Judaism that point us in this direction: *Mekilta Exodus* 21.2 – 'He should not wash his feet or tie his sandals or carry his clothing to the bath-house or gird his loins for an ascent or carry him in a litter or in a chair or in a sedan-chair, as slaves do'; *b. Ketubbot* 96a – 'all service that a slave must render to his master a student must render to his teacher, except untying his shoe.'

PART 2

Systematic Theology

6

Work as Cooperation with God[*]

MIROSLAV VOLF

In the present chapter, I will lay a foundation for such a theology of work and sketch its basic contours. The first major section deals with the ultimate *significance* of work by discussing the question of the continuity or discontinuity between the present and the eschatological orders, and with the fundamental *meaning* of work by arguing in favour of understanding work as cooperation with God. In the second major section, I will first give reasons why a pneumatological theory of work is possible. Then, in a critical dialogue with the dominant Protestant view of work as vocation developed within a protological framework, I will argue for a pneumatological understanding of work based on a theology of *charisms*, which suggests that the various activities human beings do in order to satisfy their own needs and the needs of their fellow creatures should be viewed from the perspective of the operation of God's Spirit.

Work and New Creation

The question of continuity or discontinuity between the present and future orders is a key issue in developing a theology of work.[1] The ultimate significance of human work depends on the answer to this question, for it determines whether work as occupation with transitory things and relations (*vita activa*) has an inherent value or whether it merely has instrumental value as a means to make possible the occupation with eternal realities (*vita contemplativa*).

Eschatology and the Significance of Human Work

If we leave aside the more modern – and in my view theologically and religiously not very persuasive – ethical and existential interpretations of

---

[*] This chapter is an abridged version of Chapter 4 of Miroslav Volf's *Work in the Spirit* (Eugene, OR: Wipf & Stock, 1991). Used by permission of Wipf & Stock Publishers. www.wipfandstock.com.

the cosmological eschatological statements, Christian theologians have held two basic positions on the eschatological future of the world. Some stressed radical discontinuity between the present and the future orders, believing in the complete destruction of the present world at the end of the ages and creation of a fully new world. Others postulated continuity between the two, believing that the present world will be transformed into the new heaven and new earth. Two radically different theologies of work follow from these two basic eschatological models.

Work and the Annihilatio Mundi

If the world will be annihilated and a new one created *ex nihilo*, then mundane work has only earthly significance for the well-being of the worker, the worker's community, and posterity – until the day when 'the heavens will pass away with a loud noise, and the elements, will be dissolved with fire' (2 Peter 3.10). Since the results of the cumulative work of humankind throughout history will become naught in the final apocalyptic catastrophe, human work is devoid of direct ultimate significance.

Under the presupposition of eschatological *annihilatio mundi*, human work can, of course, indirectly serve certain goals whose importance transcends the death of either the individual or the whole cosmos. One can, for instance, view work as a school for the purification of the soul in preparation for heavenly bliss. Christian tradition always insisted on the importance of work for individual sanctification. For, as Thomas Aquinas put it, it removes 'idleness whence arise many evils' and 'curbs concupiscence'.[2] One can also maintain (as Karl Barth did) that work is indirectly ultimately significant because it keeps the body and soul together, thus enabling Christian faith and service: in order to believe and serve, human beings have to live, and in order to live, they have to work.[3] According to such views, human work and its results are necessary, for without them the Christian *opus proprium* (faith, sanctification, or service) cannot take place. Yet being merely prerequisites for this *opus proprium*, human work and its results are eschatologically insignificant independent of their direct or indirect influence on the souls of men and women.

When one refuses to assign eschatological significance to human work and makes it fully subservient to the vertical relation to God, one devalues human work and Christian cultural involvement (I use the word in the broad sense inclusive of social and ecological involvement). It is, of course, logically compatible both to affirm that the world will be annihilated at the end and at the same time to strive to improve the life of individuals, to create adequate social structures, and even to be motivated to care effectively for the environment. There is nothing contradictory in wanting to use the world and delight in it as long as it lasts (or as long as human beings last in it). Because it is possible to affirm enjoyment in the world while believing in its destruction, it is also possible to consider one's cultural involvement as a way of integrally loving one's neighbour. If Bach, for instance, were annihilationist, should he have had qualms about composing his music?[4] Of course not. He could have done this out of a desire to spiritually elevate his audience and thereby glorify God.[5]

Belief in the eschatological annihilation and responsible social involvement are logically compatible. But they are *theologically inconsistent*. The expectation of the eschatological destruction of the world is not consonant with the belief in the goodness of creation: what God will annihilate must be either so bad that it is not possible to be redeemed or so insignificant that it is not worth being redeemed. It is hard to believe in the intrinsic value and goodness of something that God will completely annihilate.

And *without a theologically grounded belief in the intrinsic value and goodness of creation, positive cultural involvement hangs theologically in the air*. Hence Christians who await the destruction of the world (and conveniently refuse to live a schizophrenic life) shy away as a rule – out of theological, not logical, consistency – from social and cultural involvement. Under the presupposition that the world is not intrinsically good, the only theologically plausible justification for cultural involvement would be that such involvement diminishes the suffering of the body and contributes to the good of the soul (either by making evangelism possible or by fostering sanctification). Comfort, skill, or beauty – whether it is the beauty of the human body or of some other object – could have no more intrinsic value than does the body itself; they could be merely a means to some spiritual end. To return to our example, even if annihilationist presuppositions need not discourage Bach's work, his composing in order for people to take pleasure in his music could not be theologically motivated. He would have no theological reason for this important way of loving others. This problem would not arise, however, if Bach believed in the intrinsic goodness of creation. And he could do this only if he believed in the eschatological transformation rather than destruction.

Work and the Transformatio Mundi

The picture changes radically with the assumption that the world will end not in apocalyptic destruction but in eschatological transformation. Then the results of the cumulative work of human beings have intrinsic value and gain ultimate significance, for they are related to the eschatological new creation, not only indirectly through the faith and service they enable or sanctification they further, but also directly: the noble products of human ingenuity, 'whatever is beautiful, true and good in human cultures',[6] will be cleansed from impurity, perfected, and transfigured to become a part of God's new creation. They will form the 'building materials' from which (after they are transfigured) 'the glorified world' will be made.[7]

The assurance of the continuity between the present age and the age to come (notwithstanding the abolition of all sinfulness and transitoriness that characterize the present age) is a 'strong incentive to ... cultural involvement'.[8] For the continuity guarantees that no noble efforts will be wasted. Certainly, cultural involvement is not the most important task of a Christian. It would indeed be useless for a woman to conquer and transform the world through work but through lack of faith lose her soul (see Mark 8.36). Yet as faith does not exist for the sake of work (though it should stimulate, direct, and limit work), so also work does not exist merely for the sake of faith (though one of its purposes is to make faith possible). Each in its own way, faith and human work should stand in the service of the new creation. Not that the results of human work should or could create and replace 'heaven'. They can never do that; though, charmed with success, people often forget that simple truth. Rather, after being purified in the eschatological *transformatio mundi*, they will be integrated by an act of divine transformation into the new heaven and the new earth. Hence the expectation of the eschatological transformation invests human work with ultimate significance. Through it, human beings contribute in their modest and broken way to God's new creation.

The ascription of intrinsic value and ultimate significance to positive cultural involvement is not the only benefit of developing a theology of work within the framework of belief in eschatological continuity. In addition, such a belief gives human beings important inspiration for action when their efforts at doing good deeds, at finding truth about some aspect of reality, and at creating beauty are not appreciated. The question is not merely whether Bach would have qualms about composing music if he were an annihilationist. The question is also whether all those unappreciated small and great Van Goghs in various fields of human activity would not draw inspiration and strength from the belief that their noble efforts are not lost, that everything good, true, and beautiful they create is valued by God and will be appreciated by human beings in the new creation.

The New Testament on the Significance of Work

It might seem that discussing eschatological annihilation and transformation is a roundabout way to reflect theologically on the significance of human work. Should not the explicit New Testament statements about work determine our perspective on the issue? If they did, we would come to a rather different valuation of cultural involvement than the one implied in the idea of *transformatio mundi*. For we search in vain in the New Testament for a cultural mandate, let alone for the 'gospel of work'.[9]

Jesus left carpenter's tools when he started public ministry, and he called his disciples away from their occupations. Only indirectly did he affirm the need to work: when he said that people will be judged on the basis of their efforts to satisfy basic human needs of the poor (food, drink, clothing; Matt. 25.34ff.). Later, we find in the epistles an explicit command to work, but with the clear specification that work should serve the needs of the workers and their neighbours (see 2 Thess. 3.6ff.; Eph. 4.28). The explicit New Testament statements about work view it very soberly as a means of securing sustenance, not as an instrument of cultural advancement.

The key question is how to interpret the silence of the New Testament about the possible broader significance of human work. Is it an implicit discouragement of cultural involvement or merely an expression of a single-minded *concentration* on a different kind of work needed in a particular period of salvation history (see Matt. 9.37f.)? In answering this question, it is good to remember that in the Old Testament, the 'Scripture' for the early Christians, the purpose of work was not merely sustenance, but also cultural development, which included activities ranging from perfecting building techniques to the refinement of musical skills (see Gen. 4.17ff.). Moreover, Genesis views the diversification of employments required by such cultural development as a result of divine blessing.[10] The Old Testament view of work should caution us against concluding too hastily that a positive valuation of cultural development is incompatible with a New Testament understanding of Christian faith.

Important as this argument from the Old Testament is, it is not decisive. The answer to the question of how to translate into a Christian theology of work the silence of the New Testament about any broader significance of work than mere sustenance depends ultimately on the nature of New Testament eschatology. For the significance of secular work depends on the value of creation, and the value of creation depends on its final destiny. If its destiny is eschatological transformation, then, in spite of the lack of explicit exegetical support, we *must* ascribe to human work inherent value, independent of its relation to the proclamation of the gospel (human work and the proclamation of the gospel are each in its own way directed towards the new creation). Since much of the present order is the result of human work, if the present order will be transformed, then human work necessarily has ultimate significance. The interpretation of the explicit New Testament statements about the significance of work depends, therefore, on the eschatological framework in which they are set. So the search for a direct answer in the New Testament to the question about a possible broader significance of work than securing sustenance leads us to return to our initial discussion about the continuity between the present and future orders.

Eschatological *Transformatio Mundi*

Both explicit and implicit theological arguments can be adduced for the idea of the eschatological *transformatio mundi* and hence for the continuity between the present and the future orders.

Kingdom of God for This Earth

One can argue indirectly for the eschatological transformation of the world instead of annihilation by pointing to the *earthly locale of the kingdom of God*.[11] R. H. Gundry has argued persuasively that in Revelation the saints' dwelling place is the new earth. It is 'quite clear that the Book of Revelation promises eternal life on the new earth ... , not ethereal life in the new heaven'. In correspondence to the saints' earthly dwelling place, the promise to the church at Smyrna – 'but you are rich' (2.9) – calls for a 'materialistic reading': it refers to 'a redistribution of property ... to the saints'. Moreover, Revelation complements the economic aspect of the promise by adding a political aspect: the saints will rule as 'new kings of the earth, all of them, the whole nation of kings'.[12]

The same emphasis on the new earth as the eschatological dwelling place of God's people found in Revelation is also present in Matthew's Gospel. The prayer for the coming of the kingdom (6.10) is a prayer for God's 'rule over all the earth', and seeking the kingdom (6.33) 'means desiring the final coming of his rule on earth'.[13] Similarly, the 'earth' in the promise of inheriting the earth given to the meek (5.5) can only refer to 'the earthly locale of God's kingdom'.[14] In the *eschaton*, the resurrected people of God will inhabit the renewed earth.

The stress on the earthly locale of the kingdom of God in the New Testament corresponds not only to the earthly hopes of the Old Testament prophets (Isa. 11.6–10; 65.17–25), but even more significantly to the Christian doctrine of the resurrection of the body. Theologically it makes little sense to postulate a non-earthly eschatological existence while believing in the resurrection of the body.[15] If we do not want to reduce the doctrine of the resurrection of the body to an accidental part of Christian eschatology, we will have to insist (against Thomas Aquinas, for instance) that perfect happiness does depend on the resurrected body.[16] And if the concept of 'body' is not to become unintelligible by being indistinguishable from the concept of the 'pure spirit', we must also insist that 'external goods' are necessary for perfect happiness.[17] The resurrection body demands a corresponding glorified but nevertheless material environment. The future *material* existence therefore belongs inalienably to the Christian eschatological expectation.[18]

Liberation of Creation

Some New Testament statements explicitly support the idea of an eschatological *transformatio mundi* and indicate that the apocalyptic language of the destruction of 'all these things' (2 Peter 3.11) should not be taken to imply the destruction of creation. In Romans 8.21 Paul writes that the 'creation itself will be set free from its bondage to decay and obtain the glorious liberty of the children of God'. The liberation of creation (i.e. of 'the sum-total of sub-human nature, both animate and inanimate'[19]) *cannot occur through its destruction but only through its transformation.* As F. F. Bruce rightly points out, 'if words mean anything, these words of Paul denote not the annihilation of the present material universe on the day of revelation, to be replaced by a universe completely new, but the transformation of the present universe so that it will fulfil the purpose for which god created it'.[20] When God ushers in his final kingdom, the striving of 'everything in heaven and on earth ... after renewal' will be fulfilled.[21]

The biblical statements that affirm continuity between the present and future orders are theologically inseparable from the Judaeo-Christian belief in the goodness of divine creation. The belief in the continuity between the present and the new creation is an eschatological expression of the protological belief in the goodness of creation; you cannot have one without the other. It makes little sense to affirm the goodness of creation and at the same time expect its eschatological destruction. And goodness is a predicate not only of the original but also of the present creation, the reality of evil in it notwithstanding. God cannot, therefore, ultimately 'reject' creation, but will – as we read in the Pastorals in relation to food – 'consecrate' it (1 Tim. 4.4).

It is, of course, possible to believe that the goodness of the material creation is merely instrumental, in which case eschatological annihilation would not deny the goodness of creation. Like food, all material objects would be good because they are necessary for keeping the human body alive, and the human body would be good because it provides a temporary dwelling place for the soul. Alternatively, one can posit the instrumental goodness of the material creation by affirming that it is only a temporary means of manifesting God's greatness and glory. There is no reason to deny or denigrate the instrumental goodness of the material creation. But the material creation is more than a means; it is also an end in itself. For one, we encounter in the biblical texts what might best be described as the 'soteriological independence' of the material creation: creation too will participate in the liberty of the children of God (Rom. 8.21; see Gen. 9.10ff.). Furthermore, anthropologically we have to maintain that human beings do not only have a body; they also are body. It follows that the goodness of the whole material creation is intrinsic, not merely instrumental. And the belief in the intrinsic goodness of creation is compatible only with the belief in eschatological continuity.

Human Works in the Glorified World?

Belief in the eschatological transformation of the world gives human work special significance since in bestows independent value on the results of work as 'building materials' of the glorified world. As I have shown above, it makes theological sense to talk about human contribution to the glorified world. But is such talk logically plausible? Is it not a contradiction to ascribe eternal permanence to what corruptible human beings create?[22] A chair becomes broken in a year, bread is eaten in a day, and a speech forgotten in an hour. Most of the results of human work will waste away before they see the day of eschatological transformation.

We should not think only in terms of the work of isolated individuals, however, but also of the cumulative work of the whole human race. The work of each individual contributes to the 'project' in which the human race is involved. As one generation stands on the shoulders of another, so the accomplishments of each generation build upon those of the previous one. What has wasted away or been destroyed often functions as a ladder that, after use, can be pushed aside.

Second, although on the one hand much of human work serves for sustenance and its results disappear almost as soon as they have appeared, on the other hand, much human work leaves a permanent imprint on natural and social environments and creates a home for human beings without which they could not exist as human beings. Even if every single human product throughout history will not be integrated into the world to come, this home as a whole will be integrated.

Third, work and its perceived results define in part the structure of human beings' personality, their identity. Since resurrection will be not a negation but an affirmation of human earthly identity, earthly work will have an influence on resurrected personality. Rondet rightly asks whether Gutenberg in a glorified state would be Gutenberg apart from any eschatological relation to the discovery that made him famous.[23] One might go on to ask whether all human beings who have benefited from Gutenberg's discovery would in their glorified state be the same without his discovery. It could be argued that such an understanding of the direct ultimate significance of human work is also possible if one holds to the doctrine of the annihilation of the world. Strictly speaking, this is true. But it seems inconsistent to hold that human creations are evil or insignificant enough to necessitate their destruction and that their influence on human personality – which should be carefully distinguished from the influence the process of work has on the individual's sanctification – is good enough to require eschatological preservation.

It is plausible that the statement in Revelation about the saints resting 'from their labours (*kopōn*), for their deeds (*erga*) follow them' (Rev. 14.13; cf. Eph. 6.8) could be interpreted to imply that earthly work will leave traces on resurrected personalities. Since the preservation of the results of work is not in view in this passage, it seems that their deeds can follow the saints only as part and parcel of their personality.[24] Human work is ultimately significant not only because it contributes to the future environment of human beings, but also because it leaves an indelible imprint on their personalities.

Cooperatio Dei

In the past few centuries Christian theologians have come to view human work as *cooperation with God*. In both Protestant and Roman Catholic traditions there is agreement today that the deepest meaning of human work lies in the cooperation of men and women with God.[25] To view work as cooperation with God is compatible with belief in eschatological annihilation (one cooperates with God in the preservation of the world until its final destruction); belief in the eschatological transformation, however, is not only compatible with such a view of work – it requires it.

Depending on how we conceive of human cooperation with God in work, we can differentiate between two types of theologies of work. The one rests on the doctrine of creation and sees work as cooperation with God in *creatio continua*, the other rests on the doctrine of the last things and sees work as cooperation with God in anticipation of God's eschatological *transformatio mundi*. I will take a brief, critical look at both ways to understand human work as cooperation with God.

Cooperation in Preservation

The first way of interpreting work as cooperation with God starts with the Old Testament, especially the creation accounts. The first chapters of Genesis portray human beings, even in their mundane work, as partners with God in God's creative activity. True, the Old Testament stresses the uniqueness of God's act of original creation. No human work corresponds to divine creation *ex nihilo* (*bara*). At the same time, it draws an analogy between divine making (*asa*) and human work,[26] which seems to suggest that there is a partnership between the creating God and working human beings.

The second account of creation portrays this partnership in the most vivid manner. While giving the reason for the lack of vegetation on earth, it addresses the relation of God's creation and human work: 'for the Lord God had not caused it to rain upon the earth, and there was no man to till the ground' (Gen. 2.5). The growth of vegetation demands cooperation between God, who gives rain, and human beings, who cultivate the ground. There is a mutual dependence between God and human beings in the task of the preservation of creation. On the one hand, human beings are dependent upon God in their work. As the psalmist says, 'Unless the Lord builds the house, those who build it labour in vain' (Ps. 127.1a; cf. Ps. 65.11–13). On the other hand, God the creator chooses to become 'dependent' on the human helping hand and makes human work a means of accomplishing his work in the world. As Luther said, human work is 'God's mask behind which he hides himself and rules everything magnificently in the world'.[27]

As Luther's statement indicates, cooperation with God need not be a conscious effort on the part of human beings. In other words, work must objectively correspond to the will of God, but it need not be done subjectively as God's will. According to biblical records, God even made those whom he will later judge for the work they have done cooperate with him in accomplishment of his will (see Isa. 37.26ff.). Furthermore, cooperation with God can even occur through alienated forms of work, if the results are in accordance with God's will. Although the concept of new creation does demand striving to overcome alienation in work, such non-alienated work is not a necessary precondition of human cooperation with God.

Cooperation in Transformation

There is another, more recent, theological tradition that bases theology of work on human proleptic cooperation in God's eschatological *transformatio mundi*. It includes the essential elements of the understanding of work as cooperation with God in preservation of creation and places them in the eschatological light of the promised new creation. True, the world is presently under the power of sin and is transitory. For that reason, human work cannot create God's new world, no matter how noble human motives might be.[28] The description of the 'New Jerusalem' – the new people of God – in Revelation makes this plain.[29] The New Jerusalem is the city (which stands for 'the people') of *God* and comes 'down out of heaven' (Rev. 21.2; cf. 1 Peter 1.4; Matt. 25.34). As a divine creation it is 'a living hope' freed from all evil and corruptibility, and it infinitely transcends everything human beings can plan or execute.[30] The origin and character of the 'New Jerusalem' show that the new creation as a whole is fundamentally a gift, and the primary human action in relation to it is not doing but 'waiting' (2 Peter 3.12; cf. Matt. 6.10; Rev. 22.17).

But one should not confuse waiting with inactivity. In the New Testament the injunction to wait eagerly for the kingdom is not opposed to the exhortation to *work diligently for the kingdom*. 'Kingdom-participation' is not contrary, but complementary, to 'kingdom-expectation' and is its necessary consequence.[31] Placed in the context of kingdom-participation, mundane human work for worldly betterment becomes a contribution – a limited and imperfect one in need of divine purification – to the eschatological kingdom, which will come through God's action alone. In their daily work human beings are 'co-workers in God's kingdom, which completes creation and renews heaven and earth'.[32]

It might seem contradictory to affirm human contribution to the future new creation and to insist that new creation is a result of God's action alone. The compatibility of both affirmations rests in the necessary distinction between God's eschatological action *in* history and his eschatological action *at the end* of history. Through the Spirit, God is already working in history, using human actions to create provisional states of affairs that anticipate the new creation in a real way. These historical anticipations are, however, as far from the consummation of the new creation as earth is from heaven. The consummation is a work of God alone. But since this solitary divine work does not obliterate but transforms the historical anticipations of the new creation human beings have participated in, one can say, without being involved in a contradiction, that human work is an aspect of active participation of the exclusively divine *transformatio mundi*.

Both the protological and the eschatological understanding of cooperation with God in daily work briefly analysed above are valid theologically. One can develop a biblically responsible theology of work by using either an eschatological or a protological framework. For a number of reasons, however, I prefer the eschatological framework. Some of the reasons will become clear later, both through the critique of Luther's notion of vocation (which he developed in a protological framework) and through the reasons to be given for the proposed pneumatological understanding of work. Here I want to mention only four.

First, the eschatological nature of Christian existence makes it impossible, to my mind, to develop a theology of work simply within the framework of the doctrine of creation (protological framework). The second reason is the nature of the relation between the first and the new creation. True, because of the eschatological continuity, the new creation is not simply a negation of the first creation but is also its reaffirmation. For this reason, we cannot construe a theology of work apart from the doctrine of creation. The new creation is, however, not a mere restoration of the first creation. 'The redemption of the world, and of mankind, does not serve only to put us back in the Garden of Eden where we began. It leads us on to that further destiny to which, even in the Garden of Eden, we were already directed.'[33] For this reason the doctrine of creation as such is an insufficient basis for developing a theology of work. It needs to be placed in the broad context of the (partial) realization and of the expectation of the new creation. A proponent of an eschatological theology of work will, therefore, not treat the protological and eschatological understandings of *cooperatio Dei* as alternatives. Rather, they complement each other. Since the new creation comes about through a transformation of the first creation, cooperation with God in the preservation of the world must be an integral part of cooperation with God in the transformation of the world.

The third reason for preferring the eschatological to the protological framework is the conceptual inadequacy of 'protological' theologies of work for interpreting modern work. For them, the ultimate purpose of human work as cooperation with God is the *preservation* of the world. Although much of human work has still the purpose of preserving workers and the world they live in, by using powerful modern technology, human beings not only maintain the world as their home but also radically alter the face of the earth. Modern work transforms the world as much as it preserves it, and it preserves it only by transforming it. The static framework of preservation cannot adequately incorporate this dynamic nature of human work (unless we use the framework of preservation to radically call into question the present results of human work and limit the purpose of work to sustenance). Finally, the protological theologies of work tend to justify the status quo and hinder needed change in both microeconomic and macroeconomic structures by appealing to divine preservation of the world: as God the creator preserves the world he has created, so also human beings in their work should strive to preserve the established order.

Work and the Divine Spirit: A Pneumatological Theology of Work?

One cannot talk about the new creation without referring to the Spirit of God. For the Spirit, as Paul says, is the 'firstfruits' or the 'down payment' of the future salvation (see Rom. 8.23; 2 Cor. 1.22) and the present power of eschatological transformation in them. In the Gospels, too, Spirit is the agent through which the future new creation is anticipated in the present (see Matt. 12.28). Without the Spirit there is no experience of the new creation! A theology of work that seeks to understand work as active anticipation of the *transformatio mundi* must, therefore, be a *pneumato-logical* theology of work.

Work and the Spirit

But what does the Spirit of God have to do with the mundane work of human beings? According to most Protestant theology, very little. It has been 'inclined to restrict the activity of the Spirit to the spiritual, psychological, moral or religious life of the individual'.[34] One can account for this restriction by two consequential theological decisions. To use traditional formulations: first, the activity of the Spirit was limited to the sphere of salvation, and second, the *locus* of the present realization was limited to the human spirit. Thus when the Spirit comes into the world as Redeemer he does not come to a foreign territory, but 'to his own home' (John 1.12)[35] – the world's lying in the power of evil notwithstanding. Here, however, I want to discuss briefly the limitation of the Spirit's salvific operation on the human spirit. For my purposes, this is the crucial issue. The question of whether one can reflect on human work within the framework of the concept of the new creation and develop a pneumatological theology of work depends on the question of whether the Spirit's salvific work is limited to the human spirit or extends to the whole of reality.

We need to look no further than the Gospels to see that the exclusion of materiality from the sphere of the present salvific activity of the Spirit is exegetically and theologically unacceptable. The Gospels widely use soteriological terminology (e.g. the term *sōzein*) to designate deliverance from the troubles and dangers of bodily life.[36] More significantly, they portray Jesus's healing miracles as signs of the inbreaking kingdom.[37] As deeds done in the power of the Spirit, healings are not merely symbols of God's future rule, but are anticipatory realizations of God's present rule. They provide tangible testimony to the materiality of salvation; they demonstrate God's desire to bring integrity to the whole human being, including the body, and to the whole of injured reality.[38] In a broken way – for healed people are not delivered from the power of death – healings done here and now through the power of the Spirit illustrate what will happen at the end of the age when God will transform the present world into the promised new creation.

When the ascended Christ gave up the Spirit, he 'released the power of God into history, power which will not abate until God has made all things new'.[39] The Spirit of the new creation cannot be tied to the 'inner man'. Because the whole creation is the Spirit's sphere of operation, the Spirit is not only the Spirit of religious experience but also the Spirit of worldly engagement. For this reason, it is not at all strange to connect the

Spirit of God with mundane work. In fact, an adequate understanding of human work will be hardly possible without recourse to pneumatology.[40]

Work and Charisms

In a sense, a pneumatological understanding of work is not new. There are traces of it even in Luther. He discussed the *vocatio externa* not only in the context of the Pauline concept of the body of Christ (which is closely related to Paul's understanding of charisms) but also – and sometimes explicitly – in the context of the gifts of grace: 'Behold, here St Peter says that the *graces and gifts* of God are not of one but of varied kind. Each one should understand what his gift is, and practise it and so be of use to others.'

In recent years authors from various Christian traditions have suggested interpreting human work as an aspect of charismatic life. The document of the Vatican II *Gaudium et spes* contains probably the most notable example of a charismatic interpretation of Christians' service to their fellow human beings through work: 'Now, the gifts of the Spirit are diverse ... He summons ... [people] to dedicate themselves to the earthly service of men and to make ready the material of the celestial realm by this ministry of theirs.' To my knowledge, however, no one has taken up these suggestions and developed them into a consistent theology of work.

The pneumatological understanding of work I am proposing is an heir to the vocational understanding of work, predominant in the Protestant social ethic of all traditions.[41] Before developing a pneumatological understanding of work, it is therefore helpful to investigate both the strengths and weaknesses of the vocational understanding of work. Similarly to any other theory, a particular theology of work will be persuasive to the extent that one can show its theological and historical superiority over its rivals.

Work as Vocation

Both Luther and Calvin, each in his own way, held the vocational view of work. Since Luther not only originated the idea but also wrote on it much more extensively than Calvin, I will develop my theology of work in critical dialogue with Luther's notion of vocation (which differs in some important respects from Calvin's,[42] and even more from that of the later Calvinists).

The basis of Luther's understanding of vocation is his doctrine of justification by faith, and the occasion for its development, his controversy with medieval monasticism. One of Luther's most culturally influential accomplishments was to overcome the monastic reduction of *vocatio* to a calling to a particular kind of religious life. He came to hold two inter-related beliefs about Christian vocation: (1) *all* Christians (not only monks) have a vocation, and (2) *every type of work* performed by Christians (not only religious activity) can be a vocation. Instead of interpreting *vocatio* as a call of a select group within the larger Christian fellowship to a special kind of life, Luther spoke of the double vocation of every Christian: spirit-ual vocation (*vocatio spiritualis*) and external vocation (*vocatio externa*). Spiritual vocation is God's call to enter the kingdom of God, and it comes to a person through the proclamation of the gospel. This call is com-mon to all Christians and is for all Christians the same ('*communis et similis*').[43] External vocation is God's call to serve God and one's fellow human beings in the world. It comes to a person through her station in life or profession (*Stand*).[44] This call, too, is addressed to all Christians, but to each one in a different way, depending on his particular station or profession ('*macht ein unterscheid*').[45]

In *Kirchenpostille 1522* – a work in which Luther uses 'vocation' for the first time as a *terminus technicus* 'for a purely secular activity'[46] – Luther gives an explanation of external vocation while answering the question of someone who feels without a vocation: 'What if I am not called? What should I do? Answer: How can it be that you are not called? You are certainly in a situation (*Stand*), you are either a husband or a wife, son or daughter, male or female servant.'[47] To be a husband, wife, child, or servant *means to be called by God* to a particular kind of activity, it means to have a vocation. When God's spiritual call through the proclamation of the gospel reaches a person in her station or profession, it transforms these into a vocation. The duties of the station become commandments of God to her. In this way, Luther links the daily work of every Christian inseparably with the centre of Christian faith: for a Christian, work in every profession, and not only in ecclesiastical professions, rests on a divine calling.

Two important and related consequences follow from Luther's notion of vocation. These insights make up the *novum* of Luther's approach to human work. First, Luther's notion of vocation ascribed much greater value to work than was previously the case. As Weber rightly observed, Luther valued 'the fulfillment of duty in worldly affairs as the highest form which the moral activity of the individual could assume ... . The only way of living acceptably to God was not to surpass worldly morality in monastic asceticism, but solely through the fulfillment of the obligations imposed upon the individual by his position in the world.'[48] Second, Luther's notion of vocation *overcame the medieval hierarchy between* vita activa *and* vita contemplativa. Since every vocation rests on God's com-mission, every vocation is fundamentally of the same value before God.

Limits of the Vocational Understanding of Work

A responsible theology of work should seek to preserve Luther's insight into God's call to everyday work with its two consequences. The way Luther (and especially later Lutheranism) developed and applied this basic insight is, however, problematic. Luther's notion of vocation has serious limitations, both in terms of its applicability to modern work, and in its theological persuasiveness.

Reinterpretation of Vocation?

One might be tempted to reinterpret the understanding of work as vocation in order to free it from theological inadequacies and make it more applicable to industrial and information societies. There are, however, both exegetical and theological arguments against doing so.

1 Exegetes agree that Luther misinterpreted 1 Corinthians 7.20, the main proof text for his understanding of work. '*Calling* in this verse is not calling *with* which, to which, or by which a man is called, but refers to the state in which he is *when* he is called to become a Christian.'[49] Except in 1 Corinthians 7.20 (and possibly 1 Cor. 1.26), Paul and others who share his tradition use the term *klēsis* as a *terminus technicus* for 'becoming a Christian'. As 1 Peter 2.9 shows, *klēsis* encompasses both the call of God out of 'darkness into his wonderful light' that constitutes Christians as Christians and the call to conduct corresponding to this 'light' (see 1 Peter 1.15), which should characterize the life of Christians.[50] Thus, when *klēsis* refers not to becoming a Christian but to living as a Christian, it does not designate a calling peculiar to every Christian and distinguishing one Christian from another, as Luther claimed of *vocatio externa*. Instead, it refers to the quality of life that should characterize *all Christians as Christians*.

2 Theologically it makes sense to understand work as *vocatio externa* only if one can conceive of this *vocatio* in analogy to *vocatio spiritualis*. One has to start with the singularity and permanence of *vocatio spiritualis*, which individualizes and concretizes itself in the process of human response in the form of a *singular and permanent vocatio externa*. Even Luther himself, in a social ethic designed for a comparatively static society, could not maintain this correspondence consistently. One could weaken the correspondence between *vocatio spiritualis* and *vocatio externa* and maintain that when the one call of God, addressing all people to become Christians, reaches each individual, it branches out into a plurality of callings for particular tasks.[51]

I do not find it helpful, however, to deviate in this way from the New Testament and from a dogmatic soteriological use of *vocatio*, especially since the New Testament has a carefully chosen term – actually a *terminus technicus* – to denote the multiple callings of every Christian to particular tasks both inside and outside the Christian church. I refer to the term *charisma*.

I propose that a theology of charisms supplies a stable foundation on which we can erect a theology of work that is both faithful to the divine revelation and relevant to the modern world of work. In the following pages I will first give a theological reflection on the Pauline notion of *charisma*, and second apply it to a Christian understanding of work, while developing further the theology of charisms as the application demands.

A Theological Reflection on Charisms

In recent decades the subject of charisms has been the focus of lively discussion, both exegetical and theological. As I argue here briefly for a particular understanding of charisms, my purpose is not merely to analyse Paul's statements but to develop theologically some crucial aspects of his understanding of charisms, and in this way set up a backdrop for a theology of work.

1   One should not define *charisma* so broadly as to make the term encompass the whole sphere of Christian ethical activity. E. Käsemann has argued that the whole ethical existence of the Christian, the *nova oboedientia*, is charismatic.[52] No doubt, the whole new life of a Christian must be viewed pneumatologically, but the question is whether it is legitimate to describe it more specifically as *charismatic*. I cannot argue for this point within the confines of a book on work,[53] but must simply assert that it seems to me more adequate to differentiate, with Paul, between the *gifts and the fruit* of the Spirit. The fruit of the Spirit designates the general character of Christian existence, 'the lifestyle of those who are indwelled and energized by the Spirit'.[54] The gifts of the Spirit are related to the specific tasks or functions to which God calls and fits each Christian.

2   One should not define *charisma* so narrowly as to include in the term only ecclesiastical activities. One interpretation limits the sphere of operation of charisms to the Christian fellowship, insisting that one cannot understand 'charismatically the various activities of Christians in relation to their non-Christian neighbours'.[55] But using individual charisms as examples, it would not be difficult to show the impossibility

of consistently limiting the operations to the Christian church. The whole purpose of the gift of an evangelist (see Eph. 4.11), for instance, is to relate the gospel to *non*-Christians. To take another example, it would be artificial to understand contributing to the needs of the destitute (see Rom. 12.8) as *charisma* when exercised in relation to Christians but as simple benevolence when exercised in relation to non-Christians. As the firstfruits of salvation, the Spirit of Christ is not only active in the Christian fellowship but also desires to make an impact *on the world through* the fellowship.[56] All functions of the fellowship – whether directed inward to the Christian community or outward to the world – are the result of the operation of the Spirit of God and are thus charismatic. The place of operation does not define charisms, but the manifestation of the Spirit for the divinely ordained purpose.

3 Charisms are not the possession of an elite group within the Christian fellowship. New Testament passages that deal with charisms consistently emphasize that charisms 'are found throughout the Church rather than being restricted to a particular group of people'.[57] In the Christian fellowship as the body of Christ there are no members without a function and hence also no members without a *charisma*. The Spirit, who is poured out upon all flesh (Acts 2.17ff.), imparts also charisms to all flesh: they are gifts given to the Christian community irrespective of the existing distinctions or conditions within it.

4 The tendency to restrict charisms to an elite group within the Christian fellowship goes hand in hand with the tendency to ascribe an elite character to charisms. In widespread pneumatologies in which the Spirit's function is to negate, even destroy the worldly nature,[58] 'charismatic' is very frequently taken to mean 'extraordinary'. Ecclesiologically we come across this restricted understanding of charisms in some Pentecostal (or 'charismatic') churches that identify charismatic with the spectacularly miraculous.[59] A secular version of this 'supernaturalistic reduction' confronts us in the commonly accepted Weberian understanding of *charisma* as an extraordinary quality of leadership that appeals to non-rational motives.[60] One of the main points of Pauline theology of charisms is the overcoming of such a restrictive concentration on the miraculous and extraordinary. For this reason it is of great importance to keep the term *charisma* as a generic term for both the spectacular and the ordinary.[61]

5 The traditional view of the impartation of charisms can be described as the addition model: 'the Spirit joins himself, as it were, to the person, giving "something" new, a new power, new qualities'.[62] It might, however, be better to understand the impartation of charisms according to the interaction model:[63] a person who is shaped by her genetic heritage

and social interaction faces the challenge of a new situation as she lives in the presence of God and learns to respond to it in a new way. This is what it means to acquire a new spiritual gift. No substance or quality has been added to her, but a more or less permanent skill has been learned.

We can determine the relationship between calling and charisma in the following way: the general calling to enter the kingdom of God and to live in accordance with this kingdom that comes to a person through the preaching of the gospel becomes for the believer a call to bear the fruit of the Spirit, which should characterize all Christians, and, as they are placed in various situations, the calling to live in accordance with the kingdom branches out in the multiple gifts of the Spirit to each individual.

Work in the Spirit

But is there a connection between charismata and the mundane work? If there is, can a theology of work be based on a theology of charismata? And if it could, would such a theology of work have any advantages over the vocational understanding of work so that we could with good conscience leave the second in favour of the first? Can it be applied to work of non-Christians or is it a theology of work only for a Christian subculture? Does not a pneumatological understanding of work amount to theological ideology of human achievement? To these questions I now turn.

Theological Basis

If we must understand every specific function and task of a Christian in the church and in the world charismatically, then everyday work cannot be an exception. The Spirit of God calls, endows, and empowers Christians to work in their various vocations. The charismatic nature of all Christian activity is the *theological* basis for a pneumatological understanding of work.

There are also some *biblical* references that can be taken to suggest a pneumatological understanding of work. We read in the Old Testament that the Spirit of God inspired craftsmen and artists who designed, constructed, and adorned the tabernacle and the temple. 'See, the Lord has chosen Bezalel ... and he has filled him with the Spirit of God, with skill, ability and knowledge in all kinds of crafts ... and ... the ability to teach others' (Ex. 35.2–3). 'Then David gave his son Solomon ... the plans of all that the Spirit had put in his mind for the courts of the temple of the Lord' (1 Chron. 28.11–12). Furthermore, judges and kings in Israel are often said to do their tasks under the anointing of the Spirit of God (see Judg. 3.10; 1 Sam. 16.13; 23.2; Prov. 16.10).[64]

As they stand, these biblical affirmations of the charismatic nature of human activity cannot serve as the basis for a pneumatological understanding of *all* work, for they set apart people gifted by the Spirit for various extraordinary tasks from others who do ordinary work. But we can read these passages from the perspective of the new covenant in which *all* God's people are gifted and called to various tasks by the Spirit. In this case they provide biblical illustrations for a charismatic understanding of the basic types of human work: intellectual (e.g. teaching) or manual (e.g. crafts) work, *poiesis* (e.g. arts and crafts) or *praxis* (e.g. ruling). All human work, however complicated or simple, is made possible by the operation of the Spirit of God in the working person; and all work whose nature and results reflect the values of the new creation is accomplished under the instruction and inspiration of the Spirit of God (see Isa. 28.24–29).

Work as Cooperation with God

If Christian mundane work is work in the Spirit, then it must be understood as *cooperation with God*. *Charisma* is not just a call by which God bids us to perform a particular task, but is also an inspiration and a gifting to accomplish the task. Even when *charisma* is exercised by using the so-called natural capabilities, it would be incorrect to say that a person is 'enabled' irrespective of God's relation to him. Rather, the enabling depends on the presence and activity of the Spirit. It is impossible to separate the gift of the Spirit from the enabling power of the Spirit.[65] When people work exhibiting the values of the new creation (as expressed in what Paul calls 'the fruit of the Spirit'), the Spirit works in them and through them.

The understanding of work as cooperation with God is implied in the New Testament view of Christian life in general. Putting forward his own Christian experience as a paradigm of Christian life, Paul said: 'it is no longer I who live, but Christ who lives in me; and the life I now live in the flesh I live by faith in the Son of God' (Gal. 2.20). That Paul can in the same breath make such seemingly contradictory statements about the acting agent of Christian life ('I no longer live, *Christ lives* in me' and '*I live* my life in the flesh') testifies unmistakably that the whole Christian life is a life of cooperation with God through the presence of the Spirit. A Christian's mundane work is no exception. Here, too, one must say: I work, and the Spirit of the resurrected Christ works through me.

Since the Spirit who imparts gifts and acts through them is 'a guarantee' (2 Cor. 1.22; cf. Rom. 8.23) of the realization of the eschatological new creation, cooperation with God in work is proleptic cooperation with God in God's eschatological *transformatio mundi.* As the glorified Lord, Jesus Christ is 'present in his gifts and in the services that both manifest these gifts and are made possible by them'.[66] Although his reign is still contested by the power of evil, he is realizing through those gifts his rule of love in the world. As Christians do their mundane work, the Spirit enables them to cooperate with God in the kingdom of God that 'completes creation and renews heaven and earth'.[67]

A Pneumatological Approach to Work: Does It Solve Anything?

Here I want to show that this understanding of work is not weighed down by the serious deficiencies of the vocational understanding of work.

1   The pneumatological understanding of work is free from the portentous ambiguity in Luther's concept of vocation, which consists in the undefined relation between spiritual calling through the gospel and external calling through one's station. The resurrected Lord alone through the Spirit calls and equips a worker for a particular task in the world. Of course, neither the Spirit's calling nor equipping occur in a social and natural vacuum; they do not come, so to speak, directly from Christ's immaterial Spirit to the isolated human soul. They are mediated through each person's social interrelations and psychosomatic constitution. These mediations themselves result from the interaction of human beings with the Spirit of God. Yet charisms *remain different from their mediations* and should not be reduced to or confused with them.[68] For the Spirit who gives gifts 'as he wills' (1 Cor. 12.11) *by* social and natural mediation is not the Spirit *of* human social structures or of a person's psychosomatic makeup, but the Spirit of the crucified and resurrected Christ, the firstfruits of the new creation.

2   The pneumatological understanding of work is *not as open to ideological misuse* as the vocational understanding of work. It does not proclaim work meaningful without simultaneously attempting to humanize it. Elevating work to cooperation with God in the pneumatological understanding of work implies an obligation to overcome alienation because the individual gifts of the person need to be taken seriously. The point is not simply to interpret work religiously as cooperation with God and thereby glorify it ideologically, but to transform work into a charismatic cooperation with God on the 'project' of the new creation.

3   The pneumatological understanding of work is easily applicable to the increasing *diachronic plurality* of employments or jobs that characterize industrial and information societies. Unlike Christian calling, *charisma* – in the technical sense – is not 'irrevocable' (see Rom. 11.29). True, a

person cannot simply pick and choose her *charisma*, for the sovereign Spirit of God imparts charisms 'as he wills' (1 Cor. 12.11). But the sovereignty of the Spirit does not prohibit a person from 'earnestly desiring' spiritual gifts (1 Cor. 12.31; 14.1, 12) and receiving various gifts at different times.[69] Paul presupposes both a diachronic and a synchronic plurality of charisms.

The diachronic plurality of charisms fits the diachronic plurality of employment or jobs in modern societies. Unlike in the vocational understanding of work, in the pneumatological understanding of work one need not insist that the occupational choice be a single event and there be a single right job for everyone[70] (either because God has called a person to one job or because every person possesses a relatively stable pattern of occupational traits). People are freed for several consecutive careers in rapidly changing work environments; their occupational decisions need not be irrevocable commitments but can be repeatedly made in a continuous dialogue between their preferences and talents on the one hand, and the existing job opportunities on the other.[71]

In any case, one can change jobs without coming under suspicion of unfaithfulness. If the change is in harmony with the *charisma* given, then changing can actually be an expression of faithfulness to God, who gave the *charisma* and readiness to serve fellow human beings in a new way. There is no need to worry that in the absence of a permanent calling, human life will be 'turned topsy-turvy'[72] (as Calvin thought) or that human beings will 'spend more time in idleness than at work'[73] (as the Puritans feared). Rather, freedom from the rigidity of a single, permanent vocation might season with creativity and interrupt with rest the monotonous lives of modern workaholics.

4   It is also easy to apply the pneumatological understanding of work to the *synchronic plurality* of jobs or employments. In Paul's view every Christian can have more than one *charisma* at any given time. His aim is that Christians 'excel in gifts' (1 Cor. 14.12), provided they exercise them in interdependence within the community and out of concern for the common good. The pneumatological understanding of work frees us from the limitation of being able to theologically interpret only a single employment of a Christian (or from the limitation of having to resort to a different theological interpretation for jobs that are not primary). In accordance with the plurality of charisms, there can be a plurality of employments or jobs without any one of them being regarded theologically as inferior, a mere 'job on the side'. The pneumatological understanding of work is thus also open to a redefinition of work, which today's industrial and information societies need.[74]

Notes

1 On that issue, see H. Berkhof, *Christ the Meaning of History* (Richmond, VA: John Knox Press, 1966), p. 189; D. L. Dabney, 'Die Kenosis des Geistes: Kontinuität zwischen Schöpfung und Erlösung im Werk des Heiligen Geistes' (Th.D. diss., University of Tübingen, 1989); H. Gese, 'Der Tod im Alten Testament', in *Zur Biblischen Theologie* (München: Kaiser, 1977), p. 50; A. A. Hoekema, *The Bible and the Future* (Grand Rapids, MI: Eerdmans; Exeter: Paternoster Press, 1979), pp. 39–40, 73–5, 274–87.

2 T. Aquinas, *Summa Theologica*, II-II, Q. 187, Art. 3 (Westminster, MD: Christian Classics, 1948). See Luther, *WA. Martin Luthers Werke. Kritische Gesamtausgabe*, 56 (Weimar: Hermann Böhlau, 1883–), p. 350. For a modern Christian version of this idea, see E. F. Schumacher, *Good Work* (New York: Harper & Row, 1979), pp. 112ff. In Buddhist tradition, too, work is conceived of as a path to enlightenment (see J. Kitagawa, 'Reflections on the Work Ethic in the Religions of East Asia', in *Comparative Work Ethics: Judeo-Christian, Islamic, and Eastern*, ed. J. Pelikan, J. Kitigava, and S. H. Nasr (Washington, DC: Library of Congress, 1985), p. 38).

3 See K. Barth, *Church Dogmatics*, III/4 (Edinburgh: T. & T. Clark, 1961), p. 525.

4 See S. Williams, 'The Partition of Love and Hope: Eschatology and Social Responsibility', *Transformation* 7, no. 3 (1990), p. 26.

5 Under annihilationist presuppositions, Bach's music could not have glorified God directly because it would not have had any intrinsic value. Only the sensations of pleasantness based on a temporary arrangement of matter in the form of human hearing organs would have made Bach's organ music more beautiful and valuable than is the sound of my fingers hitting the computer keyboard.

6 *Evangelism and Social Responsibility: An Evangelical Commitment* (Exeter: Paternoster Press, 1982), pp. 41–2.

7 See Berkhof, *Christ*, p. 190.

8 *Evangelism*, p. 42. Cf. V. Samuel and C. Sugden, 'Evangelism and Social Responsibility: A Biblical Study in Priorities', in *In Word and Deed: Evangelism and Social Responsibility*, ed. B. J. Nicholls (Exeter: Paternoster Press, 1985), pp. 198–214 (208ff.).

9 Contra Pope John Paul II, *Laborem Exercens: Encyclical Letter on Human Work*, section 26.

10 See C. Westermann, *Genesis 1–11: A Commentary* (Minneapolis: Augsburg, 1984), p. 85.

11 On that notion, see J. P. Miranda, *Communism in the Bible* (New York: Orbis Books, 1982), pp. 12ff.

12 R. H. Gundry, 'The New Jerusalem: People as Place, Not Place for People (Revelation 21:1–22:5)', *Novum Testamentum* 29 (1987), pp. 258, 263.

13 R. H. Gundry, *Matthew: A Commentary on His Literary and Theological Art* (Grand Rapids, MI: Eerdmans, 1985), pp. 106, 119.

14 Gundry, *Matthew*, p. 69. In his article on work in early Christianity, Hengel states that a realistic eschatology has its roots 'in the realistic preaching of Jesus and is widespread in early Christianity' (M. Hengel, 'Die Arbeit im frühen Christentum', *Theologische Beiträge* 17 (1986), p. 194).

15 See C. H. Ratschow, 'Eschatologie VIII', in *Theologische Realenzyklopädie*, vol. 10, ed. G Krause and G. Müller (Berlin: Walter de Gruyter, 1982), p. 355.

16 Contra Aquinas, *ST*, I-II, Q. 4, Art. 5.

17 Aquinas, *ST*, I-II, Q. 4, Art. 7.

18 In his seminal work, *Theology of Hope*, Moltmann has argued persuasively for a cosmic eschatology as opposed to Bultmann's individualistic and (despite the rhetoric) present-oriented eschatology (J. Moltmann, *Theology of Hope: On the Ground and the Implications of a Christian Eschatology* (New York: Harper & Row, 1967), pp. 58ff., 133ff.). More recently he developed some of his eschatological ideas in greater detail. In relation to the problem discussed here, see J. Moltmann, *Der Weg Jesu Christi. Christologie in messianischen Dimensionen* (München: Kaiser, 1989), pp. 282ff., particularly 286.

19 C. E. B. Cranfield, *The Epistle to the Romans*, International Critical Commentary (Edinburgh: T. & T. Clark, 1975), vol. 1, pp. 411–12.

20 F. F. Bruce, *The Epistle of Paul to the Romans: An Introduction and Commentary* (Grand Rapids, MI: Eerdmans, 1963), p. 170.

21 J. Calvin, *Institutes of the Christian Religion*, ed. J. T. McNeill (Philadelphia: Westminster Press, 1977), p. 989. Some other New Testament passages that affirm continuity between the present and the future orders are: Matt. 19.28; Acts 3.19–21; Rev. 21.24–26.

22 See H. Arendt, *Vita activa oder Vom tätigen Leben* (München: R. Piper, 1981), p. 26. For a rare theological reflection on the transitoriness and permanence of work, see J. C. Haughey, *Converting Nine to Five: A Spirituality of Daily Work* (New York: Crossroad, 1989), pp. 99ff.

23 See H. Rondet, *Die Theologie der Arbeit* (Würzburg: Echter, 1954), p. 64.

24 The passage refers specifically to the works of steadfastness in faith (see R. H. Mounce, *The Book of Revelation* (Grand Rapids, MI: Eerdmans, 1977), p. 278), but there is no reason to limit the application of the statement to these works alone.

25 For Protestant examples, see J. Moltmann, 'The Right to Work', in *On Human Dignity: Political Theology and Ethics* (Philadelphia: Fortress Press, 1984), pp. 38–45, 53–7; J. Stott, *Issues Facing Christians Today: A Major Appraisal of Contemporary Social and Moral Questions* (Basingstoke: Marshall Pickering, 1984), pp. 160f. For Roman Catholic theology, cf. *Laborem Exercens*, nos. 85ff., where John Paul II takes up the theology of work developed in the Pastoral constitution *Gaudium et Spes* (nos 67ff.) of Vatican II; 'Economic Justice for All: Catholic Social Teaching and the U.S. Economy', *Origins* 16, no. 32 (1986), pp. 410–55.

26 See J. Moltmann, *God in Creation: A New Theology of Creation and the Spirit of God* (San Francisco: Harper & Row, 1985), p. 86; W. Bienert, *Die Arbeit nach der Lehre der Bibel. Eine Grundlegung evangelischer Sozialethik* (Stuttgart: Evangelisches Verlagswerk, 1954), p. 45. Differently H. D. Preuß, 'Arbeit I', in *Theologische Realenzyklopädie*, vol. 3, ed. G. Krause and G. Müller (Berlin: Walter de Gruyter, 1978), p. 614.

27 Luther, *WA* 15, p. 373. The last paragraph was taken from M. Volf, *Zukunft der Arbeit—Arbeit der Zukunft. Der Arbeitsbegriff bei Karl Marx und seine theologische Wertung* (München: Kaiser; Mainz: Grünewald, 1988), p. 115.

28 This is stressed by M. Honnecker, 'Die Krise der Arbeitsgesellschaft und das christliche Ethos', *Zeitschrift für Theologie und Kirche* 80 (1983), p. 213.

29 On the 'New Jerusalem' as people rather than a place, see Gundry, 'The New Jerusalem'.

30 See J. M. Lochman, *Marx begegnen. Was Christen und Marxisten eint und trennt* (Gütersloh: Gütersloher Verlagshaus Mohn, 1975), pp. 117ff.

31 For the expressions, cf. P. Kuzmič, 'History and Eschatology: Evangelical

Views', in *In Word and Deed: Evangelism and Social Responsibility*, ed. B. J. Nicholls (Exeter: Paternoster Press, 1985), pp. 150ff.

32 Moltmann, 'Work', p. 45.

33 O. O'Donovan, *Resurrection and Moral Order: An Outline for Evangelical Ethics* (Leicester: InterVarsity Press; Grand Rapids, MI: Eerdmans, 1986), p. 55.

34 A. I. C. Heron, *The Holy Spirit: The Holy Spirit in the Bible, the History of Christian Thought, and Recent Theology* (Philadelphia: Westminster Press, 1983), p. 154.

35 See H. Berkhof, *The Doctrine of the Holy Spirit* (Richmond, VA: John Knox Press, 1964), p. 96.

36 See W. Schrage, 'Heil und Heilung im Neuen Testament', *Evangelische Theologie* 46 (1986), p. 200.

37 See G. E. Ladd, *A Theology of the New Testament* (Grand Rapids, MI: Eerdmans, 1974), pp. 76f.

38 See Moltmann, *Der Weg*, p. 127. Without knowing the results of modern New Testament studies, Pentecostalists have rightly maintained that by experiencing healing of the body, people became 'partakers of the *bodily nature of the kingdom of God*' (E. P. Paulk, *Your Pentecostal Neighbor* (Cleveland: Pathway Press, 1958), p. 110 – italics mine).

39 C. H. Pinnock, 'Introduction', in *The Holy Spirit: Renewing and Empowering Presence*, ed. G. Vandervelde (Winfield, BC: Wood Lake Books, 1989), p. 7.

40 Similarly W. Kasper, 'Die Kirche als Sakrament der Geistes', in *Kirche: Ort des Geistes*, ed. W. Kasper and G. Stauter (Freiburg: Herder, 1976), p. 35, with reference to a theology of the world, culture, and politics.

41 See, for instance, two contemporary Protestant writers from different segments of Protestantism, D. Field and E. Stephenson, *Just the Job: Christians talk about Work and Vocation* (Leicester: InterVarsity Press, 1978), pp. 18ff; and J. C. Raines and D. C. Day-Lower, *Modern Work and Human Meaning* (Philadelphia: Westminster Press, 1986), pp. 94ff.

42 See Calvin, *Institutes*, pp. 724f.

43 Luther, *WA* 34, II, p. 300.

44 I take it that Luther's use of vocation is not limited to one's standing within the three orders but often equals the person's occupation (contra K. Bockmühl, 'Protestant Ethics: The Spirit and the Word in Action', *Evangelical Review of Theology* 12 (1988), p. 108).

45 Luther, *WA* 34, II, p. 306.

46 G. Wingren, 'Beruf II. Historische und ethische Aspekte', in *Theologische Realenzyklopädie*, vol. 5, ed. G. Krause and G. Müller (Berlin: Walter de Gruyter, 1980), p. 661.

47 Luther, *WA* 10, I, p. 308.

48 Weber, *The Protestant Ethic and the Spirit of Capitalism* (New York: Charles Scribner's Sons, 1958), p. 80.

49 C. K. Barrett, *A Commentary on the First Epistle to the Corinthians*, Black's New Testament Commentaries (New York: Harper & Row, 1968), pp. 169–70; cf. H. Brockhaus, *Charisma und Amt. Die paulinische Charismenlehre auf dem Hintergrund der frühchristlichen Gemeindefunktionen* (Wuppertal: Brockhaus, 1972), p. 224; J. Eckert, 'Kaleō, ktl.', in *Exegetisches Wörterbuch zum Neuen Testament*, vol. 2, ed. Horst Balz und Gerhard Schneider (Stuttgart: Kohlhammer, 1981), p. 599.

50 See Preston, 'Vocation', in *A Dictionary of Christian Ethics*, ed. J. Macquarrie (London: SCM Press), p. 355: the New Testament term *vocatio* 'refer[s] to the call

of God in Christ to membership in the community of his people, the "saints", and to the qualities of Christian life which this implies'.

51 See F. Wagner, 'Berufung III. Dogmatisch', in *Theologische Realenzyklopädie*, vol. 5, ed. G. Krause and G. Müller (Berlin: Walter de Gruyter, 1980), p. 711.

52 See E. Käsemann, 'Amt und Gemeinde im Neuen Testament', in his *Exegetische Versuche und Besinnungen*, vol. 1 (Göttingen: Vandenhoeck & Ruprecht, 1970), pp. 109–34; E. Käsemann, 'Gottesdienst im Alltag der Welt', in *Exegetische Versuche und Besinnungen*, vol. 2, p. 204.

53 On that issue, see Brockhaus, *Charisma*, pp. 220ff.

54 F. F. Bruce, *The Epistle to the Galatians: A Commentary on the Greek Text*, New International Greek Testament Commentary (Grand Rapids, MI: Eerdmans, 1982), p. 251.

55 Brockhaus, *Charisma*, p. 239.

56 For a similar understanding of *charisma*, see M. Harper, *Let My People Grow: Ministry and Leadership in the Church* (London: Hodder & Stoughton, 1977), p. 100; H. Mühlen, 'Charisma und Gesellschaft', in *Geistesgaben heute*, ed. H. Mühlen (Mainz: Matthias-Grünewald, 1982), p. 161.

57 H. Küng, *The Church* (New York: Doubleday, 1976), p. 246.

58 See W. Joest, *Dogmatik I: Die Wirklichkeit Gottes* (Göttingen: Vandenhoeck & Ruprecht, 1984), p. 302.

59 For a similar understanding of charisms in the New Testament, see also K. Berger, 'Charisma, ktl', in *Exegetisches Wörterbuch zum Neuen Testament*, vol. 3, ed. Horst Balz und Gerhard Schneider (Stuttgart: Kohlhammer, 1983), p. 1105.

60 For an important (but only partial) criticism of Weber's understanding of charismatic personality and its popular use in Western culture, see A. Bloom, *The Closing of the American Mind: How Higher Education has Failed Democracy and Impoverished the Souls of Today's Students* (New York: Simon & Schuster, 1987), pp. 208ff.

61 S. Schulz, 'Charismenlehre des Paulus. Bilanz der Probleme und Ergebnisse', in *Rechtfertigung: Festschrift für Ernst Käsemann zum 70. Geburtstag*, ed. J. Friedrich et al. (Göttingen: Vandenhoeck & Ruprecht; Tübingen: Mohr, Siebeck, 1975), p. 444.

62 T. Veenhof, 'Charismata: Supernatural or Natural?', in *The Holy Spirit: Renewing and Empowering Presence*, ed. G. Vandervelde (Winfield, CA: Wood Lake Books, 1989), p. 90.

63 See Veenhof, 'Charismata', p. 91.

64 The point I am making is not invalidated by the observation that the claim to Spirit's inspiration might have served Israel's kings only as a sacral legitimation of a fundamentally secular power (see G. von Rad, *Theologie des Alten Testaments I: Die Theologie der geschichtlichen Überlieferungen Israels* (München: Kaiser, 1969), p. 109).

65 See Käsemann, 'Amt', p. 110.

66 Käsemann, 'Amt', p. 118.

67 Moltmann, 'Work', p. 45.

68 For a similar differentiation between calling and mediations within the vocational understanding of work, see Bayer, 'Berufung', in *Evangelisches Soziallexikon*, 7th edition, ed. T. Schober et al. (Stuttgart: Kreuz, 1980), p. 142.

69 Paul explicates his views on charisms in the context of the understanding of the church as the body of Christ. He does not derive his views on charisms from this

metaphor of the church, but uses the metaphor to illustrate certain aspects of his teaching on charisms.

70 So industrial psychology until recently; see W. S. Neff, *Work and Human Behavior*, 2nd edition (Chicago: Aldine, 1977), p. 125.

71 Thomas Aquinas speaks of natural inclinations (caused by divine providence) to particular employments: 'Haec autem diversificatio hominum in diversis officiis contingit promo ex divina providential, quae ita hominum status distribuit ... secundo etiam ex causis naturalibus, ex quibus contingit, quod in diversis hominubus sund diversae inclunationes ad diversa officia' (*Quœst. Quodlibetales*, VII, Art. 17c; cf. E. Welty, *Vom Sinn und Wert der menschlichen Arbeit* (Heidelberg: Kerle, 1949), p. 41). As portrayed by Thomas Aquinas, the natural inclinations of different people are as static as Luther's calling and are hence equally ill-suited to modern, dynamic societies.

72 Calvin, *Institutes*, p. 724.

73 Baxter, as quoted by Weber, *Ethic*, p. 161.

74 Volf, *Zukunft*, pp. 100ff.

7

Be Fruitful and Multiply: Work and Anthropology

JAY WESLEY RICHARDS

It's obvious: we are bodily creatures. We breathe air, drink water, eat food, get dizzy if we consume too much alcohol, and grow delirious if we go three days without sleep. Modern discoveries reinforce this: we now know that our bodies are made up of the same chemical elements we find in plants, animals, and even distant galaxies.

At the same time, we all know that we are conscious agents who can make free choices that have not been predetermined by the dictates of matter.

This is the common-sense view – the view that all of us, to some degree, assume, even when we deny it. Only materialism has ever pretended that matter is all that matters, that we are *only* material beings determined entirely by blind forces of nature. And even good materialists cannot keep up the pretence for long. Whatever they officially confess, materialists act as if they are free, and act as if you are, as well. Your professor may say you are nothing but a bipedal beast, mere matter in motion, but he will hold you responsible if he thinks you voted for Donald Trump.

And yet the truth that humans are at once material and spiritual beings is hard to keep together. We incline towards one or the other side of this joint truth. We are tempted by simpler heresies. Despite the fruitful and providential interaction between the Judaeo-Christian and Graeco-Roman threads of Western culture, the early influence of neo-Platonism inclined Christians to downplay the value of the body, and sometimes to disdain physical work. Work – that is, physical work – was treated as fit only for slaves. Despite their differences, both Plato and Aristotle maintained this view, and the neo-Platonists inherited it.

At its worst, the body was treated as an imposition, and the soul as the 'true self'. Of course, Christian theology always limited how far this sort of thinking could go – and the extremes were denounced as heresies. But it was a tendency.

The tendency of our own time is in the other direction. Once material-ism became intellectual orthodoxy in the academy, some theologians and biblical scholars, such as Nancey Murphy, began to claim that Scripture knows nothing of an immaterial soul. The resurrection of the body means just that and nothing more. Any talk about an immaterial soul, they tell us, is really an imposition of Greek philosophy on to the Hebraic texts and mindset. It is, in other words, bad theology.[1]

This is a staggering claim: apparently, for 2,000 years no Christian understood the Christian view of the human person. It was only when an anti-religious materialism captured the commanding heights of culture that a few Christian scholars discovered the truth. How convenient.

Despite this embrace of fashionable materialism, however, this trend has not ushered in a new-found appreciation of work. I do not think this is a coincidence. The biblical view of work can only fully be appreciated, and appropriated, by those who maintain the biblical view of humankind as a unity of the material and immaterial.

If it were not for the relentless power of reality, the clarity of the biblical texts, and the precision of early Christian creeds, the material and spiritual unity that is the human person might easily have been lost to history. In fact, even with the testimony of reality, Scripture, and creed, the truth about humankind is still, always, at risk.

The Biblical Picture

The commitment to this unity of matter and spirit, and what it means, is perhaps nowhere clearer than in the biblical depiction of work. Indeed, it is impossible to understand the biblical view of work without the biblical view of the human person.

Of all the world's religious and philosophical texts, human work receives its highest honour in the Jewish and Christian Scriptures. To see this, it is best to start at the very beginning. John Bergsma treats the opening chapters of the Bible in detail in Chapter 2 of this volume. Here let us look at the Genesis account briefly, since it is the foundation not only for work but also for biblical anthropology.

The creation account in Genesis is known to have parallels in the ancient Near Eastern world. When nineteenth-century archaeologists discovered the Babylonian epic *Enuma Elish* etched on clay tablets, some scholars began to claim that the biblical creation epic depended on accounts such as this one. But even those scholars who insist that the biblical text is derivative still note a key difference. In the Babylonian text, Marduk kills Tiamat, splits her body in two, and uses the two halves to make the earth and the sky.

In contrast, in Genesis 1.1 God (*Elohim*) simply creates (*bara*) the heavens and the earth – that is, everything in the visible creation. In the text,

God does not have a nemesis that he must kill – let alone chop up – to construct the world. The biblical creation story lacks the vulgar mythology of the Babylonian epic. Indeed, God's creative work in Genesis seems so formal and exalted that, in the nineteenth century, European scholars, imbued with the spirit of Hegel's evolutionary philosophy, convinced themselves that this text must have been written centuries later than the text in Genesis 2 and 3, which portrays God in much earthier and more anthropomorphic terms.

Weren't these Hegelians embarrassed by the fact that God in Genesis 1 has a *work week* much like our own? In fact, he not only works during the day. He rests at night and on the seventh day. Apparently, the author of the text had his own concerns and was not interested in fitting the stereotype of abstract monotheism as imagined by German idealism.[2]

Even though God, like human beings, has a work week, God seems to exercise perfect freedom in his work. Nothing impedes him. There is no countervailing force God must overcome. There is no recalcitrant matter, as in Plato's *Timaeus*. And there is no complicated drama, as one sees in other creation stories in the ancient Near East. Again: no Tiamat, no cosmic bodies to chop up. God is the sole character in the drama for most of the chapter. Everything else comes to be because God calls it forth, pure and simple.[3]

Some biblical scholars do think the reference to 'the deep' suggests a sort of pre-existing chaos. If so, then the text would teach that God ordered the chaos, but did not create it from nothing. Is that right?

I think not. The text begins with what seems to be the preamble for everything that follows: 'In the beginning God created the heavens and the earth.' 'The heavens and the earth' is probably a shorthand for everything in creation, for the whole shebang.

Then immediately in verse 2, we read: 'The earth was without form and void, and darkness was upon the face of the deep; and the Spirit of God was moving over the face of the waters.' There is a wordplay in Hebrew that is lost in English. 'The deep' is *tehom*, and the phrase 'without form and void' is *tohu va-bohu*. Is this a reference to some primordial chaos? Perhaps. But there's no sense that this 'deep' *pre-exists* God's creative work. Quite the contrary: the text follows the preamble, which has already asserted God's unique creative work.

Moreover, the deep does not *do* anything. There is no hint that it resists God's work. In fact, the text seems constructed to rule out the idea of some contrary force. God simply says, 'Let there be', and what he commands comes to be. Whatever rumours the first audience of this text may have heard about the gods of other cultures, the true God simply commands. He creates without rival.

Incidentally, the text offers clues that while God has a work week, it is not identical to the human work week. Ours is set by the (apparent) rising and setting of the sun. In Genesis 1, in contrast, God creates the light at the beginning, separates it from the darkness, and then uses the contrast between the two to circumscribe the days of his creative work. The sun and the moon do not appear until day four of the divine work week.

Like the human beings who were the first audience for this text, God works during the day, stops working at night (marked off by 'evening and morning'), and rests on the seventh day. But unlike our work week, God's seventh day does not come to an end.

In this way, the Genesis author manages to erect a parallel between mundane human work and the supreme work of the creator, while avoiding the implication that God must toil as we do. That is quite a feat for such a short text in any age.

It is a mistake, I think, to read God's work week as an analogy of our work week. It is the other way around: the human work week reflects God's pre-eminent one. God's work is creation 'in the proper sense', as Thomas Aquinas would say. Our work week derives from God's. We only exist and work because of God's creation. We rely on light from the heavens over which we have no control. And we work with pre-existing material. Our work, then, is an analogy of God's work week, not vice versa.[4]

We are dealing here with a tightly packed theological treatise. Every detail is ordered and dense with meaning. A ten-year-old child can read it and get the gist of it. And yet a scholar can study it for a lifetime and still not discover all its secrets.

So God creates, he summons the light, separates it from the darkness, and these then set the pace for his work week. (The light and darkness here are never explained, though they are clearly not the light of our sun and the darkness of our night.) On each of the six days, God says, 'Let there be', and something comes forth. He separates the land, sky, and water. He calls forth seeds and plants and heavenly lights, as well as sea creatures and flying creatures, which he commands to reproduce. On the sixth day, he commands the earth to 'bring forth living creatures'. This creative pattern continues for six days. But on the sixth day, the pattern is interrupted by an encore. Before another evening arrives, God speaks again, this time to himself in the plural. The reason for this is provided in the text: the word for God used is a plural form *Elohim* rather than merely *El*. He says:

> 'Let us make man in our image, after our likeness; and let them have dominion over the fish of the sea, and over the birds of the air, and over the cattle, and over all the earth, and over every creeping thing that creeps upon the earth.'
>
> So God created man in his own image, in the image of God he created him; male and female he created them.

And God blessed them, and God said to them, 'Be fruitful and multiply, and fill the earth and subdue it; and have dominion over the fish of the sea and over the birds of the air and over every living thing that moves upon the earth.' (Gen. 1.26–28)

God then rests on the seventh day 'from all his work which he had done'.

Now, imagine that we had only this one text, a mere fragment from an ancient people group known as the Hebrews, and we were trying to discern their theology. What would we think? We would certainly conclude that humankind has a unique status over the rest of the visible creation. God may command the swimming and flying creatures to be fruitful and multiply. But it is only human beings that he creates in his image (*tselem*) and likeness. And so, his command to us to be fruitful and multiply will differ from his similar command to the other animals. Indeed, its meaning should, in some way, hearken to the work of *Elohim*, for the simple reason that we are created in his image and likeness.

The Hebrew term *tselem*, which we translate as 'image', is used in Scripture to refer to a resemblance, a representative figure. So it must connect in some way to what we know about God from the text. And what is that? We know that he exercises orderly creative power and freedom. Indeed, he exercises it pre-eminently. The text, therefore, suggests that we resemble God in this and perhaps other ways. God's work, and so human work, are thus connected in the biblical text from the very beginning.

This becomes more obvious in Genesis 2 and 3. As mentioned above, many source critics explain the differences between Genesis 1 and 2—3 in terms of the documentary hypothesis. The basic claim is that Genesis 2—3 are much older and more 'primitive' than Genesis 1. On this view, 'priestly' editors combined the texts sometime during or after the Babylonian exile, in roughly the sixth or fifth century BC. The evidence for this claim is that the description of God is less anthropomorphic in Genesis 1 than in Genesis 2—3, and the references to God differ in the two passages.[5] We read of *Elohim* in chapter 1. In contrast, we read of *Yahweh Elohim* – usually translated in English as 'LORD God' – in chapters 2 and 3.

The documentary hypothesis is never more plausible than it is here, since the contrasts between the passages are so conspicuous. But as a general theory to explain the Pentateuch, the hypothesis suffers several problems:

1 It quickly becomes circular and ad hoc.
2 It lacks all independent evidence. We have never found manuscript evidence of the supposed independent documents – even though they were supposed to have been written many centuries apart. We find them together – whether whole or in fragments.

3   We have no analogous evidence of other texts that are known to have been patched together in the way scholars propose for the Pentateuch. It's a hypothesis with a sample size of one.
4   The text is riddled with literary devices that exhibit its overall unity.
5   The hypothesis runs afoul of the fact that this text, as it is, has been read and studied carefully as a unified text for thousands of years.[6]

None of this means the biblical author did not use sources, written and oral, to construct the text we have. But we have every right to treat the text as we have it: as a unified narrative.

So why the contrast between the first and second chapters? When we treat the text as a unified work, the answer is simple. Genesis 1 is God-focused and treats the general creation. The word for God – *Elohim* – is the generic Hebrew word for the deity. It is very much like our generic English word 'God', which can be used to refer to the One God, as well as to the 'gods' of pagan myths and other ancient Near Eastern religions. The frame narrows slightly in every verse in chapter 1 until its climax: the creation of man. When reading even in English, we can feel the sweep from the cosmic to the particular. The action is attributed to God as creator, with the more generic word *Elohim*. This exalted tone is not lost, even though God has a work week (which might otherwise be thought of as an anthropomorphism).

Genesis 2 and 3, in contrast, are much more down-to-earth, both literally and figuratively. We do not have a precise date of origin for this text, but we do know its original audience were Israelites between the thirteenth and sixth centuries BC. In Genesis 1 the author has established that God, as creator, is transcendent, and has created all that is both freely and without rival. The author also has constructed a formal parallel between God's work in creation and humankind's work in the creation, while restraining the use of anthropomorphic expressions. Even though God has a work week, no one reading Genesis 1 would conclude, as Mormon theology does, that God has a body just as we have bodies.

Once the author has established these interpretative boundaries, he is then free to speak of God in much more intimate terms, as suits his purpose. He does just that in Genesis 2.

In chapter 2, the heavens and the earth are the background. A home for the first human couple is the foreground. Not an abstract home: a specific patch of ground intersected by four rivers: the Gihon, Pishon, Tigris, and Euphrates. Indeed, *even if* priestly editors compiled the final text after the Babylonian exile (sixth century BC), they would have had to interpret the composite narrative in just this way. Otherwise, they would have found it contradictory and so would not have combined the texts.[7]

The shift in name from *Elohim* to *Yahweh Elohim* makes a specific theological point: the creator who called forth everything that is is the same God who gave us his name at Sinai. (*Yahweh* is God's personal name, first revealed to Moses much later in the narrative, but the event is in the past for the original audience for this text.) And this same God quite intimately and uniquely created man and woman – one man and one woman.

Lest we over-spiritualize the details, the LORD God does not just create (*bara*, used in Gen. 1.1 and again in Gen. 2.3–4). He *forms* and *fashions* (*yatsar*) the man from 'the dust of the earth'. Like a potter, he forms *Adam* from the *adamah*. Unlike a human sculptor, however, the LORD God 'breathe[s] into his nostrils the breath of life; and the man became a living being'. Then the LORD God plants a garden and puts the man in it 'to till and keep it'. From that same ground the LORD God brings forth animals, giving to the man the job of naming them.

If we had only Genesis 2.4–25, without Genesis 1, it would create discomfort. That is, it would tempt the theologically astute reader to explain it away, since the language is so anthropomorphic. The effect is quite different, however, because it follows the exalted, tightly structured text of Genesis 1. Now the anthropomorphic language of Genesis 2 can do real work, rather than risk being explained away as the work of a primitive author who thought the creator had a physical body with hands and a mouth. Any reader of the previous chapter will know that the author knew better.

What is striking, for our purposes, is that God is described as a gardener who fashions dirt with his hands. He makes the man from that dirt – a human from the humus. The first thing God does is to give the man responsibility for the garden, and, in a sense, for the animals. A reader who has spent time reading, say, Aristotle, cannot help but notice the contrast. This God is no mere Unmoved Mover, contemplating only itself. And Adam is no Athenian philosopher merely contemplating the good and relying for his sustenance on the slaves in the fields. Indeed, no sooner does God place the man in the garden than he creates a helper made from one of the man's ribs. God fashions the man like a gardener, and then appoints man and woman in their original state as gardeners and herders.

If Athens protects us from imagining that God is a bearded old man in the clouds, Jerusalem protects us from imagining that God is a ghostly abstraction. Genesis 2 rubs ours noses in the dirt, just in case we miss the point.

And here is the point: work even at its most basic and laborious is part of the divine plan. It is a central part of God's mandate for us on earth. If we want to know how we resemble God, let us look to our work. The creation is, in a sense, the Garden of God, and we are the groundskeepers.[8] If we separate either the spiritual or the material part of our work, then we do violence to it, just as we do violence to ourselves when we reduce the human person either to a mere material body or to an immaterial soul trapped in matter.

Work is *not*, as some church folks imagine, part of the curse of the fall. It is right there, at the very beginning. The fall distorts and perverts our work by setting us at enmity with the ground, by turning work into toil and drudgery. But that is a distortion of a prior good – namely, work – which is part of God's original plan.

A Unique Nexus of Heaven and Earth

In both Genesis 1 and 2, human beings are set off from other animals. In Genesis 1, God makes the man and woman in his image. In Genesis 2, he gives the man his breath. Read together, it's clear that humankind is a unique nexus of the heaven and earth, of the immaterial and the material. Humankind is the dust of the earth and breath of God – lowly and exalted – at one and the same time. The man expresses this unified but hybrid nature when he does one of two things: when he reproduces after his own kind, and when he works to till the garden, purposefully to transform the earth. The text links biological reproduction with what we now think of as economic production. In the biblical picture, the two activities are more related than we might otherwise imagine. Perhaps it is no coincidence that many advanced economies not only quit producing. They quit reproducing, as well.

In any case, the treatment of human work in the rest of Scripture reinforces the picture laid down so firmly at the beginning. In contrast to the Graeco-Roman thread of Western culture, human labour is never treated as beneath the dignity of creatures made in God's image. On the contrary, work is a way in which we express our nature. From Cain and Abel, to the great leader and liberator Moses, the work of human hands is central to the human story.

The Pentateuch is traditionally attributed to Moses. But the Moses we encounter in the text is no mere bookish scholar. Though he is raised in Pharaoh's household, he spends many years in an obscure backwater, tending flocks. At the pinnacle of the united kingdom of Israel is David, a shepherd whom we first meet as boy who uses a slingshot to vanquish a foe. David prefigures the Messiah both typologically and biologically. It is from David's line that the Messiah is born.

At Jesus's birth, Matthew says that Jesus was adored by foreign dignitaries from the east, which befits a king. But Luke tells us that the *first* people to greet the Holy Family in a stable in tiny Bethlehem were humble shepherds.

Though in the Davidic line, Jesus is born into the family of a humble carpenter. In traditional Christian and especially Roman Catholic iconography, Joseph 'the worker' is often depicted holding a carpenter's square and hammer. Though Jesus is born of the virgin Mary through the Holy Spirit, Jesus did not bypass the mundane life of his family. He pursued Joseph's work until he began his public ministry. There is never any hint that this was degrading or inappropriate. Christian carpenters often feel pride by remembering that the Lord was himself a carpenter.

A superficial reading of the Gospels might suggest that the ancient Jews also saw work as degrading. When Jesus first spoke with authority in his hometown of Nazareth, it caused him trouble. Mark recounts the incident when Jesus spoke openly in his local synagogue. Those who heard him complained: '"Is not this the carpenter, the son of Mary and brother of James and Joses and Judas and Simon, and are not his sisters here with us?" And they took offence at him' (Mark 6.3).

The offence was not that he was a carpenter, though, or that he happened to have relatives. The Nazarenes were showing the provincialism of a small village. They assumed that anyone they knew as a child could not turn out to be significant. As Jesus explained, 'A prophet is not without honour, except in his own country, and among his own kin, and in his own house' (Mark 6.4).

The disciples were drawn from similar stock. Many, such as Peter, Andrew, Bartholomew, James, and John were fishermen. None were scholars, lawyers, or priests. So far as we know, the only disciple who had a scandalous job was Matthew (Levi), who was a tax collector before he left it behind to follow Jesus. Saul/Paul, who became an apostle only after the resurrection, was well educated and was even a Roman citizen. Still, he made his living as a tentmaker.

Note the pervasive unity throughout of the physical and spiritual, of body and soul. A desire to defend this unity in Jesus's person was preserved and increasingly refined in the Councils from Nicaea (AD 325) to Chalcedon (451). Chalcedon crowned the doctrine. Jesus is not God or man, not half God and half man, but *Truly and Fully God and Truly and Fully Man*.

Of course, these creeds are interested in the unity of Christ's being, rather than his work per se. The point here is that such unity is evident not just in Christ's earthly work, but in all human work portrayed in Scripture.

Returning to the biblical text and Christ's earthly ministry, the theme continues on the night before his crucifixion. In his last supper with his disciples, Jesus offers up not grains of wheat and wild grapes, but bread and wine. Almost all Christian traditions retain these elements however much they may differ on the details. The elements combine both what God has created – uncultivated wheat and grapes – and the fruit of human labour and ingenuity.

The Roman Missal (part of the Rite in Roman Catholicism) makes the point explicit. Before consecration, the priest holds up a host and cup of wine and prays, echoing the more ancient Jewish *Berakhah* prayer:

> Blessed are you, Lord God of all creation, for through your goodness we have received the bread we offer you: Fruit of the earth and work of human hands, it will become for us the bread of life.
>
> Blessed are you, Lord God of all creation, for through your goodness we have received the wine we offer you: Fruit of the vine and work of human hands, it will become our spiritual drink.

What Happens When the Balance is Lost

If the human person is a unique unity of body and soul, of the material and the immaterial, then we can predict that views that distort this truth about man will also misunderstand our work.

Consider two popular alternatives: Marxism and transhumanism.

Marxism

In the mid-twentieth century, half of the human race were subjects of a vast Marxist experiment. They suffered untold misery as a result. As an economic theory, Marxism is now dead. But it lives on in the hearty redoubts of certain humanities departments.

Karl Marx saw human beings *not* as unique sources of freedom and creativity, but as slaves of a deterministic process of matter and class conflict. What Marx called 'capitalism' was understood as simply one stage in a dialectical process in which the conflict between capital and labour predominates. According to Marx and his co-conspirator Frederic Engels, the capitalist is the person who owns 'the means of production' – the farmland, tools, and factories – and who exploits the labourers, who are the true source of economic value.

This 'labour theory of value' led Marx to make predictions about the future of capitalism that are now known to be false. In *The Communist Manifesto*, for instance, Marx and Engels predict that as capital increases – say, as factory equipment became more advanced – the wages of workers in such factories should go down. In the real world, the opposite happened. Why? Because workers who are more productive are more economically valuable to their employers. As a result, in competitive markets this allows workers to fetch higher wages for similar work. A carpenter with nail guns and power saws can do more, and will be paid more – even if his employer owns the tools – than the same carpenter who must work with wood and flint.

Marx had things backwards. Literal labour only has economic value under certain 'informational' conditions (I'll explain the phrase below). Imagine two farmers, Ernie and Bert. Ernie plants wheat seeds in furrows of rich soil, waters the field, fertilizes it with compost, protects the field from animals who might dig up the seeds, then harvests the wheat at the right time and sells it to others whom he knows will use it to make bread.

Bert works hard planting stones, which he covers with salt and sprinkles with the sacrificial blood of sparrows twice a week. Ernie and Bert work equally hard. But only Ernie creates economic value. Indeed, only Ernie really works at all. Bert is wasting time and energy.

The labour is identical, so what explains the difference? The difference is that Ernie uses his knowledge of natural processes and his knowledge of what others want and need to guide how he applies his labour. That knowledge is not itself a material object, but it has dramatic effects on the material world to which he applies it. Ernie's act is 'informational' in a way that Bert's is not.

In the same way, even in Marx's stereotypical capitalist society, the labour of the workers gains almost all its value from the fact that it is purposefully channelled towards valued ends. The more capital-intensive the labour, the more value it has. Marx, fixated as he was on the observable material part of the picture – hands sewing fabric and sowing seeds – missed the immaterial source of economic value.

Materialism and the related labour theory of value may seem to honour the physical body, but the materialist cannot honour the body for the simple reason that he denies the fact that it is a body. A body is what it is because of its form. A body can only be a *human* body if it instantiates the human form, human nature. The body is not just a jumble of parts. Nor is it merely a shell for the soul. The body expresses the soul, and the soul gives form to the body. In contrast, and strictly speaking, the Marxist and all other materialists must see the body as a mere aggregation of parts. At best, the body is a machine governed by the immutable laws of physics. So if he is consistent, a materialist like Marx does not exalt or dignify either the body or work, but rather demotes them and explains them away.

Transhumanism

No one can be a consistent materialist for long. As a world view, materialism is more unstable than carbon-15 (which has a half-life of about two and half seconds). In the information age – when we are surrounded by software and digital goods – materialism has spawned a movement that at first glance seems like its opposite: transhumanism.

The April 2017 cover story of *National Geographic* introduces the subject for casual readers. Transhumanists hold that we are now at the stage in which we will take charge of our own evolution, merge with our machines, and transcend our human form. These thinkers treat human beings as, in effect, software. Ray Kurzweil, the movement's high priest, predicts a coming technological 'singularity', in which our information technology will become more intelligent than we are. Not to worry, though, because once we can attain super-high resolution brain scans, we will be able to upload our 'minds' to much more durable hardware.

At first glance, Kurzweil seems to hold a strong form of body/soul dualism, in which the body is little more than a temporary vehicle for the soul. The soul, which is the 'true self', can persist in radically different physical substrates. Kurzweil and other transhumanists, however, are neither Gnostics nor neo-Platonists.[9] Kurzweil's 2013 book *How to Create a Mind* reveals his thinking in depressing detail. He identifies the mind not with the soul, consciousness, or a person, but with a *physical pattern in the brain.* This is the crucial premise in his argument that capturing three-dimensional brain scans will allow us to capture our mind.[10] Despite his references to information and software, Kurzweil is still stuck in the mental prison of materialism.

Since transhumanism misunderstands the truth about man, it is no surprise that it also misunderstands the nature and consequences of human work. There is now a cottage industry of books, articles, and conferences predicting that intelligent machines will soon do everything that we once imagined was the exclusive jurisdiction of man.

First, in the decades following the Second World War, the computers came for … the computers – which at the time was a job description. Claude Shannon, the founder of information theory, married a computer whom he met at Bell Labs. In the following decades, everything from travel agencies to retail stores to insurance adjusting and car manufacturing became automated. And we are just getting started. Routine assembly-line work will soon be a relic of the past. Just over the horizon are self-driving trucks and cars. Some experts plausibly predict that half of what doctors now do will be surrendered to machines in the next two decades. Certain complex physical tasks will take longer to replace, but it is not a stretch to expect humanoid robotic house and groundskeepers within our children's lifetimes.[11]

Once we create machines that are more intelligent than we are – 'strong' artificial intelligences – there will be nothing left for us to do.

Some think this end of work will usher in a hedonistic utopia wherein we party all night and sleep all day. Others see a future dystopia with a few trillionaires, along with billions of unnecessary people with nothing to do. The latter is roughly the argument of Martin Ford in his 2015 book *Rise of the Robots*.[12]

In an overreaction, a small segment of our culture seeks a simple return to the land. They call for a rejection of much of the technology that seems to come between us and the dust from which we have come, and to which we must, in the end, return.

The real problem here is not information technology, however, but the unexamined assumptions that together form the simple, transhumanist argument. It runs like this:

1 Man is a machine.
2 We build machines.
3 Our machines are mimicking more and more of the features not only of physical labour, but of intelligence.
4 Therefore, once our machines are smarter and more capable than we are, they will replace our work.

Depending on your taste, 4 is either a good or bad thing.

If 1 is false, however, then the argument goes nowhere. What if human beings, machine makers we may be, are image bearers of the creator, unique hybrids of the material and the immaterial? In that case, we should see our work, both now and in the future, in a quite different light.

Homo Faber: Man as In-former of the Material World

To do meaningful work is, at least in part, to create new economic value. As I argue elsewhere, that is always about purposefully informing 'the material and social world in more and more elaborate ways'.[13] To work is to create information.

Even work as manifestly physical as farming, fishing, shepherding, and carpentry creates economic value only to the extent that it channels the material world in ways that are valuable and meaningful and useful to oneself and/or others.

We should not overinterpret the focus in Scripture on these types of manual labour, as if these are the only kinds of work fit for human beings. These forms of work predominate in the Bible because, from antiquity until well into the modern age, the vast majority of people did one of two things: animal husbandry and farming. Moreover, it stands to reason that Scripture would portray God (in Genesis 2 and 3) as creating the world in a similar way: with his hands, as would a gardener. Genesis 1, though, keeps us from reading too much into the imagery.

This portrayal of God as a gardener has made the biblical text far more accessible to far more human beings than an abstract account of creation would have. As late as the American founding in 1776, some 95 per cent of the American population were farmers. Even at the dawn of the twentieth, half of all Americans lived and worked on farms.

Is it any wonder that Cain was a farmer, and Abel a shepherd?

At the same time, even work as abstract as computer programming is still about the purposeful input of intelligence into the material world. This is the key feature of etching a furrow in the ground to plant seeds or etching transistors in an integrated circuit.

God speaks – which is a form of meaningful communication – and the material world comes to be. Humankind acts upon that material world as a creator of new information. This is an intuitive description of the biblical picture of human beings as the nexus of material and immaterial, of heaven and earth. The immaterial sources of information are ideas in our minds that we conceive, share, and remix. (Our word 'idea' comes from the Greek *eidos*, and is a near synonym for the Latin word *informare*.) For these ideas to have social or economic meaning, though, they must touch the world of matter. The first time a person scratched a furrow in the ground to plant seeds, he *in-formed* the world. That is, he infused the physical world with information.

Consider the first man who started a controlled fire. Let us call him Prometheus. Think of the information as Prometheus intelligently chooses from a range of choices: rock rather than mud, flint rather than sand, two stones rather than one, striking them together over dry bits of grass rather than over a thousand and one other choices, and on it goes. The information is the shift from the vast range of passive possibilities to the applied know-how that yields a warm, controlled fire in a pit in a cave, roasting lamb.

Incidentally, the word *intelligence* derives from two Latin words, *inter* (between) and *lego* (to choose). To act intelligently, then, is to choose rightly among alternatives for a purposeful end. It is, in effect, how we create information. To work is to infuse information into the material and social world.

Fast-forward a few thousand years. Now whole civilizations know how to control fire. They also know how to use it to separate copper and iron and gold from ore, to melt it and mould it. They herd cattle, sheep, and goats. They cultivate fruit trees, and plant, tend, water, harvest, and grind wheat. This knowledge makes great cities possible. The know-how is no longer left to oral tradition: it can be recorded and preserved in written records.

A couple of thousand years pass. Some have found new ways to channel nature for human purposes. Water and windmills can grind grain. The harrow has been invented. Oxen and horses can now pull metal ploughs, dig deep and turn the dirt back over seeds in one clean movement. Farming is much more fruitful. Texts can now be printed. Far more people have access to books and can devote their time to texts rather than the plough. Literacy begins to spread beyond elites.

Then, in a flash, in one corner of the world, people crack the code of chemistry. They invent and improve the steam engine. They build railroads, refine oil, devise the telegraph and telephone and internal combustion engine. Electricity and lights and indoor plumbing and clean water and household appliances abound. With mass production, everyday people have access to food, shelter, and technology that the kings and queens of yore could scarcely have imagined.

Humankind has infused our world with information from the start. If we step back, though, we see a trend. When Prometheus set that controlled fire, he unleashed a bit of the power of the physical world. He did just a little more than nature could do on its own. This early act was a creative spark, a mix of matter and information, with the pre-existing structure of matter doing a lot of the work. The same is true in primitive hunting and agriculture. But over time, we have added more and more information to the mix.

In the industrial era, we built machines that could vastly exceed the work of the strongest beasts. We now construct integrated circuits and fibre optic cables from humble sand, and inform these technologies with 'software' – one part matter and a million parts information. In this way, we will build ever more powerful systems and machines. But we will not make ourselves obsolete for the simple reason that we are not machines. There will always be new work for us to do.

Work, then, is not merely toil. It is one of the ways in which we fulfil the first divine mandate, to be fruitful and to multiply. Though we have long since been cast from the primeval garden, though our work is now so often frustrated, it has not lost its original meaning. God could have hoarded all the innovation for himself. Instead, he chose to create a material world with stewards who are at the same time material and immaterial beings. God granted to them not only the dignity of causality, as Blaise Pascal wrote, but the dignity of creativity.

Notes

1 See, for example, Nancey Murphy, *Bodies and Souls, or Spirited Bodies?* (Cambridge: Cambridge University Press, 2006). For solid, biblical critiques, see John W. Cooper, *Body, Soul, and Life Everlasting: Biblical Anthropology and the*

Monism-Dualism Debate (Grand Rapids, MI: Eerdmans, 2000) and *Christian Physicalism? Philosophical and Theological Critiques*, ed. R. Keith Loftin and Joshua R. Farris (Lanham, MD: Lexington Books, 2018).

2 Scott W. Hahn and Benjamin Wiker, *Politicizing the Bible: The Roots of Historical Criticism and the Secularization of Scripture 1300–1700* (New York: Crossroad, 2013).

3 There is, of course, a pitched debate about whether Genesis 1 teaches creation from nothing as later theologians came to understand. Although I think this is implied in the text – and certainly think creation *ex nihilo* is the proper interpretation of the doctrine of creation – I do not need this point for the present discussion.

4 This is the argument of C. John Collins, *Genesis 1–4: A Linguistic, Literary, and Theological Commentary* (Philadelphia: P&R Publishing, 2005).

5 The other key piece of evidence for the documentary hypothesis is the existence of doublets in the text, in which the same or a similar event is repeated with slight variations. This is not relevant in the first few chapters of Genesis, though in a sense chapter 2 is a recapitulation of chapter 1. But they clearly are not doublets.

6 A good critique of an earlier version of the documentary hypothesis is Umberto Cassuto, *The Documentary Hypothesis and the Composition of the Pentateuch* (Jerusalem: Shalem Press, 2006). See also his two books, *A Commentary on the Book of Genesis: From Adam to Noah* (Jerusalem: Magnes Press, 1964) and *A Commentary on the Book of Genesis: From Noah to Avraham* (Jerusalem: Magnes Press, 1964). Over time, the hypothesis has grown increasingly complicated to account for critiques and inconsistencies, and is now so complex and riddled with exceptions that it fails to do what a hypothesis is supposed to do: provide a consistent, reasonably simple explanation that helps us understand the text. By that standard, the documentary hypothesis fails utterly. In its current form, it is much more a kludge that obviously depends upon the philosophical prejudices of nineteenth-century German scholarship. For an accessible, recent study of the tightly integrated literary structure of Genesis, see Eyal Rav-Noy and Gil Weinreich, *Who Really Wrote the Bible?* (Minneapolis: Richard Vigilante Books, 2010).

7 This is why it is misleading to refer to Genesis 1 as the 'first account of creation' and Genesis 2—3 as the 'second account'. It is an arrogant condescension towards the original author, editor, and/or compiler. The most basic hermeneutical task for any reader of a text is to treat it as a text.

8 Pope Benedict XVI, *The Garden of God: Toward a Human Ecology* (Washington, DC: Catholic University of America Press, 2014).

9 Another example of the paradoxical tendency of materialism to spawn its opposite: the transgender movement claims that our biological sex has no purchase on who we are. 'I' can be whatever 'gender' I identify with. And what is this gender identity, you ask? Well, that's hard to say. But in any case, it's whatever I decide it is, and it determines whether you are to refer to me as 'he', 'she', or something else. So this power to designate one's own 'gender identity' apparently has the power to override biological sex, which, until recently, was treated as biologically determined. The self, on this view, is radically independent of the body. And yet the same people who make such claims are also, more often than not, materialists who should, if they were consistent, deny the existence of such a non-bodily self.

10 Ray Kurzweil, *How to Create a Mind: The Secret of Human Thought Revealed* (New York: Penguin Books, 2013). For a contrary argument, see Jeffrey Schwartz and Sharon Begley, *The Mind and the Brain: Neuroplasticity and the Power of Mental Force* (New York: Harper, 2002).

11 For a more detailed treatment, see Jay W. Richards, *The Human Advantage: The Future of American Work in an Age of Smart Machines* (New York: Crown, 2018), ch. 2.

12 Martin Ford, *Rise of the Robots: Technology and the Threat of a Jobless Future* (New York: Basic Books, 2015).

13 Richards, *Human Advantage*, ch. 8.

8

Work and Sanctification

SCOTT B. RAE

My dad was the consummate businessman. He was one of those larger-than-life personalities, a natural sales person, visionary marketer, astute business strategist, and master manager and motivator of people. I still have vivid memories of sitting around the dinner table as a teenager when he informed us that he was taking all the money he had set aside for college for my siblings and myself, and was putting it into the company he was about to start. I wasn't all that savvy about investments at that age, but I knew that if the company didn't make it, my brother, sister, and myself were on our own for college. As it turned out, the company flourished and paid for college many times over.

My dad came to a vibrant faith in Christ a bit later in life, and he and my mom were involved for 30+ years in a strong, Bible-oriented church that taught the Bible well and faithfully. But for as long as he was exposed to the teaching of the Bible on a wide variety of subjects, he never meaningfully connected his faith to his work. Except in one particular area: he was convinced that since churches and charities *collect* revenue, they don't generate it, which meant that someone had to generate revenue for these organizations. He saw the only significant relationship between his faith and his work as instrumental, in that his work was good for making money for the church and non-profit world. The various ways in which his work could shape his spiritual life, not to mention impacting the community for good, were rarely, if ever, seriously considered by the people charged with nurturing his spiritual life.

Think about the number of hours per week that the average full-time worker spends in the workplace, as opposed to the number of hours spent in the local church. The average person spends between 40–60 hours weekly at work, and the most committed churchgoing person spends roughly 5–10 hours weekly in the church building. Simply based on the number of hours spent in the workplace, it would be reasonable to maintain the workplace is the primary crucible for the follower of Jesus to become more like him. This would also suggest the workplace is the principal arena in which followers of Jesus can fulfil the mandate to love their neighbour. It would seem the role of the church in this regard is to equip the men and women they serve who are in the workplace to be attentive to the various ways in which their sanctification is occurring by virtue of their roles and interactions in the workplace.

I got a vivid picture of how important this is as a result of a dinner discussion with my youngest son, which occurred a few days before he went off to college three time zones away from home. I was attempting to encourage him spiritually and urge him to give attention to his spiritual life before heading off to college. I asked him what he could do at college to nurture his spiritual life, and he responded with good things that revolved mainly around being involved in a local church. But as we talked, it became clear that despite being in a vibrant high school ministry at an excellent church for most of his high school years, no one had ever connected his spiritual life with that about which he is most passionate: theatre and acting. We then got to talking about his best friend from high school, who was about to enrol in a Christian college as a Bible major, intending to be a youth pastor. It became clear through the conversation that his best friend was expected to take his faith more seriously because of his occupational goals, and that since my son was not headed into pastoral ministry, he was somehow 'getting a pass' on taking his faith as seriously. Barna Research confirms the importance of connecting a person's vocational goals with his or her spiritual life. Their studies suggest that when a high school or college student's vocation is well integrated with their spirituality, they are three times more likely to remain connected to their faith and to the church.[1]

Work and the Development of Character

The predominant understanding of how faith and work relate has been a one-way relationship – that is, one brings one's faith/values to shape one's workplace. Workplace men and women often wonder how to 'bring God into the workplace', while forgetting that he is already there, and usually far ahead of us. Far less obvious and less frequently explored, however, are the ways that business can be used in a reciprocal (though not always comfortable) manner to shape *us* in positive ways. To be sure, work can also ensnare us in a variety of vices (e.g. greed, idolatry, etc.) and deform our character.[2]

Each person's experience with God shaping his or her character through business is different, with various traits/virtues being developed through involvement in specific situations. This makes it difficult to generalize. Certainly, people's responses to the challenges of work are also quite different: some find that their faith is deepened, character sharpened, and intimacy with God intensified. Others may respond to similar experiences very differently, finding that their faith is abandoned, character development is short-circuited, intimacy with God becomes spiritual complacency, or work becomes an idol that is worshipped.

What I propose here are some conceptions about character and virtue development that successful involvement in the marketplace both *requires* and *nurtures*. While the following is not meant to be an exhaustive study, I consider first how God can use business to help develop some important character traits and virtues. A later section will examine some important spiritual practices that if implemented serve as antidotes to overwork or overidentification with work, a possible 'dark side' to approaching our work as a calling (as opposed to a job or career).

Consider, first, the virtue of 'service'. Most workplaces require that people and organizations serve their constituencies well in order to thrive. Companies must be committed to serving their customers, meeting their needs, listening carefully to their criticisms, and treating them fairly. If customers are not well served, they will take their business to someone who will serve them more effectively. As George Mason University economist Walter Williams puts it, 'you don't have to like your fellow-man, but you have to serve him'.[3] Further, employees must serve their companies, team members must learn how to serve each other and become more interdependent, managers must serve those who report to them and those they manage, and executives are responsible for serving the entire organization that they lead. This notion of servant leadership has been a central aspect of much of the contemporary literature on management and leadership in the workplace.[4] If leaders and managers do not serve those who report to them well, morale suffers and employees become less productive. In general, business both requires and cultivates an orientation towards serving others.

Some of the most difficult ethical dilemmas for those in leadership involve the conflict between serving specific individuals in the organization and serving the organization as a whole. For example, when lay-offs occur, executives must balance the needs of the individual employees who have families and will need to find new jobs, with the overall health of the organization. In addition, at times, employees who are not doing their jobs or who are toxic to the organization must be let go. In those instances, it often appears that leaders are not serving those who report to them well. In reality, they are wrestling with a dilemma about whom to serve and which obligation of service takes precedence. In general, leaders are responsible to serve the entire organization, for if they don't do that well, the organization as a whole is impacted negatively, which trickles down to the lives of many individual employees.

This is not to suggest there are no limits or boundaries on one's service to any given constituency. It is true that in most contexts in biblical times, servants did not have the prerogative of setting any boundaries with their masters, because they did not have any individual rights at all, since they were the property of their owners. That's where the imagery of the servant cannot be justifiably extended, since Jesus, the ultimate servant, also put boundaries on his service, at times walking away from serving the masses in order to secure time with his disciples or personal time with God. Thus, the virtue of service and the reality of boundaries can coexist. In fact, one can make a good case that within proper boundaries, the virtue of service is actually more meaningful, since the person is serving out of choice and less out of compulsion.[5]

Flourishing in the workplace also requires and cultivates the virtues of *trust, trustworthiness, and fairness*. For the vast majority of businesses that are dependent on repeat customers for their success, trust and fairness are critical to keeping customers. Think about how quickly a person would take his or her business elsewhere if that person concluded that trust was missing and they were being treated unfairly (assuming that they have a choice of where to do business). It is not uncommon for people to go out of their way to do business with companies and individuals they trust. It is even more common for people to go out of their way *to avoid* doing business with those they do not trust. To be sure, there are many examples of companies acting in untrustworthy ways. But when that becomes public knowledge, it is common for the company's reputation to suffer, and often they lose business as a result.

Within an organization, trust (teamwork) is critical in fostering prosperity. Where trust is low, the costs of doing business increase due to, at times, costly monitoring and compliance mechanisms that are required. In addition, where trust is low there are intangible costs, such as employees being less eager to accept change, put in extra effort, or be committed to their work. The costs of low morale and high turnover suggest that treating people with *dignity and respect* is critical to good leadership and a significant part of effective management. Workplace flourishing both requires and cultivates trust, fairness, and respect.

Closely related to this is the virtue of *cooperation* that is both required and nurtured by workplace activity. It is common to hear in public debate and in social media discussions about the economy that greed or self-interest is what motivates most workplace activity, suggesting that such cooperation is not an important part of success in the workplace. Critics of business often cite Adam Smith's classic statement about how greed is good and how self-interest is what moves the economy (though most would not equate greed with self-interest). He stated, 'It is not from the benevolence of the butcher, the brewer, or the baker, that we expect our dinner, but from their regard for their own interest. We address ourselves, not to their humanity, but to their self-love, and never talk to them of our own necessities, but of their advantages.'[6] It is often inferred from this classic statement that the greed of the producer brings society its goods/services and that the pursuit of individual greed will result in the advance of the common good.

However, this segment from Smith needs to be read with his developed moral philosophy clearly in mind. Remember, Smith was not an economist, but a moral philosopher by training. And his work, *The Theory of Moral Sentiments* was written before *The Wealth of Nations*. He did not believe that human beings were egoists capable only of acting in their self-interest. He believed that human beings were motivated by what he called the 'social passions', and that justice, prudence, and benevolence were also key components to governing a person's pursuit of self-interest.

He also defended the ideas of cooperation and sympathy as part of the social passions, which he considered equally as influential on a person as self-interest. The butcher, brewer, and baker all needed *cooperation* in addition to self-interest in order to flourish. Baron de Montesquieu, one of Smith's contemporaries and fellow advocate of the free market, captured this well. He said something that sounds remarkable today: that 'commerce polishes and softens barbaric ways, as we can see every day'.[7]

It must be remembered that for much of the history of civilization, human beings often resorted to violence in order to obtain the goods and services they needed. Smith saw an economic system based on trade and mutual advantage as a great improvement over the way goods and services had been distributed in most of the history of civilization.

Workplace activity also fosters the virtues of *initiative and perseverance*. Business encourages what some call 'entrepreneurial traits, which also include *creativity*'.[8] Long-run success in the workplace requires creative solutions to complex problems. It further demands that people exercise persistence in order to accomplish significant business goals that can take months if not years to achieve. For example, men and women in sales are required to take initiative on a daily basis and persevere with the potential customers/clients until the sale is complete. This is characteristic of business in general, for if companies do not take initiative to lower their costs, increase their market share, seek out new customers, and keep their employees' morale high, they will suffer decline. Executives must be able to think creatively about bringing new products and services to the market, anticipating their customers' needs, maintaining the right level of employment, and ensuring adequate financing for their future. This kind of creativity is essential to leadership, and without it companies are ill equipped to deal with the uncertainties of the constantly changing global economy.

Perseverance is likewise critical to long-term success in business, and without it companies and individuals alike would tend to give up when persistence would enable a breakthrough to be made. For example, most start-up companies face very difficult obstacles to becoming established companies, and it is common for entrepreneurs to testify of how their determination made the difference between success and failure.

With persistence comes the *ability to deal with adversity*. With this, we move into the area of how God uses business to cultivate a person's character and relationship with him. James 1.2–5 indicates that adversity is a regular part of the Christian's life, and business is one of the primary crucibles in which both character and intimacy with God are forged, by overcoming hardships and difficulty. Anyone who has been laid off knows what this is like – and anyone who has to lay off employees or close down plants knows how painful this can be. In addition, dealing with general economic downturns provides difficult, though beneficial, opportunities to deal with adversity and to nurture the humility, wisdom and persistence that accompany it. It further develops a person's *trust in God*, enabling him or her to build reliance on God for their personal security and well-being, as well as their company's stability. A businessperson's intimacy with God often is nurtured by having to wrestle with the prospect of failure, potential lay-offs, or ethical dilemmas, both in the request for wisdom and for the strength to follow one's moral convictions. For example, in her extensive interviews of Christian CEOs, Laura Nash found that dealing with adversity or ethical dilemmas drove these men and women frequently to prayer. They cited prayer as a critical component that often emerged from these situations, and at times, the conviction that developed from those times of prayer actually provided answers to the difficult issues that were on the table at that time.[9]

Some additional virtues nourished by workplace activity can help *prevent* having to face difficult times. To be sure, many times that a businessperson or company faces adversity are due to circumstances beyond their control. But sometimes, hard times come as a result something both foreseeable and preventable. The Proverbs are clear that laziness, or a lack of diligence can contribute to economic misfortune (Prov. 6.6–11; 10.4–5; 12.11, 14, 24; 13.11; 24.30–34). Business demands *diligence and discipline*, where a person learns that 'you reap what you sow'. Popular business lecturer Stephen Covey describes 'the law of the farm' as a lesson that to succeed a person must engage in advance planning, daily attention to the work, and not put off the important work until the deadline approaches. He insists that if you ignore the law of the farm you will not reap a successful harvest.[10] Though it is true that some people succeed without hard work, that is certainly not the norm. In general, the workplace both requires and cultivates diligence and discourages laziness and a lack of discipline.

Far more frequently discussed are the ways in which marketplace activity is able to shape a person's character in negative ways. With each character trait mentioned thus far, there is the prospect of its opposite being nurtured. Take, for example, the virtue of service and its opposite: narcissism. Service assumes and promotes an other-centredness and discourages the attitude of 'it's all about me'. Yet it is quite common to hear complaints about the lack of service, consideration, and civility in the workplace and to hear that most people are only looking out for themselves. The leadership literature is replete with stories of how teams fail to function properly because individuals cannot subordinate their individual interests to that of the organization. The narcissistic personality is generally considered toxic to organizational culture, and it is not uncommon for companies to confront the dilemma that a high producer is also corrosive to the chemistry of the organization. It is widely recognized that many charismatic leaders have narcissistic personalities that actually inhibit them from taking their organizations to reach their full potential. For example, leadership expert Jim Collins maintains that the primary character trait separating good from great leaders is *humility*: the ability to see oneself realistically and to consider the interests of the organization ahead of one's own personal agenda.[11]

We also mentioned the importance of trust and trustworthiness as critical virtues nurtured and required by marketplace activity. But there the workplace brings regular temptations to deception and various ways of misleading clients, employees, and co-workers. The ethical dilemmas around bluffing and truth-telling suggest that the opportunities to shade the truth, mislead constituents, and outright lie to them are commonplace. The well-publicized accounts of the origin of Borland Software, which began with an elaborate bluff designed to mislead an advertising sales person,[12] to the myriad scandalous Ponzi schemes ranging from Barry Minkow's ZZZ Best Carpet Cleaning to Bernie Madoff, all illustrate the ease with which one can fall into the temptation to deception in the workplace. Even bluffing, which can be morally neutral under the right conditions, in which both parties know that they are in the equivalent of a poker game, is most successful precisely when one party does not know that bluffing is considered 'part of the game'.[13]

The virtue of cooperation, essential for workplace harmony and efficient productivity, also has a dark side – a temptation that is well documented in the workplace. According to recent Gallup polling, roughly two-thirds of US employees in the workplace are either disengaged from their work or *are actively undermining* their companies.[14] The figures for workplaces outside the United States are even more discouraging. The motives for such behaviour vary widely, but are generally grounded in levels of discontent with one's work, which manifests itself most commonly in withdrawal and can even bring about behaviour which is counterproductive to the organization's mission and goals. When the trust level in an organization is low, it is not unusual to find employees unwilling to embrace change or 'go the extra mile' to accomplish important organizational objectives. They may even actively subvert needed changes, redirect work to others, or fail to cooperate in those 'all hands on deck' moments when a company is experiencing stress or deadlines.

The virtues of perseverance and initiative have their own corresponding temptations: to laziness and restlessness. Not only are employees disengaged from their work, many employees simply do the minimum their jobs require and get by. The temptation to laziness and sloth comes from a variety of sources, some due to demotivating organizational dysfunction and others to personal character issues that would likely manifest regardless of the organizational setting. This temptation can also manifest itself in restlessness under the guise of ambition.[15] Rather than persevere in difficult times and take initiative to make and see through improvements, it can be a symptom of laziness to simply move on to another job, and then to another. Of course, fulfilling one's goals might mean moving to another more challenging job, or finding another job that is a better fit for one's gifts, skills, and talents. Or it may mean moving to a job in a better structured and better run organization, or to a boss with whom you will have fewer conflicts. It is not uncommon for people to change jobs regularly, though it is more difficult to determine how frequently those job changes reflect restlessness and an unwillingness to persevere in one's current job situation. When the economy is contracting and the prospect of finding another job is more difficult, the virtue of perseverance is that much more important.

The virtues of diligence and discipline are closely related to perseverance, and relate as well to workplace engagement. But the opposite of those manifests itself a bit differently than one might expect. It is true that the temptations in the workplace to laziness, lack of focus, and boredom are ubiquitous. But a lack of diligence can also manifest itself in busyness, which allows a person the appearance of discipline but actually keeps him or her from focusing attention on the most important aspects of the job.[16] Busyness can be a means of avoiding engagement with the more challenging parts of one's job, and can often divert great energy into doing things that are unimportant as a way of avoiding difficult aspects of the job.

To summarize the way in which workplace activity both requires and nurtures virtues essential to one's character and spiritual life, consider the New Testament teaching on the fruit of the Spirit and deeds of the flesh (Gal. 5.19–25) and how those might be applied to the workplace.[17] Consider which set of traits would make someone more employable. Vices such as jealousy, discord, rage, selfish ambition, dissension, and others would clearly disqualify someone from being hired, and would be grounds for termination in many contexts. By contrast, the fruits of the Spirit, which include kindness, patience, self-control, gentleness, and faithfulness, are virtues that are in high demand in most workplaces. What's ironic about this is that it is rare in our churches that a person would hear any application of these virtues and vices to life in the workplace. Yet given the amount of time spent in the workplace in a person's life, it makes sense to conclude that the workplace is the primary place where we would expect to see these virtues and vices on display.

Work and Intimacy with God

However, there's more to the connection between work and spirituality than these virtues, as important as they are to the development of someone's character. Workplace activity is also the crucible for cultivation of someone's intimacy with God, both in gratitude for success and dependence on him in times of difficulty. Take, for example, an executive who must lay off employees, always a difficult and painful decision that cannot be done callously or insensitively. Those decisions that affect people's lives and families are often made with deliberation and care, and leaders often learn quite a bit about themselves in the process. Similarly, dealing with business failures often drives believers to Jesus in dependence and asking him for wisdom to deal with very difficult circumstances. Business adversity frequently surfaces uncomfortable things that must be faced in order for someone to grow and mature, things that often send men and women to prayer and reliance on God.

Consider the following example. An executive in the telecommunications industry with a long history of turnaround success was hired to turn around a troubled company that required a move to another country and learning a variety of cultural factors that complicated his ability to lead the company. Though he came into the situation with justifiable optimism and had a first year that went very smoothly, he soon realized he was in for the biggest challenge of his career. Many arrangements that he thought were solid turned out to be fleeting, and he was faced with the prospect that the entire operation could fail spectacularly.

As he reflected on that difficult time, he understood that God was powerfully at work, using the challenges of his business life to shape his soul. In thinking back on it, he realizes that this time was one of the most significant times of spiritual growth in his life. He said, 'So as I was in these very, very challenging circumstances, God was showing me what was really going on. As painful as the dramatic business failure was, it paled in comparison to the anguish in my soul. God showed me in the midst of the pain, and continuing in the solitude of the ensuing months, the reason I was so distraught and in such a spiritual funk. I had made achievement my god. It wasn't until the achievement went away, that I realized a part of my god also went away.'

With the benefit of five years' perspective, he describes the experience this way:

Through that painful experience, God completely reoriented my perspective of time. He showed me that my call was not to live in my plans for the future or memories of the past, but to be fully present to the present moment. I began to see each moment as a sacrament. It became a kind of second conversion for me. The remarkable part was that after coming into this recognition and confessing that I had made achievement my god (which took months to recognize), I came into a place of profound joy and freedom. The truth was I *had* made achievement my god. I lived for the adrenaline rush of success, but I had been blind to this truth for decades. As God revealed this reality to me through the pain and the failure, it set me free. As much as I pleaded for him to do otherwise, God didn't deliver me from my circumstances. He delivered me through them.

He adds this spiritual perspective. 'But through our surrender to him, Jesus draws us into this profound intimacy with him and a freedom and joy I had heard about but had never really tasted. Out of a darkness that grew blacker than black for me, God brought me into a freedom and a lightness of soul I didn't know were possible. It is a country I'd only rarely visited before, and, if I had it was only for brief periods. Nothing the world has to offer compares to the inexpressible joy that comes from experiencing the tender intimacy with God for which we are designed.'

He summarizes it this way, 'My career has been the crucible for the formation of my soul … For me, part of the pruning shears that God has used (to shape my soul) have been the challenges of my involvement in business.'[18] Involvement in the workplace is an arena in which many important character traits are nurtured, and in which a person's daily intimacy with God is cultivated.[19]

Work and Spiritual Practices

While our work can be used as a crucible to develop our faith, spirituality, and character, we have seen that it can also shape us in negative ways. Consider the widely discussed vices of greed, consumerism, and materialism, which have the capacity to hinder a person's sanctification and give the illusion of security in one's net worth rather than in God's provision. Other vices that play out regularly in the workplace include pride/arrogance (which often manifests itself in the abuse of power), envy of the successes of others, anger expressed inappropriately, lust and sexual temptation, and as already mentioned, laziness/sloth, busyness, restless-ness/discontentment, and deception in one's business dealings.[20] Most people see these regularly in their workplaces, and if they are honest with themselves, in their own behaviour in the workplace as well.

In addition, there is a side to seeing our work as a calling that opens the possibilities of *overwork*, leading to neglect of other important life pri-orities, and of *overidentification* with work, whereby our work becomes our identity. For example, the research of Amy Wrznesiewski and her colleagues suggests that 'people with a calling find their work inseparable from their life'. While the overall effects are positive (i.e. higher job and life satisfaction), those with callings also tend to put in longer hours.[21]

As an antidote to overwork and overidentification with work, the Bible mandates that we *'remember the Sabbath'* (Ex. 20.8–11; Deut. 5.12–15). *It is the primary spiritual discipline designed to put work in perspective.* From the beginning, the Bible instituted the Sabbath as a means to nur-ture the spiritual practices of rest, leisure, and worship, and to remind the people of God that there is more to life than work. To keep work from becoming an idol that is worshipped, or that in which someone finds their security and identity, the Sabbath practice was designed to enable people periodically to disengage from work and remove occupational obstacles that would prevent someone from unhindered time to connect with God. Though we've defended the idea that in the workplace God gets our attention, nurtures character, and connects intimately with his people, sadly, that experience is not the norm for most people today. Even if that experience were the norm, there is a place for rest, leisure, and time with God that is unhindered by workplace responsibilities and pressures. Thus, the Sabbath mandate is still important, and even though the people of God are not under the Mosaic law today, remember that the Sabbath originally was grounded in the order of creation (Gen. 2.1–2). This sug-gests that the need for rest and leisure is part of the human constitution from creation, though it is not a rigid or legalistic requirement today.

There are some important differences between the world of work in the ancient world and today that have a bearing on our understanding of the Sabbath. First, there was little separation between the workplace and the home in biblical times. There was not much of a dichotomy between work and home, since most work occurred in or around the home. Agriculture and trades dominated the ancient economy, and parents did much of their parenting on the job. As a result, balancing work and family was not that difficult, since there was so much overlap between the two. With the Industrial Revolution, however, work became increasingly separate from home, as people (mostly men) left home during the day to go to work.

More recently, as women have entered the workforce in unprecedented numbers, they too wrestle with the dual demands of work and family. More women are working, but the demands of parenting are still there for them. It is well documented that in dual-career families, women bear more of the burden for the 'second shift' of domestic responsibilities.

Further, with more and more people working from remote locations, and being constantly reachable by technological devices, people are finding that drawing a boundary between work and home can be more difficult than ever. It may be that work is actually returning to look more like it did in ancient times, with less separation between home and the workplace.

A second difference has to do with the way leisure was viewed in the ancient world vis-à-vis work. For example, the classical Greeks related work and leisure in a way quite different from today. Aristotle, in his *Nicomachean Ethics*, insisted that leisure was primary and work was subordinate to it.[22] This is quite different from the contemporary view that leisure is what you do when you are not working. In both classical and contemporary periods, leisure is preferred over work, and is actually the goal for which work is simply a means. The Greek term for leisure is *schole*, from which we get our words 'scholarship' and 'school'. Work was defined as *the absence of leisure*, and the Greeks used the term *ascholia* to define it. That is, work was secondary to leisure and was something to be done when one was not at leisure. This is an important difference between the view of work and leisure in the ancient world and today. Today, in much of the developed world, we largely view work as primary and leisure as secondary – that is, we define leisure in terms of work, not the other way around.[23]

The Scripture spoke into this background of the ancient world when it addressed these critical notions of work and leisure. From the beginning, God designed human beings to live their lives in ways that would contribute to their flourishing. One of the primary concerns addressed early in Scripture, as early as Genesis 1—2, is the need to bring work and leisure together. Both are essential to becoming the person God designed human beings to be. Although handed down as one of the Ten Commandments, it was intended as and often received as a gift. God instituted a Sabbath day in order to ensure that people kept their work from taking over their lives. In Exodus 20.8–11, God ordained a rhythmic pattern of one day in seven for human beings to rest – that is, to stop working and give attention to other aspects of life, namely the contemplative and worship components, and to put aside all the occupational obstacles that get in the way of nurturing one's soul and one's relationship to God. The term in Hebrew, *shabbat*, simply means 'stop and rest'. God intended through observing the Sabbath that people put away their 'to do' lists and do those things that refresh them, giving particular attention to worship, reflection, and one's relationship to God.

The Bible repeats this command periodically throughout Israel's history (Lev. 23.3; Neh. 13.22; Isa. 56.2; Ezek. 20.12, 20; Mark 2.27). For example, in the book of Deuteronomy, when God repeated all the Ten Commandments just before Israel entered the promised land, God reissued the Sabbath command, but with a different basis. In Deuteronomy 5.12–15, God reminded Israel of the Sabbath, but this time it was based on their experience of slavery in Egypt. God encouraged them to 'remember that you were slaves in Egypt and that God brought you out of there with a mighty arm and outstretched hand. Therefore, the Lord your God has commanded you to observe the Sabbath day' (Deut. 5.15). Because of their 400 years of slavery in Egypt, God commanded them to keep the Sabbath.

What is the connection between their sojourn in Egypt and the need to keep the Sabbath? When they were slaves in Egypt, there was no rest from work – it consumed their lives, and they never got a break. In fact, when they requested rest, their taskmasters put even more taxing demands on them, requiring even more time and effort. God is affirming to the Israelites that they were no longer slaves, and they should not live as though they are. Refusal to keep the Sabbath meant that people were enslaved to their work. *The Sabbath command was designed to remind them that they are not to live like they are enslaved to their jobs.* Moreover, it should be noted that the Sabbath was not created in the service of work. In other words, Sabbath observation was not for the purpose, so commonly accepted today for taking time off, of 'recharging our batteries' or becoming more effective workers. It was, and is, simply a gift to be received.

Keeping the Sabbath was also an exercise of faith. Refusal to keep it meant that people were not willing to trust God for their income. In Exodus 31.12–17, God indicates that the Sabbath is a sign of his covenant with Israel – that by keeping it, they communicate that they trust God to take care of them, according to their covenant relationship. God emphasizes this even more strongly when he specifies that the Sabbath must be kept even during harvest and planting times (Ex. 34.21). In an agricultural society, these were the two busiest times of the year, when taking time off would mean loss of income.

The point of the Sabbath command is a loving reminder that there's more to life than work; we are more than labourers. Of course, for people who do not like their jobs or are just grinding away at them, there is little temptation to work too much. But for many who are driven to succeed, or for people who work in demanding, high-stress occupations, the pressure of work can be overwhelming. This is especially the case for those who consider their work a calling, something to which they are devoting their lives. This is all the more so as people are more frequently expected to be constantly available to work, even when not in the office, and increasingly often even while on 'vacation'. The Sabbath command reminds us that *we are not our work*, and that work, though a significant part of our lives is not that which ultimately defines us, nor the primary place from which we derive our identity. The ability to take regular time off affirms to ourselves and to our community that life is bigger than work. We are called to more than our work, and our vocation is not reducible to our occupation. The Sabbath gift affirms the notion that we have multiple vocations (defined simply as *'arenas of service* to which we are called'). For example, I have a vocation as a husband, father, neighbour, professor, church member, all of which I am responsible for maintaining simultaneously.

The book of Ecclesiastes commends the enjoyment of all of life, including both work and leisure, as God's good gift. For example, Ecclesiastes 8.15 puts it this way: 'So I commend the enjoyment of life, because nothing is better for a man under the sun than to eat and drink and be glad. Then joy will accompany him in his work in all the days of the life God has given him under the sun.' We would suggest that passages like this one teach that we should keep life in proper perspective, with commitments to enjoy both work and leisure, without either one defining who we are.[24]

But Sabbath rest is not the only spiritual practice relevant to the workplace. There are other spiritual disciplines that can be employed during the workday at one's particular place of work. Take, for example, the discipline of *prayer* and how it can be regularly employed at one's work. Prayer should pervade our work days, rather than being a spiritual discipline that is somehow reserved for one's private time with God. Prayer is not only beneficial to bring perspective, but it also is necessary in the midst of the difficulties one encounters in the workday. Prayer for dealing with difficult people in the workplace, prayer for tense meetings one is anticipating, prayer for contentment in the midst of boredom and restlessness, prayer for colleagues who are in pain and hurting, prayer for wisdom to make challenging decisions and resolve ethical dilemmas – all can be a regular part of one's workday.

In addition, the discipline of *solitude* will often accompany these times of prayer. They may be brief, but, in the midst of a busy workday, taking moments for solitude, away from one's phone, email, or other communications, can be moments to cultivate intimacy with God and hear his voice throughout the workday. This is especially the case with employees who commute or who travel to various locations to conduct business, such as sales persons. The times in the car going from place to place are potentially precious moments of solitude in which one can connect with God. Further, many workplaces have areas which are conducive to a break in the workday routine, in which employees can retreat and have solitude, if only for a brief time, occasionally throughout the day.

The discipline of *gratitude* also has a place in the workplace. Stopping to give thanks for having a job that supports oneself and dependants, often over many years, is easy to overlook. Giving thanks for the good things about a person's workplace, the good people they work with, the meaningful work they have to do, the way in which their work serves the community and enables them to love their neighbours, all are appropriate avenues for gratitude. Of course, a person may also practise gratitude for the wisdom and grace to deal with the difficult aspects of their work, the difficult people, or the challenging situations and ethical dilemmas that need resolution.

The discipline of *confession* may also be appropriate for the workplace, since, as we have acknowledged, some of the difficult situations that occur in the workplace may be the result of our mistakes or short-sightedness. In addition, some of the difficult people in the workplace may be ourselves. We may treat employees or co-workers unfairly at times, for which confession, at least privately if not also to the person, is required. We may respond in the midst of pressure in ways that are ungracious or involve harsh words that we might later wish to take back. We may succumb to lack of diligence and not do our best work, for which confession is required. We make mistakes and sometimes even intentionally harm others and our organization, for which private confession is appropriate.

These disciplines are not only for our private time alone with God or for Sabbath worship. Since those who work full time spend the vast majority of their waking hours at work, it would be a bit odd to think that such a large segment of life would somehow be compartmentalized from the spiritual disciplines that constitute such a significant part of a person's spiritual life. Particularly given the theology of work articulated in this volume, that one's work constitutes service to God and that all believers, regardless of the place from which they derive a pay cheque, are in full-time Christian service, underscores the importance of framing one's work and one's relationship to God accordingly. As Dallas Willard taught, exercising spiritual disciplines enables us to weave the presence of God throughout the texture of our work, 'in the name of the Lord Jesus, giving thanks through him to God the Father' (Col. 3.17).

Conclusion

Business is an environment that both reveals and refines a person's character and spirituality. We have argued that involvement in business both requires and nurtures virtues such as service, trust, and perseverance. It further functions as a crucible in which sanctification occurs. The workplace both requires and nurtures a variety of virtues essential to character growth, and provides an arena in which God can get a person's attention, drive him or her to further dependence on him, and move the person to a greater intimacy in relating to God. All of this assumes that the person is attentive to what God is doing in the workplace to shape him or her spiritually. One of the important aspects of pastoral ministry in the church is to help workplace men and women to 'get their antennae up' so they can better perceive what God is doing to form them spiritually through their workplace interactions and responsibilities. In order to maximize the role of the workplace in a person's spiritual formation and to realize its limits, we have suggested the practice of Sabbath and ways of thinking that help place work in perspective with other important aspects of life and keep work from being the source of one's identity.

Notes

1 Barna Research, 'Making Space for Millennials', 2014. Full report available at http://barna.org/spaceformillennials.

2 For further reading on how work can bring both opportunities to honour God and temptations to immorality, see Wayne Grudem, *Business for the Glory of God* (Wheaton, IL: Crossway, 2003).

3 Cited in John Stossel, *Give Me a Break* (New York: Perennial Currents, 2005), p. 244.

4 See, for example, Robert K. Greenleaf, *Servant Leadership: A Journey into the Nature of Legitimate Power and Greatness* (Mahwah, NJ: Paulist Press, 2002).

5 For further discussion of the place of boundaries with the virtue of service, see Henry Cloud and John S. Townsend, *Boundaries* (Grand Rapids, MI: Zondervan, 1992).

6 Adam Smith, *An Enquiry into the Nature and Causes of the Wealth of Nations*, ed. R. H. Campbell and A. S. Skinner (Oxford: Oxford University Press, 1976), I.ii.2.

7 Baron de Montesquieu, *The Spirit of the Laws*, 81, cited in Ruth Chadwick and Doris Schroeder, *Applied Ethics: Critical Concepts in Philosophy*, vol. 5 (New York: Routledge, 2002), p. 296.

8 For further discussion of this, see Robert Sirico, *The Entrepreneurial Vocation* (Grand Rapids, MI: Acton Institute, 1999).

9 See Laura L. Nash, *Believers in Business* (Nashville: Thomas Nelson, 1994) for further discussion on this.

10 Stephen A. Covey, *The Seven Habits of Highly Successful People* (New York: Free Press, 1989).

11 Jim Collins, 'Level 5 Leadership: The Triumph of Humility and Fierce Resolve', *Harvard Business Review* 79 (January 2001), pp. 66–76, 175. See also the discussion of this in Collins, *Good to Great: Why Some Companies Make the Leap ... and Others Don't* (New York: Harper Collins, 2001).

12 Robert A. Mamis, 'Managing by Necessity', *Inc.* (1 March 1989), pp. 31–4.

13 See the discussion of bluffing and truth-telling in Scott B. Rae and Will Mes-

senger, 'Truth, Honesty and Deception in the Workplace: An Overview', Theology of Work Project, available at www.theologyofwork.org/key-topics/truth-deception.

14 Annmarie Mann and Jim Harter, 'The Worldwide Employee Engagement Crisis', *Gallup Business Journal* (7 January 2016), available at www.gallup.com/businessjournal/188033/worldwide-employee-engagement-crisis.aspx.

15 R. Paul Stevens, *Taking Your Soul to Work: Overcoming the Nine Deadly Sins of the Workplace* (Grand Rapids, MI: Eerdmans, 2010), pp. 56–61.

16 Stevens, *Taking Your Soul to Work*, pp. 44–9.

17 See Stevens, *Taking Your Soul to Work*, pp. 67–120 for further discussion of the fruit of the Spirit in the workplace.

18 Personal interview with Barry L. Rowan, 7 April 2009. All subsequent quotations from Mr Rowan come from this interview.

19 For further reading on this important topic, see Nash, *Believers in Business*.

20 For further discussion of the vices of the workplace, in the general framework of the seven deadly sins and the fruit of the Spirit, see Stevens, *Taking Your Soul to Work*. See also Grudem, *Business for the Glory of God*, for aspects of the workplace that provide temptations to dishonour God.

21 Amy Wrznesiewski, Clark McCauley, Paul Rozin, and Barry Schwartz, 'Jobs, Careers and Callings: People's Relations to Their Work', *Journal of Research in Personality* 31 (1997), pp. 21–33 (at 22).

22 Gilbert C. Meilander (ed.), *Working: Its Meaning and Limits* (Notre Dame, IN: University of Notre Dame Press, 2000), p. 7.

23 For historical material on the relationship between work and leisure, see Josef Pieper, *Leisure: The Basis of Culture* (New York: St Augustine's Press, 1998).

24 This section is not intended to be an exhaustive study of the Sabbath institution. For further reading on this, see Marva Dawn, *Keeping the Sabbath Wholly: Ceasing, Resting, Embracing, Feasting* (Grand Rapids, MI: Eerdmans, 1989); Dawn, *The Sense of the Call: A Sabbath Way of Life for those who Serve God, the Church and the World* (Grand Rapids, MI: Eerdmans, 2006); Mark Buchanan, *The Rest of God: Restoring Your Soul by Restoring Sabbath* (Nashville: Thomas Nelson, 2006).

9

Being God's People by Working on God's Mission

GREG FORSTER

Who are these strange people called God's people, and what are they up to in this very strange world? A sound theology of work is essential to understanding the closely interdependent questions of ecclesiology ('Who are these people?') and missiology ('What are they up to?'). Without a sound theology of work, God's people tend to lose track of their mission in the world; when that happens, they tend to lose track of their identity as God's people. The Great Commission and the Great Commandment unite to show us that God's people are those whom he empowers through the gospel not only to *receive* but also to *reflect* his holy love – through our witness and worship, but through our work as well, which takes up a far greater portion of our lives. God creates, sustains, and reforms his covenant people by working *in* them in such a way that he also works *through* them to bless all the nations of the world in their work, witness, and worship.

The recent movement in the church championing the theological significance of work arises – often unconsciously, sometimes very consciously – in response to the perplexing social conditions of advanced modernity. These conditions are creating an existential challenge for the church. The faith and work movement represents a promising response to this challenge. However, it raises key ecclesiological questions that would benefit a great deal from more systematic attention. This chapter reviews the changing conditions that have raised this ecclesiological challenge and lays out a possible approach to a systematic-theological response that starts with the Great Commission and the Great Commandment.

A Small Dose of Fussy Methodological Throat-Clearing

This chapter is not ecclesiology so much as meta-ecclesiology: it describes a challenge to ecclesiology that is arising from other theological developments. It will not offer a constructive ecclesiology, nor assert a position on the field's standard controversies. We will not address whether one ought to be a Roman or a Reformer, a Presbyterian or a Pentecostal, a credo-baptist or a cradle-baptizer.

Instead, this chapter will assert that ecclesiology in our time must take account of the theological significance of work. Christians of every ecclesiology ought to confront this challenge. They will benefit enormously if they are aided in this task by systematic theologians specializing in this discipline.

Ecclesiology must account for work because, as we will argue, the theological significance of work is intrinsically important in any time and place. However, our main point in this chapter is that contemporary developments have made it especially urgent in our time for the church to connect its understanding of itself to its understanding of work. The social conditions of advanced modernity have made what was always an important issue an existential issue.

This chapter begins not with Scripture but with the present situation of the church. We could just as easily work in the other direction. Scripture is of course the authoritative source of our understanding of the church, as of all doctrinal questions. Systematic theology can and must centre on the question 'What does Scripture mean?'

However, systematic theology does not take place in a vacuum. We cannot make sense of Scripture except by relating it to our understanding of ourselves and our situation, including not only the history of interpretation but the contemporary situations that shape those questions and needs to which we seek to apply Scripture. Both our history and our current situation powerfully shape the way we formulate the questions we bring to the text. To interpret Scripture with integrity, we must be open to reformulating our questions when our formulas are challenged by Scripture. But we must be *self*-aware in addition to being *Scripture*-aware, so we know what questions we are asking. As Calvin says at the beginning of his *Institutes*, our understanding of God and our understanding of ourselves are interdependent.[1]

This chapter begins with self-awareness, because the current social situation of the church has changed radically in ways that the church does not yet well understand. In the long run, however, it does not much matter whether we begin with self-awareness or Scripture-awareness, as long as we are always moving to include both, such that our awareness of each is always increasing and deepening our awareness of the other.

Gregg Allison defines ecclesiology as the area of systematic theology that is addressed to two questions: 'What is *a* church?' and 'What is *the* church?'[2] As he notes, these questions reflect the fact that God's people 'consists of two interrelated elements', local churches and the universal church.[3] In this chapter we begin by considering God's people as a universal reality, and then draw conclusions for local churches on this basis. We do so because the challenge to ecclesiology arising from changing social conditions in advanced modernity is most easily grasped in general terms. But this, again, is a method that could be reversed. All our concepts of 'the universal church' are abstractions that generalize from the concrete realities of particular local churches. This is not to say that the universal church is not a real thing; it is to point out that the universal church only exists because local churches exist, specifically in a certain relation to one another that establishes the church's universality.

An Existential Threat to the Church's Identity in Advanced Modernity

One especially valuable aspect of Allison's formulation of the central question of ecclesiology ('What is the church?') is that it focuses our attention on the church's identity. Since the Reformation, most of the attention in ecclesiology has been taken up by competing accounts of the church's chief characteristics or 'marks', its discipline, its polity, and its ordinances. Its identity is covered, but has often received short shrift especially since a discussion of the church's *identifying* characteristics or marks is often all we get concerning the *identity* of the church, when much more could and should be said. The really juicy historical battles have been: Are Rome and its affiliates the one true church? Should bishops rule? How are doctrinal controversies to be settled? How should we understand the sacraments?

As soon as someone nailed Brother Martin's 95 theses to the Wittenberg church door, the main question became: 'Who has the right to speak and act with the church's authority?' 'What is the church?' has not been a focal point.

'Who speaks for the church?' may have been the right question to ask in early modernity. Now, a shift of focus to 'What is the church?' is welcome. In the advanced modern world, changing social conditions are making it far more difficult for any kind of group or institution to maintain a stable identity, and religious identity has been hardest hit.

The dominant social change in advanced modernity is increasing choice. This occurs because pluralism creates an ongoing condition of 'cognitive contamination' in which previously isolated social worlds are now in daily contact.[4] For centuries, more and more beliefs and moral commitments that used to be taken for granted are now a matter of choice. Will I believe in God or live a secular life – or both? If I am religious, which religion will I follow – or will I be 'spiritual but not religious'? Who should rule the civil community, and what ideas of justice should the law enact? What kind of work will I do amid the enormous and ever-proliferating variety of vocational paths? Whom will I marry and will I have other sexual partners, and if so, how many and of what kind?

The important point for our purposes is not whether this change is good or bad. It has facilitated many good and many bad developments. Nor is it relevant to consider which of the various contributing causes is the most important source of this change. The Reformation, Renaissance humanism, and the rotation of crops all contributed, among other developments.[5] Peter Berger has suggested that advanced modernity owes a great deal to Protestant evangelicalism, but it is also in some respects a very long-term side effect of the transition of the world's largest civilizations from traditional polytheism to more mature monotheistic and pantheistic religions in the eighth to third centuries BC.[6]

Some of the causes of modernity were good (religious freedom, economic development). Some were bad (humanistic and rationalistic philosophies). Some were difficult to classify. Much ink has been spilt over which is 'primary' or 'the most important', which is probably a question with no meaningful answer.

The important point for our purposes here is the cumulative effect of this expansion of choice on the stability of identity, especially religious identity.[7] In advanced modernity, I can choose to identify myself as Christian, but what does the choice to identify as Christian mean in an environment of ever-expanding individual choice? Does it commit me to any particular doctrine? To any particular moral virtues, rules, or purposes? To submit to or support any particular institution or authority? As a functional matter, the answer given to all these questions is increasingly 'no'. For each of these issues, an increasing number of people reject the historic implications of Christian identity (e.g. that it commits me to the Trinity, or to opposing homosexuality, or to meaningful membership in a local church). In the environment of radical individual choice, it becomes extremely difficult to make it plausible that people who identify as Christians yet reject these commitments are not 'really' Christians. We can say that they are not Christians, but our saying this has little practical effect.

That is not all. At a deeper level, even the meaning of the individual's choices *for himself* is destabilized. I may choose to adhere to historic Christian commitments in doctrine, morals, and life. But I know all the while that I am adhering to them only by choice. They are not cosmic certainties like the stars in the sky, which are what they are whether I like them or not. They are more like the books I have chosen to put on my own bookshelf. Sure, I like them – but do I like them because they're actually the best books? Don't I like them mainly because I chose them? Have I found what is really true, good, and beautiful, or have I simply created a comfortable bubble for myself? Where do I turn to find anything really certain, since the certainty of everything in my life depends upon my own capacity for making good choices – and, whatever comforting lies I may tell myself, I really know that my capacities are frail and limited?

For institutions other than the church, unstable identities aren't always a problem. Tiffany's began by selling stationery, but was unable to turn a steady profit; it changed its identity when more sustainable opportunities emerged in the jewellery business, and everyone was better off. Most of the great Western universities were founded as theological schools, then changed their identities to liberal arts institutions. Of course there are many complaints – many just complaints – about what these institutions do now, but there were also many just complaints about what they did when they were theological schools. The change itself was not intrinsically wrong, unless we think the liberal arts are somehow intrinsically inferior to theological learning.[8]

In fact, when identities are shaped by injustices, they *ought* to be destabilized; this is why the social environment of advanced modernity has enabled much that is very good and just. For example, Martin Luther King, Jr argued that both blacks and whites were harmed by the false identities inculcated in them by segregation. 'Segregation distorts the soul and damages the personality. It gives the segregator a false sense of superiority and the segregated a false sense of inferiority.'[9] Long-term peace, justice, and happiness, King argued, required all people to destabilize their false identities and adopt new ones that harmonized with universal goodwill and mutual recognition. This point, suitably reframed in the legal context, had been substantially the reasoning of the US Supreme Court in ruling that segregation was inherently unconstitutional.[10] To the extent that the old, unjust identities were in fact destabilized, it was only the social environment of advanced modernity that permitted this destabilization. One couldn't have pulled off anything similar in any ancient or medieval society, or even in early modernity – quite the reverse.

But this same environment raises serious challenges for the church. Within certain limits, of course, the church's sense of identity can and must change. As the church grows in theological understanding and in practical wisdom, its sense of identity as the church will correspondingly deepen. And as social circumstances around the church change, the church inevitably changes its understanding of how it relates to those circumstances, which to some degree must involve questions of its own identity. For example, the social environment of religious freedom works a significant change in the church's sense of identity; giving up its historic alliance with the state has forced the church to a new understanding of itself.[11]

Beyond a certain point, however, an unstable identity becomes an existential threat for the church. It calls into question the church's status as God's people. The church cannot switch what Jesus it follows or what gospel it preaches in the same way Tiffany's switched from selling stationery to selling jewellery. 'For if someone comes and proclaims another Jesus than the one we proclaimed, or if you receive a different spirit from the one you received, or if you accept a different gospel from the one you accepted ...' (2 Cor. 11.4).

The proper mission of a business is to provide economic goods and services that advance human flourishing, so it can change what goods and services it provides without abandoning its deeper mission. The proper mission of a school is to cultivate the knowledge, wisdom, and capacities of students; it, too, can change what kinds of knowledge, wisdom, and capacities it cultivates without abandoning its mission.

By contrast, the church claims to be the embassy of an invisible kingdom, supernaturally created by Christ's life, death, and resurrection and entrusted with the continuing presence of his power (2 Cor. 5.18–20). It is not what it claims to be if it is not being formed supernaturally by that power (see e.g. John 14.15–26; Rom. 12.1–8; 1 Cor. 12.1—13.13; 1 John 1.5–10).[12]

Persuading people that you are an ambassador of an invisible, supernatural kingdom is hard enough under the best circumstances. If the church has no stable identity, it becomes effectively impossible.

A church that is unable to make plausible and socially effectual claims about who is or is not a Christian will have a greatly reduced ability to form its members in Christlikeness. Churches can respond by offering versions of 'Christlikeness' that are superficially attractive to the popular consumer market. This leaves them rushing constantly from one 'transformative' fad to another in search of market share. Or they can give up the task of identity formation as hopeless, leaving their people relatively unchanged in whatever secular identities they had when they first walked in the church door.

Both these options leave the church unable to present to the world a highly credible claim that it is the embassy of an invisible, supernatural power. Unfortunately, this is all too accurate a summary of the state of formation in much of the church around us today.[13]

When changes in the church's sense of identity flow organically from its growing wisdom and its continuing effort to relate itself rightly to its social circumstances, this does not undermine its basic claim about what it is. When its identity changes because it is *captive* to the destabilizing forces of advanced modernity, rather than because it is responding to those forces from a clear position of its own, the situation is gravely different.

The church must exist before we can argue over ecclesiology's traditional questions, such as who gets to use its authority and how. In the recent past, when social conditions were more favourable to stable identity, the existence of the church was more or less taken for granted, at any rate within the geographic area understood to be 'Christendom'. It was only on the margins, along those borderlines where Christian populations found themselves adjacent to other populations or in those rare cross-cultural circumstances where Christians encountered those from distant cultures, that the identity of the church was fundamentally challenged. Today, the boundary is everywhere, and we live in a state of perpetual boundary-crossing.

Thomas Aquinas wrote one *summa* to defend the existence of the church to outsiders, and another *summa* to tell the church how to arrange its own life. That distinction has now collapsed. In the destabilizing environment of advanced modernity, the whole earth is a permanent mission field.

Living by Hope: Connecting Who We Are to What We Do

It is important to recognize that this challenge is also an enormous opportunity. In advanced modernity, we are surrounded by people who are searching for stable identity and a secure ground for moral formation. This hunger is palpable and growing.

Consider this testimony from a speech by *New York Times* columnist David Brooks:

I spend much of my time at great colleges all around the country, and I teach at a great, great college where I'm very honoured to teach, Yale University. And my students are wonderful, but most of the secular institutions I visit, whether it's in education or anywhere else, do not integrate the soul, the heart and the mind. They have, in most of these places, people have an overdeveloped self and an underdeveloped soul ...

A lot of them have been raised with conditional love; their parents love them, and are also extremely anxious about them, and when the kids do something that the parents think will lead to worldly success, the beam of love is a little stronger. When they do something their parents disapprove of, the beam of love is withdrawn. The wolf of conditional love is at the door, and it makes them terrified that the elemental love of their life will be withdrawn if they don't do the right thing ...

My students are so hungry for spiritual content, and one of them said to me: 'We are so hungry.' ... What I see when I go to Christian institutions is a vocabulary, a method and an approach to life – whether it's a chapel service, spiritual disciplines, curriculum – that lives it out. You have the gospel, you have the example of Jesus Christ, you have the beatitudes, you believe in a personal God who is redeeming this world at this moment, you have the exemplars.[14]

The Bible promises that the Holy Spirit will build the church. We should face the conditions of advanced modernity with hope, not fear. We are being transformed by a power that transcends the conditions of human culture and civilization. If the church grasps the nature of its present situation and turns to the Bible for answers (as well as for a deeper understanding of the questions) it will find the means that God will use, through our obedient action, to stabilize and renew its identity. This, in turn, will position the church to shine like a star in the darkness.

The need to stabilize the identity of the church under conditions of permanent destabilization implies a need for ecclesiology to recognize its interdependence with missiology. We cannot separate who we are from what we do.

If the identity of the church is not yet a sufficient focus in systematic theology, the mission of the church is conspicuous mainly by its absence. Widely used systematic theology textbooks typically contain no significant treatment of the church's mission in their sections on ecclesiology.[15]

It must be stated emphatically that connecting ecclesiology to missiology does not mean disconnecting ecclesiology from doctrine, morals, history, etc. On the contrary, under the social conditions of advanced modernity, a connection to missiology is the best hope to *strengthen* the role of doctrine, morals, history, etc. in ecclesiology. In a destabilized social world, the only churches that are likely to remain committed to their doctrine, morals, history, etc. will be the churches with a strong sense of mission that is grounded in those very commitments. The church can retain its historic formative commitments if it helps its people live every area of their lives out of them; that is, teaches people to drive trucks as if God is holy love in the Trinity, to make sandwiches as if God became a man, to write reports as if Jesus died and rose for us and is coming back. Luther's notorious sermon illustration on what it means to change a dirty nappy in light of the doctrine of justification by faith is one of many examples showing how this can be done.[16]

Even the pagan sages have known, at least since Aristotle's *Poetics*, that character cannot really be disentangled from plot. Oedipus accepts the Sphinx's challenge because he is daring; he is daring because he accepts the Sphinx's challenge. Character and plot go together like the chicken and the egg; which came first is a question to which there is no answer. We see the same principle in Aristotle's complex analysis of the relationship between virtue and action in the *Nicomachean Ethics*.

Long before Aristotle, though, the Old Testament bore witness to this connection. It taught that the identity of God's people was interdependent with the arrangement of all their life activities. Its account of God, God's people (Israel), and God's place (the holy land) draw theology, identity, relationships, institutions, laws, and routine practices together into a seamless web. The way the Israelite was to do his or her daily work was comprehensively shaped by membership in the people of God and location in the land of God. Ploughing a field or baking a meal, the Israelite was at all times to act for God's purposes, conform to God's law, and look forward to God's return; his or her understanding of who God is was to permeate and reshape all aspects of life. Christopher Wright refers to this deep interconnectedness of theology, social relationships, and economic activities as an 'ethical triangle'.[17]

This ecclesial/missional connection is maintained in the New Testament. Identity as God's people and the organization of all life activities remain interdependent. Peter says those who call on God as Father and have been purified by the blood of the Son should 'be holy in all your conduct' (1 Peter 1.13–21). Paul says to 'God's chosen ones' who have 'the peace of Christ' and are 'called in one body': 'whatever you do, in word or deed, do everything in the name of the Lord Jesus, giving thanks to God the Father through him'; and again, 'Whatever you do, work heartily, as for the Lord and not for men, knowing that from the Lord you will receive the inheritance as your reward. You are serving the Lord Christ' (Col. 3.12–24).

After Pentecost, however, with God's people being built among the nations rather than in a single chosen nation, a new tension has emerged. God's people are now living in a social world whose structures (other than the church) are not in redemptive covenant relationship with God. Christians must organize both their lives in the church and their lives in the world.

Hence the New Testament has much to say about local church life, and also much to say about how households are organized. Concern for the ecclesiastical community exists side by side with a number of 'household codes' demonstrating detailed concern for how the rest of life is organized (see Eph. 5.22—6.9; Col. 3.18—4.1; 1 Tim. 3.1–13; Titus 2.1–10; 1 Peter 2.13—3.7). The household is of such importance that failure to meet its needs is described as worse than unbelief (1 Tim. 5.8).

The New Testament's intense concern for households has far-reaching, transformative implications that are easily overlooked by modern readers. We must understand that in premodern civilizations such as those of the New Testament world, 'households' included not only what we now call family life, but also all that we now call jobs, commerce, and economic life.[18] Even law and government were exercised by households, because authority was invested not in bureaucratic offices that were then in turn *held* by individuals, as in our modern states. Political authority was held by individuals directly and sometimes, by extension, their families (i.e. dynasties); authority rested in individuals as individuals rather than in offices *occupied* by a changing series of individuals. Bureaucratic organization of public power separate from the household is a hallmark of the modern world.[19]

When Scripture calls us to order all of our lives for God, this is often understood as 'ethical'. It is that, but also more. Ethics cannot be reduced to a set of rules or of virtues. Ethics requires purpose: motive or intention. This is true of particular ethical judgements, because the ethical goodness or badness of an action depends in large degree on its motive. It is also true of ethics as a whole, for the question 'What are all these rules and virtues *for*?' requires an answer if the rules and virtues are going to be justifiable or even intelligible. ('Which homicides should be considered murders?' is a question we cannot answer until we first know why we prohibit murder.)[20]

Hence ethics leads us to mission, and to the connection between ecclesiology and missiology. In the disintegrative conditions of advanced modernity, ecclesiology requires Christian ethics – a renewed sense of *what we are called to do* to ground our sense of *who we are*. Christian ethics, in turn, presupposes missiology, which answers the question 'What is the "calling" that grounds our account of what we are "called" to do?' In renewing our understanding of the church's mission (missiology) we can renew our understanding of what it means to live a Christian kind of life (ethics), which in turn can renew our understanding of what it means to be the church (ecclesiology).[21]

We have already observed that other kinds of institutions (businesses, schools) have wide latitude to change identities because the kinds of missions they are (properly) devoted to permit this. And we have stated that the church's mission is of such a nature that it cannot endure a similar instability of identity without calling into question the authenticity of its own mission. We must now look more closely at how the church's mission shapes its identity, and vice versa.

The Faith and Work Movement as Ecclesiological/Missiological Response

In this light, the growth of the faith and work movement takes on a new significance. The movement can be seen as a missiological response to the breakdown of Christian identity in advanced modernity. Theologians should consider how the missional emphasis of this movement arises from an intense desire to integrate all of one's life around Christ – an imperative that has at least as much ecclesial as missional significance.

The desire to integrate all of one's life around Christ has been a consistent theme in theology of work resources and meetings for a generation. There is no space here for a detailed review of this breathtakingly vast popular movement, which has produced without exaggeration tens of thousands of local organizations and hundreds of thousands of books. In his authoritative history of the movement, David Miller identifies three 'waves' of the movement across the twentieth century; the current wave is distinguished from earlier ones primarily by its focus on the integration of all of life around Christ.[22]

That this intense desire for *integration* is a response to the *disintegrative* social conditions of advanced modernity is not a difficult case to make. Some leaders in the movement have even made this a key theme. For example, Timothy Keller and Katherine Leary Alsdorf frame their discussion of how the gospel reconstructs our understanding and practice of work as a response to the specific dysfunctions and 'idolatries' of modern and postmodern culture.[23]

Unfortunately, the movement has often applied this insight missiologically but not ecclesiologically, seeing the significance of work for what we are called to do, but not for who we are as God's people. And in some cases it is badly *misapplied* ecclesiologically, as some in the movement have appealed to the theological significance of work to justify anticlerical and anti-ecclesiastical tendencies.[24]

This is now changing, with the emergence of literature and leaders who intentionally make the role of pastors and local churches central, and even pursue constructive ecclesiological reforms in light of the theological significance of work.[25] The questions being raised by this new direction in the movement, which we will consider below, represent an opportunity for academic ecclesiological scholars to serve the church by contributing the clarity and insight made possible by deep study.

Commissioned to Work and Worship

This chapter can only begin to scratch the surface of a challenge that will require much more effort from diverse theologians fully to canvas. We can, however, sketch one possible systematic-theological response to the ecclesiological challenge outlined above. What follows is offered not as a resolution of the problem but as a first step that hopefully will prompt much more investigation from systematic theologians.

The passage traditionally known as the Great Commission, the charge Jesus gives to his disciples just before ascending to heaven (Matt. 28.18–20), provides one promising place to examine the connection between ecclesiology and missiology. Here, Jesus tells his people who they are and what they are to do.

'Work' as such is not mentioned. However, we cannot in fact apply the Great Commission's call to discipleship and obedience without confronting the theological significance of work. This would be true in any time, but it is especially true in our time.

The traditional label 'commission' is well chosen, and points to the simultaneously ecclesiological and missiological significance of the passage. A commission formally endows its recipient with a particular mission. But it also formally establishes that recipient as possessing a certain status, defining characteristics, authority, polity, and ordinances by virtue of its having received this mission. A police 'commissioner', or the 'commissary' on an Army base, or the Federal Communications 'Commission' are called that because they have been formally endowed with a certain mission. But the same formal act that grants each of them a mission also *constitutes* each of them: it creates an office or institution that exists because of that mission, and has specific marks, rights, responsibilities, and rules as a result.

The Great Commission points most broadly towards four characteristics or imperatives that define the identity and mission of God's people. The church is grounded in the gospel, called to discipleship among all nations, washed by the water of the Trinity, and learning how to obey its Lord.

The commission is bookended by statements that ground it in the gospel. 'All authority in heaven and on earth has been given to me' points to the cosmic dimension of the gospel, the worldwide availability of salvation and sanctification in the present age, and its directedness towards eschatological fulfilment in the second coming (when Jesus's authority over all things will be fully manifested). 'Behold, I am with you always, to the end of the age' points to the personal dimension of the gospel, the immediate presence of Christ to us – individually and as a church community – as our forgiving and transforming saviour and Lord.

The commission proper (the part that is a main verb rather than a participle) begins with the call to 'make disciples of all nations'. The primary mission of the church is to help people become students ('disciples') of Jesus Christ through the gospel, even as they continue to participate in the life of their nations.

Here we find the central connection to work. It is the theological significance of work that makes the key difference between real discipleship and mere consumer Christianity, as diverse figures ranging from David Wells to Dallas Willard have stressed.[26] Authentic discipleship to Jesus Christ requires that all areas of our lives and all our activities become modes of discipleship. Without this imperative to transform all of life into an arena of spiritual learning and service, 'discipleship' tends to become identified merely with the consumption of religious goods and services.

Work, including work in the home, on the job, in neighbourhoods and in every context, takes up the overwhelming majority of our waking hours. This is by divine design, for we were made to work as well as worship; we were made to worship in large part by working. Work and worship are inseparably connected throughout Scripture, even at the linguistic level.[27] The gospel restores us to worshipful work, both today and in eternity; we will glorify God for eternity in worshipful work as well as in contemplation.[28]

We are, of course, made for more than just work; we are made for relational intimacy and for contemplation. And we are finite creatures who must rest. Restlessness and sloth are both closely associated with godlessness; the godly are to avoid both doing too much work and too little. This is not primarily a function of the *quantity* of work we do (although that matters) but of quality. We are to live integrated lives in which work and rest unite to glorify God in a whole life that centres on loving God and neighbour.[29]

But if we do not regard our daily tasks in our work as arenas of discipleship, then by definition 'discipleship' is something we do as a leisure-time activity during the relatively small number of hours each week when we are not working. In such a case, we have given up the overwhelming majority of our lives to being formed by the world and its standards, reserving only a tiny fraction of our lives to be formed by God.

One of the primary focal points of the faith and work movement is the idea of 'whole-life discipleship'. Mark Greene, an internationally recognized movement leader and the popularizer of this phrase, has stressed that the church's failure to regard work as important is only a symptom of a much deeper problem: a failure to regard *all of life* as significant.[30] The faith and work movement is really, at bottom, a discipleship-in-all-of-life movement. Work is just the most obvious or most urgent place that has become disconnected from discipleship in Christians' lives generally.

The second imperative in the Great Commission is 'baptizing them in the name of the Father and of the Son and of the Holy Spirit'. Here we find the clearest affirmation of the institutional church with its ordinances or sacraments. An institution specifically devoted to the ministry of the word is needed. While the imperative to discipleship demands that we take our daily work captive to Christ, we are to be formed for discipleship in our daily work by ecclesial leaders; that is, people whose 'daily work' is to steward the mystery of the gospel.

Baptism is in the name of the Father, Son, and Spirit because these ecclesial activities point us towards the mystery of the Trinity, and the holy love that is among the three persons who are God. Their holy love for one another, first extended to us in creation, now washes us of our sin in redemption through justification and sanctification.[31]

Yet the holy love of God also leads us back out to the world of our daily work, and so should the life and ordinances of the local church. This much becomes clear as we pass to the final imperative of the Great Commission.

Commanded to Work and Worship

The third of the Great Commission's three imperatives is 'teaching them to observe all that I have commanded you'. We must be learning to obey the commands of Jesus if we are to be God's people. These commands centre on love. Just as we are washed by the holy love that is God in the Trinity, we are to extend the holy love that we have received from God back to God, and to others.

Asked to summarize the law of God, Jesus said to love God and neighbour (Matt. 22.34–40; Mark 12.28–34). This is traditionally called the Great Commandment, drawing on Jesus's own language in these passages.

In his classic book *Christian Mission in the Modern World*, John Stott framed whole the dilemma of modernity for the church in terms of this connection between the two 'Greats'. He pointed out that when the Great Commission is understood in a narrow way that excludes the world of work, focusing only on verbal evangelism and church activities, it is difficult to relate the demands of the Great Commission to the demands of the Great Commandment. We may strive to obey both, but without a way to relate the two we will constantly have difficulty setting priorities among them. Stott identified this as one of the church's most critical challenges in the modern world.[32]

Willard likewise took the church to task for its neglect of 'teaching them to observe all that I have commanded you'. This neglect had become so extensive that Willard titled one of his books *The Great Omission* to confront us with the seriousness of the problem. The omission of the Great Commission's call to obedience leaves the church with a mission too narrow to help us live our lives as if we were really living in the kingdom of God today.[33]

The best solution, as Stott and Willard both suggested, is to widen our understanding of the Great Commission – of the mission of God – to encompass all of life. The Great Commission includes the institutional church and verbal evangelism, but is not limited to them. This allows us to relate the Great Commission to the Great Commandment and harmonize them. The Great Commandment tells us what God wants from our lives, and the Great Commission tells us how we are to pursue it: the gospel of justification and sanctification giving us transformative power for discipleship in all of life, church life and life in the world alike.

In one of the popular books produced by the faith and work movement, Lester DeKoster has emphasized two ways in which the love of God acts through our daily work. Our ordinary, daily work is one of the primary ways in which God provides for and takes care of the needs of his world;

it is also one of the primary ways he shapes Christians into people who are characterized by love.[34]

Overcoming the Formation/Work Dichotomy

Christian leaders are currently experimenting with two inadequate responses to the challenge of modernity. They are inadequate not because they are wrong as such, but because they are incomplete halves: the ecclesiological and missional halves. In isolation from one another, these two emphases tend to go wrong. An approach that embraces both and connects them, relating them to one another and harmonizing them, would be far more effective in confronting the challenge of modernity.

One approach, as we have already seen, is the faith and work movement. If our challenge is to connect the Great Commission and the Great Commandment, we can see the faith and work movement as having begun from the Great Commandment side. Its purpose is to empower Christians to practise the holy love of God in the way they do their daily work. At its best, the movement does not stop there, but makes the connection between the Great Commandment (putting love into action) and the Great Commission (being the church and doing what the church is to do).

However, as we have also seen, the movement is not always at its best. One of its most important weaknesses has been its disconnection from local churches and the clergy. This is not always because of conscious anti-ecclesialism or anticlericalism; it is as often a result of unconscious neglect. For reasons of history that were mostly beyond direct human control, the movement first began and long grew in parachurch structures. The institutional church and the clergy were sometimes actively disliked, but more often they were simply viewed as occupying a different, parallel sphere of responsibility that was not highly important for the movement either as a potential partner or as a rival.

In a private conversation, the author of this chapter once made an argument for the importance of the clergy to an internationally famous faith and work leader. The leader gave this reply: 'Pastors only give 52 sermons a year, and they have a lot they have to cover. Realistically, how often are they going to preach about work? This movement has to belong to the laity, because we're the ones who have the time to do it.' This comment revealed no active hostility to the clergy and the local church, but it did reveal a tragic lack of vision for the vital role they play in helping people develop discernment and power in their spiritual lives. Out of every 52 sermons, we should expect 52 to help us put the holy love of God into action through our daily activities, which are mostly work!

The other approach doubles down on the things that have been emphasized by the traditional, narrower reading of the Great Commission. This approach hopes to counteract the disintegrative tendencies of advanced modernity by focusing on the formative role of the institutional church, spiritual disciplines and what used to be called 'religious works'.[35]

These things are clearly needed. Character formation is indispensable to discipleship – in some ways it simply *is* discipleship, conforming our character to Christ's through the gospel. But in the chaotic and choice-driven environment of advanced modernity, character formation can only happen through conscious design and sustained, intentional effort. Character formation requires people to acknowledge not only that they have free will and can make their own choices, but that their existing character is not all that it ought to be, and therefore their choices are not what they ought to be. The religious ordinances and disciplines of the church are indispensable both to helping people realize this latter insight, and helping them understand how to change.

However, this emphasis on formation and the institutional church goes wrong if it is not directed at formation *for the purpose of living out Christlike character in all of life, in every area of human activity, out in the world beyond the walls of the local church*. If character formation in the church is not referred outward to life in the world, it becomes merely circular and empty of meaningful content.[36] We engage in the disciplines in order to become Christlike, but 'Christlike' comes to mean 'engaging in the disciplines'. As Hunter has noted, this ultimately produces a church whose only mission is 'to be itself', which is a self-referential void.[37]

This is why Willard, perhaps the foremost champion of spiritual disciplines in the twentieth century, constantly emphasized that spiritual disciplines must not become ends in themselves – and that this fate could only be avoided if the purpose of spiritual disciplines is to empower us for Christlike life in our daily activities. *And this, he said, primarily means work.* A key passage in *The Divine Conspiracy* is devoted to this subject, as are multiple chapters of his posthumous *The Divine Conspiracy Continued*.[38]

So, again, at its best the church movement that emphasizes spiritual formation begins with the Great Commission but does not stay there. It has striven to connect the Great Commission and the Great Commandment. And, again, a failure to strive for this connection is an important source of the trouble on those occasions when we find this movement going wrong.

A more complete solution to the dilemma of advanced modernity will be available to the church when we realize that, like chocolate and peanut butter, the spiritual formation movement and the faith and work movement are two great tastes that taste great together.

GREG FORSTER

A Fresh Vision of What It Means to Be the Church

When we do connect ecclesiology and missiology, the Great Commission and the Great Commandment, we are required to rethink each in light of the other. This need not mean radical departures from traditional commitments on either side. It could, however, be the first step to a fresh vision of what it means both to be the church and to do what the church is called to do in the world – a fresh vision that would have the power to sustain the church by the Holy Spirit through the challenges and opportunities of advanced modernity.

The traditional foci of ecclesiological inquiry – the marks, discipline, polity, and ordinances of the church – should be rethought in light of the theological significance of work. This could start with a heightened awareness of what Abraham Kuyper called the precedence of 'the church as organism' over 'the church as institution'; the church exists as an *organic* spiritual body before it exists as an *organization*.[39] To use other language for the same thing, we must ensure that the life of the 'church gathered' is not an end in itself (leading into a self-referential void) but directs us towards being and acting as the 'church scattered'. The directedness of Sunday towards Monday is suggested in passages like Ephesians 4.12 (ecclesial leaders are appointed to 'equip the saints for works of service') and Hebrews 10.24–25 (Christians should be 'not neglecting to meet together, as is the habit of some', and the reason given for the imperative to meet together is 'to stir up one another to love and good works' and 'encouraging one another').

This rethinking will be different in different traditions, and it is hard to generalize. Presbyterians and Pentecostals will come to different conclusions about how to rethink the sacraments or church discipline in light of this challenge. Nonetheless, numerous liturgical and even structural reforms that are already being adopted by churches across a wide variety of traditions point to the need for all traditions to engage in this rethinking. These include:

- Services to publicly commission the laity to their work, the same way 'missionaries' are commissioned to their areas of service;
- Monthly liturgical focus on particular vocational sectors (health care one month, commerce another, government, education, etc.), sometimes combined with commissioning;
- Formation groups specific to vocational sectors to contextualize Christian mission and ethics to each sector;
- New member processes that ask people about their vocational capacities as they join the church, building a knowledge base of available

talents in the congregation for use in discerning opportunities for missional initiatives;

• Questions being raised about how local churches relate to the increasing ethical challenges facing Christians in their workplaces, for example, diaconal support for those who lose their jobs for the sake of kingdom faithfulness, or the role of church discipline in promoting workplace integrity.[40]

Such reforms should not be adopted without being accompanied by serious ecclesiological reflection. Some churches may conclude that some of these reforms are inconsistent with their ecclesiology. They will need further ecclesiological reflection to discern how they can connect Sunday worship to Monday work in ways that express their convictions about what it means to be the church.

A similar rethinking is of course needed and has already begun on the missiological side. In academia, approaches to missiology stemming from the thought of Lesslie Newbigin and others have emphasized the connection to ecclesiology. Note that Newbigin's *Foolishness to the Greeks* begins with a chapter entitled 'Post-Enlightenment Culture as a Missionary Problem' and ends with one entitled 'What Must We Be? The Call to the Church'.[41] His *The Gospel in a Pluralist Society* famously states that we must see 'the congregation as a hermeneutic of the gospel'; less well remembered is his statement that this means the church must be 'a community that does not live for itself but is deeply involved in the concerns of its neighbourhood', a statement that points straight to the theological significance of work.[42]

Indeed, what is the faith and work movement but an extension of Newbigin's principle, seeking to make 'the church scattered' as much a hermeneutic of the gospel as 'the church gathered'? This helps explain the faith and work movement's increasing engagement with local churches. The influence of leaders like Amy Sherman and Tom Nelson is forcing the movement to take Christian identity and the local church more seriously.[43]

In a chapter of this kind it is possible to become too 'never before in history-ish'. The challenge of being faithful disciples in a fallen world, bringing God's holy love into the world's unholiness, remains the same in every age. Nonetheless, the destabilizing social environment of advanced modernity raises unique questions about what it means to be the church and to do what God calls us to do. If we wish to remain the strange people called God's people, and to be doing his work in this very strange world, ecclesiology will need to connect the church's historic commitments – doctrine, morals, history and all the rest – to God's mission in the world around us.

Notes

1 See John Calvin, *Institutes of the Christian Religion*, ed. John T. McNeill, trans. Ford Lewis Battles (Louisville, KY: Westminster John Knox Press, 2006), pp. 35–9; see also H. Richard Niebuhr, *Christ and Culture* (New York: Harper, 1951), pp. 1–44; Charles M. Wood, *The Formation of Christian Understanding* (Eugene, OR: Wipf & Stock, 1993); David H. Kelsey, *Proving Doctrine* (Harrisburg, PA: Trinity Press International, 1999); and Gary T. Meadors (ed.), *Four Views on Moving Beyond the Bible to Theology* (Grand Rapids, MI: Zondervan, 2009).

2 Gregg R. Allison, *Sojourners and Strangers* (Wheaton, IL: Crossway, 2012), pp. 19, 29.

3 Allison, *Sojourners*, p. 29.

4 See Peter Berger, *The Many Altars of Modernity* (Boston: De Gruyter, 2014), pp. 5–9.

5 A few samples from this truly huge literature: on the Reformation as a cause of modernity, see Alister McGrath, *Christianity's Dangerous Idea* (New York: Harper-One, 2008); on secular philosophy (including Renaissance humanism among much else), see Allan Bloom, *The Closing of the American Mind* (New York: Simon & Schuster, 1987); on technological development (including large increases in food production due to improved crop rotation), see Joyce Appleby, *The Relentless Revolution* (New York: W.W. Norton, 2010), pp. 56–86.

6 Berger, *Many Altars*, pp. 17–32, 59.

7 See Berger, *Many Altars*, pp. 8–9; James Davison Hunter, *To Change the World* (New York: Oxford University Press, 2010), pp. 205–10.

8 They are not.

9 Martin Luther King, Jr, 'Letter from a Birmingham Jail', available at www.africa.upenn.edu/Articles_Gen/Letter_Birmingham.html (accessed 28 March 2017).

10 *Brown v. Board of Education of Topeka*, 347 U.S. 483.

11 See Berger, *Many Altars*, pp. 34–49.

12 See Graham Cole, *He Who Gives Life* (Wheaton, IL: Crossway, 2007), pp. 209–41.

13 See Amy Sherman, *Kingdom Calling* (Downers Grove: InterVarsity Press, 2011), pp. 15–23; Dallas Willard and Gary Black, Jr, *The Divine Conspiracy Continued* (New York: HarperOne, 2014), pp. 1–11; David Wells, *God in the Whirlwind* (Wheaton, IL: Crossway, 2014), pp. 15–39.

14 David Brooks, 'An Evening with David Brooks', Trinity International University, 10 February 2016; www.youtube.com/watch?v=IljLS1mcl6c (accessed 17 March 2017).

15 Consider for example Wayne Grudem, *Systematic Theology* (Grand Rapids, MI: Zondervan, 2000); Michael Horton, *The Christian Faith* (Grand Rapids, MI: Zondervan, 2011); and Millard J. Erickson, *Christian Theology*, 3rd edition (Grand Rapids, MI: Baker, 2013).

16 See Martin Luther, 'The Estate of Marriage' (1522), available at www.1215.org/lawnotes/misc/marriage/martin-luther-estate-of-marriage.pdf (accessed 28 March 2017).

17 See Christopher J. H. Wright, *Old Testament Ethics for the People of God* (Downers Grove: InterVarsity Press, 2004), pp. 17–20.

18 See Keith Reeves, 'Family, Land and Household in the Old Testament', Oikonomia Network newsletter, 11 November 2015; and Keith Reeves, 'Households

and Economic Injustice in the Old Testament', Oikonomia Network newsletter, 8 December 2015.

19 See Francis Fukuyama, *The Origins of Political Order* (New York: Farrar, Straus & Giroux, 2012).

20 See Scott B. Rae, *Introducing Christian Ethics* (Grand Rapids, MI: Zondervan), pp. 19–32, 50–61.

21 Logically, there is no reason we couldn't also start with either ecclesiology or ethics and argue our way towards the others; the order we follow here is selected as the one most likely to serve the contemporary church the most effectively, given the present social conditions in which identity is unstable and ethics intensely contested.

22 See David W. Miller, *God at Work* (New York: Oxford University Press, 2007); and David W. Miller, 'God Bless Us, Every One: The Past, Present and Future of the Faith and Work Movement', Oikonomia Network Faculty Retreat, 7 January 2016, available at http://oikonomianetwork.org/resources/god-bless-us-everyone-the-past-present-and-future-of-the-faith-and-work-movement/ (accessed 29 March 2017).

23 Timothy Keller and Katherine Leary Alsdorf, *Every Good Endeavor* (New York: Dutton, 2012), pp. 140–52.

24 The Faith@Work Summit, one of the largest and most prominent conferences in the movement, at its meeting in October 2016 dedicated an entire plenary session, with six speakers, to publicly repenting from these tendencies and expressing a commitment to value the role of pastors and local churches. That such a session was felt to be necessary indicates the extent of this problem in the movement. See www.fwsummit.org (accessed 17 March 2017).

25 See for example Sherman, *Kingdom Calling* and Tom Nelson, *Work Matters* (Wheaton, IL: Crossway, 2011).

26 See Dallas Willard, *The Divine Conspiracy* (New York: HarperOne, 1998), pp. 283–7; and Wells, *God in the Whirlwind*, pp. 219–32.

27 See Seong Hyun Park, 'Working and Keeping', Oikonomia Network newsletter, 20 February 2014.

28 To select once again from a truly vast literature, see Darrell Cosden, *A Theology of Work* (Eugene, OR: Wipf & Stock, 2004).

29 See Chris Armstrong, 'Vocation? Whatever!', Oikonomia Network, available at www.youtube.com/watch?v=5rm-ICqhGVY (accessed 29 March 2017).

30 Mark Greene, 'Mark Greene and Lausanne Conference 2010', The Lausanne Movement, 2010, available at www.youtube.com/watch?v=Owuab_M5L3Y (accessed 29 March 2017).

31 See Wells, *God in the Whirlwind*.

32 John Stott, *Christian Mission in the Modern World* (Downers Grove: Inter-Varsity Press, 1975), pp. 25–54.

33 See Dallas Willard, *The Great Omission* (New York: HarperOne, 2006).

34 Lester DeKoster, *Work: The Meaning of Your Life* (Grand Rapids, MI: Christian's Library Press, 2015).

35 Prominent examples include James K. A. Smith, *Desiring the Kingdom* (Downers Grove: Baker, 2009); and Rod Dreher, *The Benedict Option* (New York: Sentinel, 2017).

36 See Luma Simms, 'The Benedict Option Can't Save Your Faith or Family', *The Federalist*, 28 March 2017.

37 Hunter, *To Change the World*, p. 219.

38 See Willard, *Divine Conspiracy*, pp. 283–7; and Willard and Black, *Divine Conspiracy Continued*, pp, 25–84, 201–86.

39 Abraham Kuyper, *Rooted and Grounded* (Grand Rapids, MI: Christian's Library Press, 2013).

40 For specific examples of these and many other reforms see Sherman, *Kingdom Calling* and the many resources linked on the 'TOW for Pastors and Churches' page of the Theology of Work Project website (www.theologyofwork.org/tow-for-pastors-and-churches, accessed 28 March 2017).

41 See Lesslie Newbigin, *Foolishness to the Greeks* (Grand Rapids, MI: Eerdmans, 1986).

42 Lesslie Newbigin, *The Gospel in a Pluralist Society* (Grand Rapids, MI: Eerdmans 1989), p. 229.

43 See Sherman, *Kingdom Calling*; Nelson, *Work Matters*; and especially Tom Nelson, 'The Importance of the Workplace-Church Connection', Faith@Work Summit, 29 October 2016 (video forthcoming at fwsummit.org).

10

Work and the New Creation

DARRELL T. COSDEN

Most theological reflections on the meaning, value, and purpose of human work begin with reflections on the narrative of creation found in Genesis 1—3. God is a creator/worker, and God created us in God's own image to be workers. A doctrine of work, therefore, is built both from and within the doctrine of (initial) creation. Work's theological meaning is found in being a creation mandate or an order of creation.[1] Creation as a doctrine is then juxtaposed with the doctrine of redemption. In the 'order of redemption' we find the good news, the 'gospel mandate' in which the narrative of Jesus and salvation are explicated within the doctrines of Christology, soteriology, and ultimately eschatology. Work, when it is discussed in the contexts of these doctrines at all, tends to receive mention simply as what Christ did as a carpenter before his ministry of salvation began, or as a form of obedient service subsequent to and distinct from salvation.[2]

Typically, work is given its theological locus within protology, the doctrine of the initial creation. On this view (which finds expression, for example, within Lutheran two-kingdom theology), work becomes strictly part of our earthly calling or vocation to love God through concrete acts of serving and thereby loving our neighbour. It is theologically important as an order or ordinance of creation. Work is thus seen as only indirectly corresponding to redemption, as an obedient response to it. Within Reformed circles, work as vocation is described as a creation mandate (Gen. 1.28) that is again juxtaposed to a redemption mandate (Matt. 28.18). Work is at best penultimate in relation to Christ and eternal salvation. Work here is a common rather than redemptive grace, and, as now fallen, it serves only to provide the context for sanctification and becomes a discipline that is good for the soul, as the Puritans preached.[3]

Within most of the Catholic tradition work theologically is located primarily within the natural order as prescribed by natural law. Again, when biblically discussed, natural law and work find their moorings in Genesis and protology. In Catholic thought, work's Christological meaning is an addition of grace to nature. In work, Christ the carpenter identifies with all working people, and then through suffering within work we become caught up in Christ's suffering and redemptive work of the cross.[4] Work itself, however, is common to all and undertaken within the order of and constrained by the parameters of natural law.

For most of the tradition, work is integral to creation and the created order. Reflection upon it derives primarily from the doctrine of creation, here meaning the doctrine of the initial creation. This is not wrong as such. However, orienting work in this way and making protology its locus and point of orientation leaves work at best only tangentially or penulti-mately related to the centre of the Christian faith: Christ and his eternal salvific purposes.

Different than a theology of vocation, creation ordinances, or natural law, a theology of work as a comprehensive theological reflection on work itself is a quite recent invention. Marie-Dominique Chenu, in the context of rebuilding Europe after the Second World War and in an attempt to secure the Christian faith's place within that process, was one of several Catholic thinkers probing for a methodology for thinking theologically about 'secular' things.[5] He is credited with coining the term a 'theology of work'. While several thinkers since have offered tentative explorations towards a theology of work, Miroslav Volf is the first theologian to attempt a comprehensive theology of work.[6] He took pneumatology rather than protology as his doctrinal starting point and oriented work eschato-logically towards the new creation, rather than protologically towards the initial creation. In this chapter, the trajectory of Volf's proposal will be followed and defended. Indeed, my own proposal for a theology of work takes its bearings from and builds upon Volf's proposal.[7]

Work: Mere Instrumentality?

Volf begins with the understanding that all of God's purposes are eschato-logical, oriented towards the goal that we call 'new creation'. Taking his cue from Moltmann's eschatological framework initially expressed in *Theology of Hope*, Volf grasps that all doctrine, including the doctrine of creation, leans towards eschatology. This means that theologically all doc-trines are thinking about God and God's economy (creation) as pointing forward towards the eschaton. Doctrinally, then, eschatology integrates such doctrines as protology, Christology, and soteriology into the doc-trine (rather than doctrines) of the church. In this way, creation is not thought of as complete or yet established. Nor is it a doctrine distinct from or other than the doctrine of the new creation. Creation as a whole is a work in process directed towards bringing about the good of establish-ing community and creating something of eternal value both to God and to ourselves. The work of creation (initial, continual, and new) includes humankind creating through work to bring about the good. Likewise, given the conditions of human finitude as well as sinfulness, all of human life and activity require God's redemptive and transformative action.

Herein lies work's meaning theologically for God and for us. Volf states it succinctly: 'For the significance of secular work depends on the value of creation, and the value of creation depends on its final destiny.'[8] The rest of this chapter unpacks this thesis and in so doing argues that eschatology rather than protology is the doctrinal starting point for understanding human work.

Work's theological meaning and value is derived from, bound up with, and ultimately depends upon the value of creation, in its material and immateriality. Ultimately creation's value to God as well as to people, therefore, lies in its goal more than in its utility value.[9] This is not to diminish the instrumental value of work, which shortly will be discussed. Rather, it is to start by placing work and its utility within a wider trajectory of meaning than is typically done by society at large, and even within economic discussions of work.

Generally, what does society perceive to be the value of creation and thus work? Admittedly, I am painting here in broad brush strokes, generalizing, and doubtless overstating things without sufficient nuance. Nevertheless, there are generally observable tendencies in Western culture that warrant comment.

For many living in information societies, a materialist and utilitarian understanding of the value of creation, work, and its material products seems to dominate. This populist notion pervades even among those whose experience of work might itself at times suggest something less reductionistic. Here, nature is seen primarily as a resource at the disposal of humans for manipulation and consumption according to our needs and desires. This is an anthropocentric understanding of nature which certain environmentalists seek to challenge. The existence of the environmental movement itself suggests that such an instrumentalist view of nature predominates. In a utilitarian mindset, nature is seen as inert and neutral as a tool. It is not understood as creation, which is a decidedly theological concept implying stewardship and responsibility.

Likewise, human work is not celebrated as noble or virtuous in itself, but is often depicted as an unfortunate but necessary means for acquiring life's necessities and wants. Here, possessing and consuming ultimately defines the good life. Making and trading commodities is good to the extent that doing so makes acquiring and consuming higher levels of goods increasingly possible. Work is valued only to the degree that it makes acquiring more of these goods possible. In this sense nature (creation) is valued as a commodity. Again, this materialist or utilitarian mindset and understanding of work and the economy is consumerist in nature. It implies that the good life consists of indulgent consumption and is what the Greek philosophers and the Stoics argued, for their own reasons, is an inhuman or animalistic way of living. To them such a life is pre- or subhuman. Clearly a theological anthropology and understanding of work and the good life stands in opposition to a consumption-oriented understanding of the good life.

This populist attitude is reinforced in much advertising, as well as in much public and political discourse. It is advanced in economics by beliefs like Milton Friedman's infamous notion that the business of business is business with no teleological ordering to anything but itself. It is advanced politically when economic growth and spending are touted as the assumed goal of the political process and policy. When the value and virtue of work and nature/creation is reduced to a means of acquisition and consumption, and, when indulgence becomes a virtue, then the notion of the good life is reduced to an animalistic level of existence and society begins to deteriorate.

Similarly, this utilitarian attitude towards work and nature often is comprehended as indistinguishable from the structures of free markets and capitalism. This is entirely understandable, and in practice quite often is the case. Many utilitarian thinkers even promote such ideas. Increasingly in our information societies, those using free market and capital tools do so to the end of consumption and growth for growth's sake, believing that human flourishing and the good life consist in consumption for its own sake. We see this reflected in much of today's marketing, which is driven by and drives this particular vision of anthropology and flourishing. Yet to equate the mechanisms of free markets and capital to these underlying ideologies is mistaken. Abstractly, markets *are* neutral. Markets as mechanisms do not value or believe anything. They are simply vehicles for exchange. Of course, beyond theory, when actual people engage in market activities, markets become more than a collection of individual transactions. They become, take on, and create a culture and thus develop a kind of life of their own. This culture then affects people's beliefs, attitudes, and values, which in turn direct their exchange of goods while setting the subjective value of things. If people as a culture think about work and nature in a reductionist and utilitarian way, the markets negatively will reflect this. Thus, the plea for and use of free markets and capital can seem to be, and often is, a plea for consumerism and crony capitalism.

The point of this diversion into a discussion of populist anthropology and economics is to show that it is possible for creation and work to be valued instrumentally (or merely as a utility) and in entirely unhealthy ways. This need not, however, invalidate the instrumental or utility value of work and the creation. As stated earlier, while ultimately creation's value to God as well as to people lies in its eschatological goal more than in its present utility, creation and work's value does include its instrumentality. It is simply an instrumentality directed towards and bracketed by a different vision of the good life. It is likewise built upon a quite different anthropology. This utility is directed towards God's eschatological purposes, which makes creation and work's instrumentality both more human and theologically significant.

For work to be work, and not another important human activity that we call play, work must serve as a means to an end.[10] Work *is* about acquiring the goods necessary for life. Work is about loving our families and our neighbour through providing goods and services. Work within and upon creation does create value for ourselves and, when excess is created, for others (and, as shall become clear, for God's ultimate use). Working itself does provide a context for disciplining and focusing our frequently unbridled desires. It does build in us character and virtue. All of these things are good. The theological tradition, with Catholics emphasizing work and Christ's sufferings and the Lutheran and Calvinist impulse to thrift, discipline and service have not been wrong to emphasize and show the importance of work's and creation's instrumental nature and value.[11]

It is likewise true that in creation, work is central to the proper and healthy building of relationships, community, and culture. Work done poorly can destroy relationships. Work done well builds personal and social cohesion. Through work and in workplaces many of life's important interpersonal relationships are forged and grow. Its products make possible families, and its processes build family legacies. Likewise, interdependent relationships between institutions are created and developed through work, and thereby through interconnected webs, cultures and societies are built.[12] Work is vital instrumentally to healthy relationships and societies. Work does more instrumentally than simply provide for the economic needs of individuals. It does more than simply build character in the worker. It makes relational goods and social goods possible. The instrumental or utility value of work is good, and structurally its utility lies in creating and building relationships towards building societies and culture.

Yet without grounding or directing these various instrumental goods towards a larger, transcendent *telos*, the value of creation and work remains untethered. It becomes arbitrary, especially with debates about what constitutes the good life undermining their utility good. For Christians, if work and creation are not oriented Christologically, soteriologically, and thus ultimately eschatologically, the notion of the *intrinsic* goodness of work and of creation remains tenuous. As Volf says, 'without a theologically grounded belief in the intrinsic value and goodness of creation, positive cultural involvement hangs theologically in the air'.[13]

Work: Intrinsic Significance in God's Creation

As this chapter's thesis suggests, the intrinsic value and ultimate goodness of creation and the goodness of work done therein depend upon creation's destiny. This raises the question, however: Ought human work and God's creation be bound so closely together? Some argue, and not without good cause, that it is human work that threatens to destroy the creation. Should we not simply leave creation alone and 'let it be'? Doesn't our work harm God's wonderful creation?

Within the context of an eschatological framework and when prodded by these questions, notions of God as a worker and us as workers in God's image begin to find a deeper meaning than otherwise possible. I will explain this claim to a 'deeper' meaning in what follows.

To begin, I want to clarify a few terms. What Volf states about the value of 'secular' work depending upon creation's destiny, I will call 'ordinary work'. I use the adjective 'ordinary' somewhat awkwardly to contrast it with what is sometimes called 'spiritual work', meaning the work of pastors, missionaries, and so on whose work revolves around the ministry of the word and sacrament, the care of souls, and traditional forms of mission and evangelism. I say awkwardly since the division of work into categories of sacred and secular, ordinary and spiritual, is both artificial and highly problematic given the argument developed in this chapter and indeed the paradigm developed throughout this book.

Theologically, with an eschatological point of orientation as its starting point, ordinary work is not seen as extrinsic to, as incidental to, or as an imposition upon creation. It is, rather, integral to it. Work is part of the creation itself in virtue of being inexorably linked with creation's *telos*. Work is ontological in this sense.[14] This is true both of created humans as well as of the broader non-human creation. Consider the following brief case study in the theological use of Scripture.

The canonical shape of Scripture begins with Genesis and ends with Revelation. The narrative structure of Scripture we might say proceeds from 'in the beginning' to the end – meaning here its *telos*. As a single narrative, we read the diverse and polyphonic tests as an unfolding story that ultimately reveals an unexpectedly complex and beautiful tapestry in the end. However, when we build our theology in that same order, proceeding from the beginning to end, adding together layer after layer and discrete part by part, we run the risk of missing the canonical shape of the plot line. While each book or section of Scripture has its own discrete structure and meaning, when the canonical shape is observed, a larger story emerges which subsumes the parts.

To illustrate, consider the Genesis 1—11 narrative and a few of its details. Scholars suggest that these texts historically serve as a mirror and counter-narrative to the cosmogonies of the larger and more powerful nations surrounding and threatening to engulf Israel. On their own they offer a theological and social critique of 'the nations' and their cosmo-logical anthropologies and political ideologies and structures. God as creator in Israel's texts is not, as such, a claim to our theological question which suggests possibly a creation *ex nihilo*. That idea is at best an impli-cation of the text, and at worst is possibly forced into it. The text is silent on this point for that is not the question it is addressing. Rather, the point is to show how God brings order out of chaos, that which always threatens to destroy creation, and to show how despite appearances, Israel is central to God's purposes. God does not create like the gods of other nations, by violence and through imposition. Rather, God works as a loving and nurturing gardener, bringing order and creating the conditions for the luxurious flourishing of creation. Likewise, humanity is depicted as an invited partner in the process. Unlike the nations who understand human-ity as worker-slaves, blindly forced to follow the arbitrary will of the gods, Yahweh makes humans to correspond to himself. God makes humans to be workers like himself who nurture and bring order to this grand project of creation. Israel, the heirs to this plan, are not insignificant even though they are small, marginalized, and lack the 'power' of the nations.

The Genesis 1—11 text is wonderful in its vision and details, and it is important for a theology of work. However, without the canonical con-text (and the eschatological orientation this provides), these texts, while grounded and sufficient for Israel in her context, hang in the air for us. They do not tell us to what end God created. They lead us to understand that God chose Israel to bless the nations, but what will that look like and why? Why are we created like God to work? Why does God want a creation? While Israel's *telos* is clearer, what is the goal or *telos* of creation in itself?

It is the eschatological orientation given by Revelation's claim that God is making all things new, that God wants to dwell permanently and not simply 'in the cool of the day' in creation, that gives the Genesis narra-tive and theology its context and thrust. If we fail to see how the Genesis narrative fits as part of the direction of Scripture's overall narrative, we run the risk of missing the larger point or misappropriating the texts them-selves. Let me illustrate with one small detail.

In Genesis we see that humans are created in God's image. That is, humans are created to be like God who is a worker and to do ordinary work. When the Western church tells this story, it suggests that human-kind started out in God's image and that the human task is to retain it primarily by being obedient. God says to work so work is a matter of obedience. The fall is often portrayed as Adam desiring to be like God, in a lack of humility. Yet how is wanting to be like God a sin if our whole design is to be like God? Are we condemned for wanting to be who we are? Also, where does the text's central theme of work fit into this?

Grasping the canonical and eschatological thrust of Scripture, the Eastern church, following Irenaeus, tells the story differently. They suggest that humanity was not created as already in the image, but created with the purpose to grow into and become it. That is, humanity's creation starts with an eschatological orientation. Humans work to realize and grow into who they were created to be. This is a larger purpose than obedience. Obedience to the task and to pursue it in God's way and in fellowship with God is vital. Obedience is not, however, the point. The sin of Adam was something like impatience, or knowing better than God how to become who he was created to be rather than wanting to be who God created him to be in the first place – namely, like God.

The point of this illustration is to show that without understanding the eschatological *telos* of both humanity and creation, our understanding of human life and work's purpose for us and for the creation can become skewed. Revelation 20—21 tells us God's ultimate goal for creation is for it to become his eternal home. The purpose of ordinary human work that creates value, that preserves and transforms, and that distributes goods is to build and shape, together with God, that future home. This continues to be a narrative of bringing order out of chaos. Equally and simultaneously, God uses our work to build and shape us and human culture, personally and socially, into those who are fit to live forever in creation with God. Importantly, that home is the earth itself, ultimately built, transformed, healed, and perfected. We call this the new creation.

Work, God's and ours, is therefore integral both to God's plan for humans and God's plans for the shaping of the wider creation. It is integral likewise to God's plan for himself. Work is not a primarily a trial, test, curse, or imposition upon creation, though we often make it into these. It is not conceptually a violence done to creation, even though we often do destroy the creation and ourselves in our working. Theologically, ordinary work, done in cooperation with God, is built into creation's design by being essential to its *telos*. It is, as I have said, ontological in this way.

This eschatological and canonical vision gives the Genesis narrative a trajectory that includes its meaning for Israel but that also sets it within a wider horizon. It explains why creation's own destiny matters. Indeed, it provides creation with its own *telos*, a *telos* with an inherent purpose or goal: to become the flourishing dwelling place of God with us. Eschatology also places our understanding of ordinary and spiritual work theologically together within a broader horizon that makes creation and work matter more, and in ways that protological accounts of creation and work cannot.

As part and parcel of creation, our ordinary work is integral to God's overarching eschatological and salvific purposes. It thus is invested with ultimate and not simply penultimate meaning. Our work matters because our destiny matters, together with and within creation's destiny.

The reason we are created to work and commissioned to work includes necessarily all of work's instrumental and relational dimensions, and these matter for life here and now. Work's meaning and purpose must include these ordinary and mundane dimensions in order to count as *work*. Neither the instrumental nor the relational dimensions can be pursued or exercised to the exclusion of the other, however, if our work is to line up with its eschatological purposes. Left- and right-leaning ideologies are shown inadequate. Economic concerns, as well as wider societal well-being, are anchored together and put into a right reciprocal relationship with this vision. Yet the eschatological point of orientation transcends these dimensions as well by placing work within a wider eschatological trajectory. Ontologically our work is one way of being human. It thus becomes an end in itself. It is a means to many ends, but it is not only utilitarian in nature. Since the goal of creation is God's eternal Sabbath, our work too finds its place within this playful and celebratory vision. Eschatologically we are shown through our work to have become like God as we were always intended to be. Working and work are thus a part of our nature and creation's nature.

Of course, this vision only attains if we understand that creation's destiny is transformation rather than annihilation and replacement. This important point is highlighted by Volf:

> If the world will be annihilated and a new one created *ex nihilo*, then mundane work has only earthly significance for the well-being of the worker, the worker's community, and posterity – until the day when 'the heavens will pass away with a loud noise, and the elements, will be dissolved with fire' (2 Pet. 3.10). Since the results of the cumulative work of humankind throughout history will become naught in the final apocalyptic catastrophe, human work is devoid of direct ultimate significance.[15]

Volf concedes that an annihilationist eschatology and a commitment to current social engagement and transformation can be logically compatible. One can still work now for the good and flourishing of creation while believing that one day God will discard and replace everything. His point, however, is that while logically compatible such a view is 'theologically inconsistent'.[16] To expect creation to be annihilated and replaced by God is hardly goodness that moves beyond a very restrictive utilitarian sense. Were God not to redeem creation, its declaration as good would lose any transcendent meaning. As Volf says, 'it is hard to believe in the intrinsic value and goodness of something that God will completely annihilate'.[17] Thus, 'without a theologically grounded belief in the intrinsic value and goodness of creation, positive cultural involvement hangs theologically in the air'.[18]

As we have seen, alternatively a transformational eschatological vision imbues creation and our work within it with intrinsic value and thus ultimate meaning. A transformative eschatology suggests that our work itself, when perfected and transformed within the renovation of creation, becomes the 'building materials' from which the glorified world will be established.[19]

Work as Agent of Transformation

But what is the theological justification for understanding God's work eschatologically to be transformative rather than annihilationist? Here eschatology is both Christological and Trinitarian.

Beginning with the Christological vision, consider Easter and Christ's resurrection. John 11.25 states that Jesus is the resurrection and the life, and John 14.6 says he is the way, the truth, and the life. Jesus is thus more than the means of salvation. He is salvation, its embodiment and actualization. Thus Jesus in his bodily resurrection is the paradigm for salvation. Romans 8 suggests that this prototypical role is not just for himself, but for those in Christ and indeed for the whole of creation, in that order. What this means is that Christ's salvation is our salvation. What we see of Christ's materiality, of his body in his resurrection, becomes true of us in our resurrection. First Corinthians 15 explicitly makes this argument. In Christ's resurrection we see his materiality, the material creation, taken up and transformed 'in him'. He embodies God but simultaneously, according to Romans 8, embodies nature. Christ is a microcosm, as Maximus the Confessor argued. Thus, his future is our future. His future is creation's future. Rather than an annihilated and replaced body, in Christ we see healed, transformed, and perfected bodily existence. Thomas is invited to see and touch his very scars. The meaning could not be clearer: Christ is risen and transformed, we will be raised and transformed, and creation will participate in the resurrection by becoming itself transformed.

The reading of 2 Peter 3 that suggests to readers an annihilation of creation rather than its redemption is misguided. It is based upon both questionable translation and an odd textual variant that is inconsistent with the point and flow of its own argument. Contrary to teaching of creation's destruction, even 2 Peter teaches the deeply penetrating nature of God's healing and transforming love.

The future of creation and all therein is subject to the transformative experience that Christ himself experienced. This includes our ordinary work as well, for it is as much creation as we are ourselves. At this point Christology and eschatology are indistinguishable. Christ's materiality, his bodily existence as the second Adam, gathers up the protological account of creation in Genesis but also expands its horizon. Christ is God's 'yes' to creation. Creation is good and worth preserving and transforming. Creation's goodness is thus shown to be intrinsic and ultimate, inasmuch as Christ's embodiment is eternal rather than temporary. Christ's body was not just of instrumental value, to be cast off once his important 'spiritual' work was done. Rather, Christ's bodily resurrection and ascension is the guarantor of creation's ultimate worth and value to God. That Christ thus lives literally in creation and that the fullness of the triune God in Revelation 21—22 resides in his eternal home which is the new creation are of one piece. They both declare the same thing: God has pronounced his eternal 'yes' to creation's intrinsic value in incarnation and glorification.

The Value of Work and Our Final Destiny

The significance of work does depend upon the value of creation, and the value of creation does depend on its final destiny. Its final destiny is secured Christologically, being proclaimed and demonstrated in Christ's incarnation, resurrection, and ascension. The Spirit consummates creation with the coming to creation of the fullness of the triune God who will be all in all. God will dwell eternally in the creation he initially made, continually makes, and will finally make. This consummation is God's final work, before his Sabbath rest, of bringing order out of chaos for creation's eternal flourishing. The Spirit accomplishes this throughout the entirety of the creation project, from initial establishment through to completed fulfilment. The final judgement purifies, transforms and perfects the creation that has come to be. God does this together with us and through us using resources supplied by our ordinary work that builds, shapes, preserves and thereby brings into being that which is. It is this entrepreneurial and eschatological orientation that makes our being co-workers with God a form of freedom rather than a sentence to futility, frustration, and slavery as Israel's neighbours had imagined. Herein our being co-workers with God finds its deeper meaning. The best that protology alone can offer is a glimpse of this through our appointment to work. It hints to our being co-workers with God but does not reveal the depth, the goal, or end to which that concept is directed. The eschatological orientation confirms that our intuition was right from Genesis that we are in fact what the New

Testament calls co-heirs and joint heirs with Christ and thus co-workers in Christ with God empowered by the Spirit. We are not obedient slaves.

Conclusion

Importantly, this theology of work is neither a spin-off or marginal doctrine within theology. Nor is it relegated simply to an application of 'real' doctrine. Rather, it takes us to the heart of what Christians have always and everywhere believed and proclaimed about who God is and what God is doing. It takes us to the heart of the doctrine of the Trinity as expressed in the creeds. It takes us into the centre of what some have called the beatific vision.

By way of drawing together the various strands of argument made in this chapter, in what remains I will recount this eschatological orientation as more traditionally presented and highlight within some ways that creation and our ordinary work lie at the heart of and participate in God's eternal purposes. This should be read as an abstract or manifesto for an eschatological grounding for a theology of work.

The Christian hope is for the resurrection of the dead to the 'new creation' where all creation experiences God's full and unending presence such that creation itself is included within the relationship of love between the Father, Son and Spirit. This historic hope is the promise that in Christ the creation itself, including what God and humanity have made, will be transformed and set free to be what God intended. To realize this promise of renewal to a 'new heavens and new earth' is creation's *telos*. As such, its goal and purpose is fully to become itself in fellowship with God, thereby bringing it into harmonious relationship within itself, as well. This can be described as creation flourishing as itself in Christ. This *telos* of flourishing was always creation's calling (vocation) but as a result of sin, creation came to require deliverance, salvation from death and destruction. This need includes all human life and action, including our life projects that we call work.

For creation to be 'saved' and so to flourish requires the inclusion of both human and non-human created reality. A salvation including people but excluding non-human and material creation would not be full salvation to the new creation (even for people) as Scripture promises.

The new creation, as shorthand for this comprehensive salvific vision, is the content and orientation of Christian eschatology since it is the goal of all God's works and purposes and ultimately through God's sovereignty, of all human work and purposes. Therefore, the direction and an orienting principle of theology becomes the new creation, wherein creation's *telos*, material content, and means of being renewed all mirror and flow from the loving nature of the triune God: decreed from the Father, made present in Christ Jesus, and brought about by the Holy Spirit.

It follows that 'the good life' is indeed only truly good when finding its purpose, meaning, and activities oriented towards this new creation where God dwells forever with us and the whole of creation in our fully renewed materiality (referred to in Scripture as the new heavens and new earth). It also follows that as a perennial human activity, if human work is to be part of a good life and find meaning for ourselves and others, if it is to find its place within God's creation, it too must find its goals and methods, as well as its very products, oriented towards and actually participating in some way in God's salvific purposes to the new creation.[20]

For working men and women to experience the fullness of the human vocation, as beloved of God, we need to grasp how our ordinary lives, including our life projects (work), participate with God within God's eschatological goals. Our work is a product of, and in significant ways is bound up with, who we are and are becoming as persons. Our working reflects but also shapes our very identities. Beyond ourselves, its 'products' become part of the reality (identity) of the actual world. As such, work both is integral to who we are and part of 'the fabric of this world'.[21] Since work is neither a result of sin, nor simply incidental to our identity, if we are to be saved, our work and working selves must be saved too. If creation is to be saved, our work and working must be saved too since they have now become part of the world's particularity.

These bold claims about work's inclusion in human and creation's salvation could seem on the surface to run counter to Christian belief about salvation where faith and human work(s) are often depicted antagonistically and as antithetical. Yet these claims are consistent with, and necessarily implied by, our fundamental Christian beliefs about salvation derived from Scripture and as historically expressed, for example, in the Apostles' and Nicene creeds. To this end we have developed the claim that at the heart of Christian eschatology, Christology, Trinitarian theology, soteriology, and pneumatology, lies ordinary human work and working, including their material as well as immaterial products and processes. The argument does not remotely suggest that our work and working in any way save us. Rather it is that we are saved not by, but with our work. Our work is saved by God along with us, as a part of us and as a part of creation itself.

Notes

1 Emil Brunner, *The Divine Imperative: A Study in Christian Ethics,* trans. Olive Wyon (London: Lutterworth Press, 1937), book III, section 3; Dietrich Bonhoeffer, *Ethics,* trans. Neville Horton Smith (London: SCM Press, 1955), pp. 73–8, 254–8.

2 Pope John Paul II, *Laborem Exercens: Encyclical Letter* (1981), section 26. Also, Gustaf Wingren, *The Christian's Calling: Luther on Vocation,* trans. Carl Rasmussen (London: Oliver & Boyd, 1957).

3 Ian Hart, 'The Teaching of the Puritans about Ordinary Work', *Evangelical Quarterly* 67, no. 3 (1995), pp. 195–209.

4 *Laborem Exercens,* section 27.

5 Marie-Dominique Chenu, *The Theology of Work: An Exploration,* trans. Lilian Soiron (Dublin: Gill & Son, 1963).

6 Miroslav Volf, *Work in the Spirit: Toward a Theology of Work* (Oxford: Oxford University Press, 1991).

7 A project more fully carried out in Darrell Cosden, *A Theology of Work: Work and the New Creation* (Carlisle: Paternoster Press, 2004).

8 Volf, *Work in the Spirit,* p. 93.

9 Cosden, *A Theology of Work,* pp. 10–13, 181–2.

10 Volf, *Work in the Spirit,* pp. 10–14; Cosden, *A Theology of Work,* p. 10.

11 Max Weber, *The Protestant Ethic and the Spirit of Capitalism,* trans. Talcott Parsons (London: Unwin University Press, 1930).

12 James Davison Hunter, *To Change the World: The Irony, Tragedy, and Possibility of Christianity in the Late Modern World* (New York: Oxford University Press, 2010).

13 Volf, *Work in the Spirit,* p. 91.

14 Cosden, *A Theology of Work,* pp. 13–18, 184–7.

15 Volf, *Work in the Spirit,* p. 89.

16 Volf, *Work in the Spirit,* p. 90.

17 Volf, *Work in the Spirit,* p. 91.

18 Volf, *Work in the Spirit,* p. 91.

19 Volf, *Work in the Spirit,* p. 91.

20 For a fuller development, see Cosden, *A Theology of Work.* See also Darrell Cosden, *The Heavenly Good of Earthly Work* (Peabody, MA: Hendrickson Publishers, 2006).

21 Lee Hardy, *The Fabric of This World: Inquiries into Calling, Career Choice, and the Design of Human Work* (Grand Rapids, MI: Eerdmans, 1990).

PART 3

Practical Theology

Economics and the Theology of Work

JÜRGEN VON HAGEN

The God of the Bible is God at work. God might have chosen to sit on a throne and simply will things into being. Instead, he chooses to be active and at work.[1] The gods of the ancient Greeks were believed continually to rest in contemplation.[2] The Greek philosophers, therefore, had a very low view of work. For them, work stood in the way of one's freedom to live a happy life and should be left to slaves who, by definition, had no freedom and were unable to live such a life.[3] In contrast, the God of the Bible is constantly working at creation and its maintenance, upholding his covenants, and redeeming his people. The Bible depicts his activities in terms of human work in agriculture and all ancient crafts, and frequently calls creation, humankind, and the people of Israel the 'work' of God's 'hands' (e.g. Job 3.19; Ps. 8.7; 19.2; 102.26; Isa. 60.21). If humankind is created in the image of God, work is part of our nature. Indeed, work is part of the economic order of creation (Gen. 2.5), and it will be part of the order of the new creation after the end of history (Isa. 65.17, 21–22).

The Vulgate translates Job 5.7 as 'Man was made to work as the bird to fly', a dictum which is also attributed to Martin Luther.[4] It implies that human beings find fulfilment in and glorify God by their work.[5] The Bible affirms that our work is successful only if it is blessed by God: 'Unless the Lord builds the house, they labour in vain who build it' (Ps. 127.1). Psalm 90 asks God to 'confirm the work of our hands' for otherwise it does not stand. In the same vein, Martin Luther wrote: 'It is our role to do hard work, but we must know that our labour does not suffice. We are to till the ground, to sow, and if it ripens, to harvest; nevertheless, we are to confess and say: "Unless the Lord had given it, all our work would have been in vain, dear Lord, it is your gift."'[6] Ecclesiastes 5.5 warns us that God may destroy the work of our hands if we anger him by foolish speech and oaths not taken seriously.

In our work, therefore, we experience our complete dependence on God. This includes both the experience of our inability to accomplish anything without God's help, which proves our lowliness compared to God, and the experience that God blesses us by blessing our work. It is particularly interesting that, in the social laws of Deuteronomy, God combines the command to treat the poor and underprivileged well and to provide for them with the promise of blessing human work.[7] God also uses our work as an instrument to build, shape, and maintain his creation and to accomplish his will in this world.[8] As Martin Luther put it, our work is 'God's mask behind which he hides himself and rules everything magnificently in the world.'[9]

Christian faith and theology thus have a deeply positive view of work. This is demonstrated and discussed at length in the other chapters of this book, and it is not the task of this chapter to repeat it. Instead, the purpose of this chapter is to draw out some implications of the theology of work for economics. Work, of course, is a key concept in economics too – so much so that the classical economists of the late eighteenth and early nineteenth centuries and Marxian economists regarded work as the sole source of economic value. Even if this is no longer the case in modern economics, work is still regarded as an indispensable input to all production. Furthermore, in all modern economies, incomes derived from work are the largest part of the income of society as a whole and the main determinant of social inequality in modern societies. Work is, therefore, a topic where theologians and economists naturally meet and find common interests.

The textbook approach of economics to human work, however, stands in stark contrast to the positive view theology of work has of it. It regards work as painful and something we would rather avoid; we only work because we are forced to do so in order to acquire the things necessary for living. Economists speak of the 'disutility of labour' or work, meaning that working reduces our happiness. The founder of classical economics, Adam Smith, equated work with 'toil and trouble'.[10] John Stuart Mill, who like all classical economists used the term 'political economy' for what we now call economics, wrote: 'Political Economy ... makes entire abstraction of every other human passion or motive; except those which may be regarded as perpetually antagonizing principles to the desire of wealth, namely, aversion to labour, and desire of the present enjoyment of costly indulgences.'[11] Mill continued: 'Political Economy presuppose(s) an arbitrary definition of man, as a being who invariably does that by which he may obtain the greatest amount of necessaries, conveniences, and luxuries, with the smallest quantity of labour and physical self-denial with which they can be obtained in the existing state of knowledge.'[12] Similarly, according to William S. Jevons, one of the founders of neoclassical economics:

labour is the beginning of the processes treated by economists, and consumption is the end and purpose. Labour is the painful exertion which we undergo to ward off pains of greater amount, or to procure pleasures which leave a balance in our favour… . The problem of Economics … is *to satisfy our wants with the least possible sum of labour.*[13]

While this resembles very much the Aristotelian view of work, Jevons did recognize that work may itself be a source of pleasure and satisfaction. However, he argued that this could only be so 'in a limited amount and most men are compelled by their wants to exert themselves longer and more severely than they would otherwise do'.[14] Marshall, another founder of neoclassical economics, followed Jevons and defined 'labour as any exertion of mind or body undergone partly or wholly with a view to some good other than the pleasure derived directly from work'.[15] He added: 'Most people work more than they would if they considered only the direct pleasure from work; but, in a healthy state, pleasure predominates over pain in a great part even of the work that is done for hire.'[16] Modern economics textbooks simply disregard the possibility that work might give pleasure at all and treat it as something people would avoid if they could.

Whence this difference between the theological and the economic approaches? This is the question I discuss in the first section of this chapter. At the heart of this discussion is the distinction between work and labour, which, though introduced already by John Locke, is generally overlooked. Based on that, I discuss the notion of labour markets in the second section. Finally, I discuss some implications of the theology of work for labour market policies, with conclusions to follow.

The Labour of our Bodies and the Work of our Hands[17]

Speaking of the work of our hands links the concept of work to the creative process of making something. This is illustrated in the substantive use of the word: we speak of a 'work of art', a 'day's work', or a book as a 'writer's work'. In this sense, artists, artisans, and craftsmen are the epitome of people engaged in work. This is the creative aspect of work, and it is this that is the focus of the theology of work. In its original meaning, work is a process involving deliberate human effort that results in the making of an object that can be used to achieve some purpose, or that can be enjoyed for its own sake. Work engages the whole person: body, mind, imagination. Work requires planning and the careful execution of plans until the desired object is finished, and, when it is, we can be pleased with the work of our hands. For this reason, work can be regarded as one of the key elements of a happy life and is not limited to paid employment.[18] That the early economists thought of this object as a durable one is clear from the fact that Locke argued that work is the origin of and the ultimate reason for private property. Both the classical and Marxist economists regarded services as unproductive, since, being consumed in the process of production, services yield no tangible, durable objects. Therefore, they did not regard the production of services as proper work.

Labour, in contrast, is the simple exercise of the brute physical strength of the human body.[19] In Aristotle's terms, labour is what slaves and tame animals do as they 'with their bodies minister to the needs of life'.[20] Marx coined the term *Arbeitskraft* for it, which in this context is perhaps best translated as *manpower*, for it served Marx to separate the pure physical effort of the human body delivered by the individual worker to the factory from the value-generating process of work which all workers of the factory together are engaged in under the command and control of the capitalist owner.[21] In this sense, manpower is a substitute for electrical or other power.

Clearly, all human work requires some amount of labour as an input. However, not all instances in which labour is exerted qualify as work. In ancient times, slave labour did not. Nor does labour in the context of modern industrial production. As Marx rightly pointed out, industrial workers (or, rather, labourers) sell their *labour*, not their *work* to the entrepreneur who employs them. The workers are remunerated for a certain amount of time spent in the process of industrial production and for the effort they exert, but they never own the work of their hands, the object to the making of which they contribute. In fact, being confined to a single and more or less narrow stage of the production process, they may never even see that object. As a result, they derive neither joy nor satisfaction from it; they are, as Marx put it, 'alienated' from it.[22] A hundred and fifty years after Marx, we know that this was equally true for industrial production in socialist systems.

Work emerges as a result of the specialization of individuals on certain crafts. By specializing in the making of a certain type of object, say shoes or tables, craftspeople develop their skills and become experts at it, making more and better objects than a single person trying to make all things.[23] But in modern, industrialized economies, labour emerges as a result of an ever finer division of labour, in which the contribution of each individual worker to the production process becomes limited to minor tasks and any particular skills they might have lose their value.[24] Adam Smith argued that decomposing the work process into a multitude of menial tasks each assigned to different individual workers facilitated mass production and greatly increased productivity. In the early twentieth century, the introduction of the assembly line by Henry Ford and of Frederick W. Taylor's 'Scientific Management', which consisted of breaking up production processes into many tiny and precisely measurable segments, brought this development to perfection. Increased productivity and efficiency came at the cost of transforming work into labour.

Adam Smith, who praised the benefits of the division of labour as the source of the *wealth of nations*, also clearly saw the negative consequences it had for those engaged in labour:

> In the progress of the division of labour, the employment of the far greater part of those who live by labour, that is, of the great body of the people, comes to be confined to a few very simple operations, frequently to one or two. But the understandings of the greater part of men are necessarily formed by their ordinary employments. The man whose whole life is spent in performing a few simple operations, of which the effects are perhaps always the same, or very nearly the same, has no occasion to exert his understanding or to exercise his invention in finding out expedients for removing difficulties which never occur. He naturally loses, therefore, the habit of such exertion, and generally becomes as stupid and ignorant as it is possible for a human creature to become.[25]

Furthermore,

> [The common people] have little time to spare for education. Their parents can scarce afford to maintain them even in infancy. As soon as they are able to work they must apply to some trade by which they can earn their subsistence. That trade, too, is generally so simple and uniform as to give little exercise to the understanding, while, at the same time, their labour is both so constant and so severe, that it leaves them little leisure and less inclination to apply to, or even to think of, anything else.[26]

In the same vein but even more starkly, Whately wrote:

> [O]ne result of the division of labour when carried to a great extent [is] the evil of reducing each man too much to the condition of a mere machine, or rather of one part of a machine; the result of which is, that the mind is apt to be narrowed – the intellectual faculties undeveloped, or imperfectly and partially developed, through the too great concentration of the attention on the performance of a single, and sometimes very simple, operation.[27]

While work contributes to the development of our intellectual capacities, industrial labour destroys them. While we find our dignity in our work, industrial labour turns us into small machines subject to the speed and timing of a much larger one, as Charlie Chaplin perfectly illustrated in *Modern Times* (1936). Labour robs us of our human dignity. Marx expressed this insight saying that the capitalist mode of production forces workers to sell their labour as a commodity, implying that one worker's manpower is equal to any other worker's manpower and therefore has the same price.[28] Capitalists buy manpower, like any other commodity used as a production input, at the lowest price possible. But since the worker's manpower is inseparably connected to their body, the worker's body effectively becomes a commodity.

The first sentence in Studs Terkel's 1970 study of 'what people do all day and how they feel about what they do' runs like this: 'This book, being about work, is, by its very nature, about violence – to the spirit as well as to the body.'[29] It goes on: 'it is about daily humiliations'.[30] Terkel reported interviews with all kinds of workers in the United States. The interviews document work environments that are physically exhausting and painful in which workers are treated in ways that are degrading and humiliating. A study of working conditions in the United States conducted by the US Department of Health in 1973 concluded: 'And significant numbers of American workers are dissatisfied with the quality of their work lives. Dull, repetitive, seemingly meaningless tasks, offering little challenge or autonomy are causing discontent among workers at all occupational levels.'[31]

In addition, the (almost) perfect substitutability of one person's labour for another's also implies a high degree of economic uncertainty for the worker, who is easily replaced by another. Whately recognized this: 'I wish first to call your attention to another inconvenience which may result from a high degree of division of labour: I mean, the additional liability to the evil of being thrown out of employment.'[32] Clearly, labour is not compatible with a Christian view of human beings and their work.

Standard economic analysis deals with labour, not work. It considers labour as an input into production, which, in modern societies, the majority of people sell in order to obtain the monetary income they need to purchase consumption goods and services in their markets. The consumption of such goods and services and the time spent in leisure are the sole sources of 'utility' or 'happiness' for which people strive. In this view, time spent working is time not spent in leisure. Since labour is painful, people will work only if they get paid for it and they will work more and harder if the price of labour – that is, the wage rate – increases.[33] Individual 'labour supply' – that is, the decision how much time to spend on labour – is ultimately conceived as a trade-off between leisure and consumption goods and services bought for money. In this trade-off, the wage rate determines the quantity of consumption goods and services an hour of labour can buy, and it is the only determinant of labour supply both at the level of the individual and of society.

Marx and Engels expected that, due to its dynamic laws and logic, the capitalist mode of production would eventually encompass the entire economy and suck in the entire population except for a small group of capitalists. As capitalist firms grew larger and larger, small producers and craftsmen would lose their competitiveness and become labourers themselves.[34] 'Work' in its proper sense would disappear completely to be replaced by labour, and wages would be the only motivation to supply labour.

Evidently, however, Marx's and Engels's prediction has turned out to be false. In a globalized world, manufacturing production based on mere labour has moved from the developed to the developing world, where labour is cheaper. Labour-protection legislation, the result of union activities in all developed countries, has turned labour into a 'quasi-fixed factor' protecting workers (to various degrees, depending on the country) against lay-offs and the economic uncertainty related to them.[35] Responding to consumers' taste for diversity, mass production of standardized, uniform consumer products like 'model-T' cars has increasingly been replaced by the production of differentiated and complex products. To facilitate flexible responses to changes in market conditions, such production is often organized in self-directed teams of workers with well-defined missions.[36] This allows each individual team member to appreciate better their contribution and to see the product of the joint work. With more complex products and production processes, individual skills become increasingly valuable and rewarded instead of losing value, and training plays an increasing role at work.[37] A large proportion of the workers in modern industries and services, which today make up between 80 and 90 per cent of economic activity in the developed countries, find their work intrinsically rewarding.[38]

All this suggests that labour is no longer the dominant paradigm of production, at least in the modern, developed world.[39] In the post-industrial economy, the theology of work can find its place and relevance again.

Extrinsic and Intrinsic Motivations to Work

Building on the labour paradigm and the leisure-consumption trade-off, economists have long argued that financial incentives can be used to improve work effort and performance. In the most extreme form of performance-related pay, piece-rate pay, a worker is paid per unit of output rather than by the hour or day. The more pieces he produces, the more money he gets. More moderate forms of performance-related pay include mixtures between a fixed compensation per hour or day and a variable compensation depending on individual output, premiums for overtime or for output quantity, quality exceeding some standard, prizes for high performance, or promotions. Operating on a leisure-consumption trade-off, workers increase their effort in response to monetary rewards. This implies that employers can control their performance and improve productivity through financial incentive systems.[40] Empirical evidence broadly confirms that performance-dependent pay increases worker productivity. However, the picture is more nuanced than the simple leisure-consumption trade-off would suggest. Empirically, it seems that the mere existence of any performance-related elements in individual compensation schemes increases productivity, but that this effect does not depend much on how strong the link between performance and pay actually is.[41] This is inconsistent with the leisure-consumption trade-off.

Furthermore, recent management and economics literature argues that financial incentives can be ineffective or even lead to inferior performance. There are numerous, interesting examples for this:

A former White House economist reported that he and others on his team used to voluntarily spend many Saturdays at work designing and improving the economic policies of the US President. When the President ordered them to be paid for their overtime, many of them quit showing up on Saturdays.[42]

The Boston fire department had a problem with firemen calling in sick on Fridays and Mondays. In order to make them show up more regularly, the department ended a policy of unlimited sick days, cutting firemen's pay if they had more than six sick days. Instead of reducing the number of sick days, the firemen responded by claiming more of them.[43]

Giving machine operators the opportunity to develop the skills it took to repair their machines rather than relying on repair staff to come in resulted in the operators developing strategies to reduce downtimes and prevent machine failures, thus increasing overall productivity and efficiency.[44]

Empirical evidence also suggests that financial incentives for managers do not necessarily result in better business performance. Kohn argues that financial incentives work when better performance means an increase in quantity rather than quality of output, suggesting that they work for simple but not for complex types of work.[45] Furthermore, financial incentives seem to stifle creativity and efforts to seek for innovations.[46]

These findings have led to the distinction between *extrinsic* and *intrinsic* motivations to work. Financial incentives are extrinsic. They rely on the leisure-consumption trade-off. Intrinsic motivations are based on the worker's own, non-monetary valuation of what he does. Survey-based research found that the principal motivation for good work performance is job enjoyment in the sense that employees have positive feelings about what they do and their role at the workplace. Base pay came in second, but financial incentives topping off base pay were found to play only a minor role in motivating employees.[47]

Intrinsic motivation to work relates to what Douglas McGregor, in his 1960 path-breaking book, called *The Human Side of Enterprise*. Realizing the limits of financial incentives and management by command and control for increasing productivity, McGregor argued that management should learn how to use the talents of the people working for them and create a work environment in which people flourish and their creative potential can be activated.[48] Contrary to the paradigm of a labour–leisure trade-off, McGregor's argument rests on the assumption that work is as natural to human beings as playing and resting.[49] Management can improve the productivity of its workforce by aligning their workers' individual goals with the goals of the company.

Daniel Pink points out three basic elements of intrinsic motivation: autonomy, mastery, and purpose.[50] Autonomy is the freedom to make choices about what to do at the workplace and when and how to do it. It gives workers a sense of responsibility for their own performance. Mastery refers to the opportunity to develop one's skills and expertise at the workplace, to become an expert and to develop improvements of the production process or the product itself. Purpose refers to the feeling or experience that one's work contributes to an important and good cause. It gives workers a sense of pride in what they do. Intrinsic motivation can also stem from the social aspect of work; that is, the feeling of being a valued member of a team working together for a common goal. For example, Ladley, Wilkinson, and Young report that compensation schemes rewarding teams of workers for good performance were more effective in raising productivity than schemes rewarding individuals.[51] Worker–employer relationships may also involve elements of reciprocal gift-giving: this happens when employers pay a group of workers collectively more than the market wage for a given type of job and the workers reciprocate by above-standard work performance.[52] Designing jobs and workplaces in ways that promote such intrinsic factors has been found to improve work performance and productivity.

Should economists pay attention to this? One might argue that economics should continue to focus on labour and extrinsic motivations alone, leaving intrinsic motivations to other social sciences and theology.[53] This would be justified if intrinsic and extrinsic motivations worked separately and independently; that is, if the effectiveness of the former did not depend on the latter and vice versa. Empirical research, however, has shown that this often is not true. Specifically, increasing extrinsic incentives may reduce the strength of intrinsic incentives. This is what the examples of the White House economists and the Boston firemen suggest. Both groups were likely driven by a strong sense of working for the public good. When the President started paying the economists for working on Saturdays, the financial reward put a price on their Saturday labour and implicitly down-graded their intrinsic motivation. The economists interpreted the extra pay as a signal showing that the President regarded their work as labour, and that reduced their willingness to show up on Saturdays. Similarly, by putting a price tag on sick days, the Boston fire department implicitly communicated to the firemen that it regarded their efforts for the public good as mere labour, a commodity. The firemen reacted by reducing their effort.

This possibility of extrinsic incentives crowding out intrinsic ones implies that economists must worry about both and their interaction. Economic advice on the design of jobs, workplaces and compensation schemes neglecting such interaction is bound to produce adverse results. To the extent that the Christian faith gives rise to intrinsic motivations for work, economic analysis should take the theology of work into account. A lot of interesting research remains to be done in this area.

Labour Market Analysis and Policies

The traditional economic analysis of labour markets is based on the labour paradigm. It regards labour as a homogeneous commodity, implying that all labour receives the same wage. The focus of the analysis is on the total amount of employment and the wage rate that emerge in a labour market equilibrium, defined as the wage rate for which the workers' total labour supply and the employers' total labour demand equalize. As explained above, labour supply is derived from a leisure-consumption trade-off and depends positively on the wage rate. Labour demand is a negative function of the wage rate.[54] This analysis can be cast into a simple diagram (Figure 11.1).

In Figure 11.1, the wage rate is plotted on the vertical axis, the amount of employment on the horizontal axis. The upward sloping curve illustrates the supply of labour: the larger the wage rate, the larger the number of people who wish to work and the larger the number of hours they wish to work. The downward sloping curve illustrates the demand for labour. The larger the wage rate, the lower the amount of labour employers wish to hire. The labour market equilibrium occurs at the intersection of the two curves. At this intersection, the equilibrium wage is w1 and equilibrium employment is e1.

We use this simple framework to explore the importance of intrinsic motivations for work such as the Christian faith. Suppose that the work-

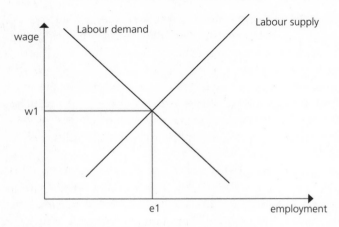

Figure 11.1 Traditional labour market analysis

ing population consists of two groups: Christians, who value their work over and above the fact that they get paid for it, and non-Christians who, for simplicity, have no intrinsic motivation for work.[55] Let this be the only difference between the two groups. An intrinsic faith motivation for work implies that Christians are willing to work more than non-Christians at the same wage rate; that is, faith motivation makes the labour supply curve of Christians lie to the right of the labour supply curve of non-Christians. If the labour supply curve above belongs to the sum of both groups, the labour supply curves of the two groups are to the left of the combined curve and they are steeper than the combined one. This is shown in Figure 11.2.

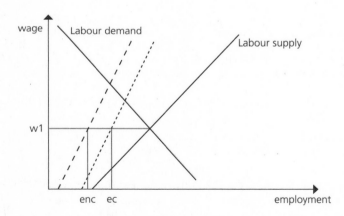

Figure 11.2 Plotting intrinsic motivation

Here, the broken labour supply curve belongs to the non-Christians, while the dotted curve belongs to the Christians. Note that the exact position and distance between the two depends on the shares of the two groups in the total workforce. Assuming that employers cannot distinguish between the two types of workers, the equilibrium wage must be the same, w1, for both. Combined employment remains the same, but we can see how it is split up between Christians and non-Christians. Not surprisingly, at the wage w1, there are more Christians employed than non-Christians.

Suppose now that for some reason the Christian motivation to work becomes weaker and eventually disappears. This means that the labour supply curve of Christian workers shifts to the left until it becomes the same as the labour supply curve of non-Christians. Figure 11.3 shows the effects. The combined labour supply curve shifts to the left. This means that, due to the vanishing faith motivation to work, total labour supply is now less than it was before at each wage rate. A new labour market equilibrium emerges at which the wage rate, w2, is higher than before and employment, e2, is less than before. Due to the higher wage, more of those who were previously non-Christians are willing to work and are employed. Thus, non-Christians benefit from the disappearance of Christian faith-motivated workers in the labour market.

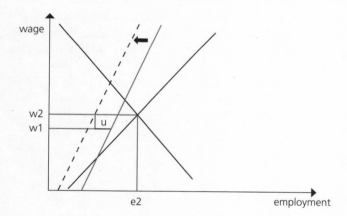

Figure 11.3 Labour supply curve absent Christian workers

Things are more complicated for Christian workers who lost their faith motivation to work. Recall that their new labour supply curve now falls exactly on that of the non-Christians, the broken line in Figure 11.3. To see what happens, I have plotted their old labour supply curve as a thin solid line in that figure. The figure shows that some Christian workers remain employed and benefit from the higher wage. Others, however, lose their jobs, because the higher wage demands a higher level of productivity which they do not deliver. As a result, employment of Christian workers falls by the amount corresponding to the line segment 'u' in the figure. For Christian workers, the vanishing of faith motivation results in an insider–outsider division. Those who remain in employment benefit, while those who lose their jobs remain unemployed.

Recent research on the fate of the American working class suggests that this analysis has some relevance for the American society.[56] This research documents meticulously the social decline particularly of the poorly educated working class in America; that is, people with at most a high school diploma. This decline is marked by masses of people out of employment and who have left the labour market for lack of prospects to get jobs, high rates of alcohol and drug abuse, instability of families, high rates of birth out of wedlock, and dwindling church attendance and membership. Case and Deaton show that life expectancy of middle aged people has fallen significantly since the turn of the century in this part of society, whereas life expectancy has increased for all others. They attribute this to the increasing number of what they call 'deaths of despair', deaths of middle aged people related to alcohol and drug abuse, drug overdoses, and suicides. Murray considers a longer time span and documents the economic and social decline of the same segment of American society, a segment which until the 1980s enjoyed jobs, home ownership, and stable families.

It is difficult to identify the causes of this social and economic decline. However, both Case and Deaton and Murray point to the fact that the poorly educated part of the American working class lost its religious commitments and values from the 1970s onwards. Vance presents plenty of anecdotal evidence supporting the point that poorly educated workers who stayed involved with their Christian religion fared much better than those who did not. If the loss of religious commitments implied a loss of faith-related intrinsic motivation for work, the above analysis gives an interpretation for what the research documents, and the latter shows that the consequences of vanishing intrinsic work motivations can be devastating.[57] Traditional economic analysis would miss that point, observing only that wages have increased for those who stayed in the labour market.

Furthermore, this interpretation indicates that more generous welfare policies would not help. Giving the people affected by these developments more money might just increase their spending on alcohol and drugs and accelerate further decline. Instead, it would seem necessary to rebuild their value systems and to help them improve their skills to enable them to re-enter the labour market. Clearly, Christian churches ministering to them have an important task here.

Going back to our previous labour market analysis, assume now that employers can distinguish between Christian and non-Christian workers so that there are two separate labour markets. For simplicity, let the labour demand curves be the same in both markets. Figure 11.4 illustrates that scenario. The broken line is the labour supply curve of non-Christians, the dotted line the labour supply curve of Christians. There are now two equilibrium wages, one for non-Christians, wnc, and one for Christians, wc. Due to the Christians' intrinsic motivation for work, wc is lower than wnc. At the same time, employment for non-Christians, enc, is lower than employment for Christians, ec. The figure is consistent with the observation that employers attracting Christian workers such as charities or religious organizations often pay lower wages than others.

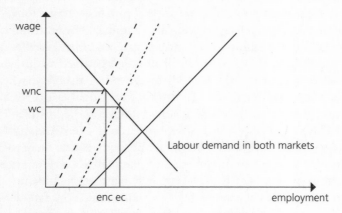

Figure 11.4 Christian and non-Christian equilibrium wages

Assume now that the government imposes a minimum wage policy requiring that wages cannot be lower than wc. Traditional economic analysis would predict that such a policy has no effect on equilibrium employment and wages. The discussion in the previous section, however, points to the possibility that this could be wrong. Specifically, assume that by imposing a minimum wage, the government causes Christian workers to pay more attention to their extrinsic motivation and less to their faith-related, intrinsic motivation. This implies that the labour supply curve of Christians shifts to the left. The wage rises in their labour market and employment falls. In the end, those Christian workers who remain employed benefit from the policy, but others lose their incomes permanently. The example shows that the design of labour market policies requires knowledge about the interaction between intrinsic and extrinsic work motivations.

Matching Individual Workers and Employers

This analysis still rests on the assumption that labour is a homogeneous commodity traded in a competitive market. More recent approaches to labour market analysis emphasize heterogeneity; that is, the fact that workers are individuals with individual skills, attitudes, and personal histories, and employers offer jobs requiring specific skills and experiences. These approaches are based on models of search and matching.[58] Workers who are not employed search for jobs. Employers who need additional workers search for employees. Different workers have different skills and other characteristics influencing their productivity such as intrinsic motivations for work, implying that their attractiveness as employees differs. Different employers offer different wages and work environments, implying that the attractiveness of working for them differs from the point of view of potential employees. Employers have imperfect information about the characteristics of the workers and workers have imperfect information about the employers. Therefore, both sides search for their best opportunities in the market. Each period, pairs of potential employers and potential employees meet, negotiate bilaterally and decide to enter or not to enter into an employment contract. If they agree, the worker stays with that employer. If they do not agree, both continue to search in the next period. Finally, every period some existing employment contracts are ended so that some workers switch from employment to unemployment and begin to search for new jobs.

The role of the labour market is to produce good matches of workers and employees; that is, situations in which an employer and a worker agree on a contract. Search is costly for both. It is costly for an employer because, if he does not employ a worker this period, he cannot produce as much as he would like to and thus forgoes profit opportunities. Furthermore, there are costs of posting vacancies. Search is costly for a worker because, if he does not accept a job offer this period, he is left without an income from work and forced to rely on alternatives such as welfare payments or simply to enjoy leisure. The combination of heterogeneity and imperfect information implies that the labour market is imperfectly competitive. Workers and employers in different matches can agree on different wages; therefore there is, in every period, a distribution of wages rather than a uniform equilibrium wage. A labour market equilibrium is characterized by the condition that the number of successful matches each period equals the number of jobs terminated, so that, all other things equal, the number of workers in unemployment and the number of vacancies remain the same.

Recognizing that workers are individuals with specific characteristics and in individual economic circumstances, this approach can explain why there are different labour market outcomes for different types of employees. It is also more consistent with the Christian view of the individual underlying the theology of work than treating labour and, hence, employees, as a commodity.

One of the characteristics of this approach is that the labour market is characterized by important externalities, such as the fact that the behaviour of one side has effects on the other side that are neither taken into account by either one nor reflected in the wages. This is where intrinsic work motivation comes in. Suppose that there is a significant group of workers in the market with an initially strong Christian work motivation. When unemployed, such workers will search more intensively than others and accept wage offers that would be rejected by others. Given the number of vacancies and employers searching for employees, their behaviour would make it harder for those without such intrinsic motivation to find jobs, implying that they stay in unemployment for longer. If the Christian work motivation vanishes over time, unemployment in this group would increase and unemployment in the other group would fall. To what extent such effects play a role empirically would be an interesting research topic.

Welfare Policies

As explained above, traditional economics assumes that human beings derive utility or happiness from leisure and the consumption of goods and services purchased in the market. They work only to gain an income and afford consumption. This implies that individuals would be happier if they could afford the same bundle of consumption goods and services without working than if they have to work for it. This assumption is the foundation of welfare policies in modern societies. Welfare policies aim at a more equitable distribution of happiness or 'welfare' in society than the distribution resulting from market processes without government intervention. Since happiness is derived from consumption and leisure, unacceptably low happiness is equated with unacceptably low income, which may be due to an individual's inability to work (because of handicaps, chronic illnesses, old age, or other circumstances) or lack of sufficient earning capability (because of low education or other circumstances). To achieve a more equitable distribution of happiness, therefore, governments tax those with high incomes and happiness and pay transfers to those with low incomes and happiness. In this logic, such transfers must not become too generous if the recipients enjoy more leisure than those who work and pay taxes, since too many people would choose to be without work and rely on transfers otherwise. Transfers are also often combined with financial or other penalties for staying out of work for too long in order to prevent people from having a free ride on society.

Christian theology of work, in contrast, teaches that work is an essential condition for human beings to live a happy life. This implies that individuals would be less happy consuming the same bundle of goods and services without working than with working, and that they would rather work and receive a lower income than not work and receive a given transfer from the government. If this is true, equating low levels of income with low levels of happiness is no longer justified. Welfare policy must take into account the loss of happiness resulting from being without work and take measures to keep people employed.

An extreme way to achieve that would be to legislate a 'right to work'; that is, a basic right to have employment, as it exists today in Article 23 of the United Nations Universal Declaration of Human Rights, though this is not a right that can be enforced in practice.[59] Such a right, however, would translate into a duty of employers to employ people who cannot find work otherwise and thus constitute a significant infringement of their private property. Short of that, it would force the government to make sufficient jobs available, which would be equally undesirable since it would lead to excessive growth of government and public employment.

A more practicable way to preserve employment would be to pay employers subsidies for hiring people who cannot find work otherwise. This would cause free-riding problems on the part of employers, but welfare policies face free-riding problems anyway and measures can be designed to reduce them. Furthermore, the government could provide opportunities for training to allow unemployed persons to improve their earnings capacities and find suitable jobs. Abolishing forced retirement ages and leaving the choice of when to retire to the individual equally falls under such policies.

Still, a realistic welfare policy must recognize that there are people who cannot find paid work in the market economy at all. This does not imply, however, that they cannot work at all, since the concept of work underlying the Christian theology of work is broader than paid employment. Even without pay, such people can be given work that they find fulfilling and gratifying. If Christians take seriously what their theology of work teaches, Christian churches and charities have a duty to care for such people. The rising number of 'deaths of despair' witnessed in the United States since the turn of the century indicates that they have not done a sufficiently good job in that regard.

Conclusion

Work is a natural place for theologians and economists to meet and discuss. In this chapter, I have argued that economics has traditionally focused on labour rather than work. This has hampered the dialogue between the two disciplines. However, changes in the productive structures of developed countries have brought work back to the forefront of business practices and economic research and policies. Given these developments, economists can no longer disregard the importance of intrinsic motivations for work such as the Christian faith. A large and interesting research agenda and fruitful dialogue lie ahead of us.

Notes

1 David J. Jensen, *Responsive Labour: A Theology of Work* (Louisville, KY: Westminster John Knox Press 2006); Friedrich Kiss, 'Die menschliche Arbeit als Thema der Theologie', in *Mitarbeiter der Schöpfung: Bibel und Arbeitswelt*, ed. Luise Schottroff and Willy Schottroff (München: Chr. Kaiser, 1983), p. 20.

2 Aristotle, *Politics*, trans. B. Jowett (Oxford: Clarendon Press, 1920).

3 Hannah Arendt, *Vita Activa oder Vom tätigen Leben* (München: Piper Taschenbuch, 2002), pp. 22ff.

4 Kuratorium Singer der Schweizerischen Akademie der Geistes- und Sozialwissenschaften (ed.), *Lexikon der Sprichwörter des romanisch-germanischen Mittelalters* (Berlin: De Gruyter, 1999), p. 200.

5 David S. Lim, 'The Doctrine of Creation and Some Implications for Modern Economics', *Transformation: An International Journal of Holistic Mission Studies* 7 (April–June 1990), p. 31.

6 Martin Luther, 'Sermon on Matthew 6:24–34', in *Die Werke Luthers in Auswahl*, ed. Kurt Aland, vol. 8 (Göttingen: UTB Vandenhoeck, 1991), p. 361.

7 Frank Crüsemann, '"... damit er dich segne in allem Tun deiner Hand ..." (Dtn 14,29). Die Produktionsverhältnisse der späten Königszeit, dargestellt am Ostrakon von Mesad Hashavjahu, und die Sozialgesetzgebung des Deuteronomiums', in *Mitarbeiter der Schöpfung: Bibel und Arbeitswelt*, ed. Luise Schottroff and Willy Schottroff (München: Chr. Kaiser, 1983), p. 88. See e.g. Deut. 12.7, 18; 14.29; 15.10, 18; 16.15; 23.21; 24.19.

8 Miroslav Volf, *Work in the Spirit: Toward a Theology of Work* (Oxford: Oxford University Press, 1991), p. 90.

9 Martin Luther, *Werke Kritische Gesamtausgabe*, vol. 15 (Weimar: Hermann Böhlau, 1883), p. 373.

10 Adam Smith, *An Inquiry into the Nature and Causes of the Wealth of Nations*, 5th edition (London: Methuen & Co., 1776), I.5.1.

11 John Stuart Mill, *Principles of Political Economy*, 7th edition (London: Longmans, Green & Co., 1909), V.38.

12 Mill, *Principles of Political Economy*, V.46.

13 William S. Jevons, *The Theory of Political Economy*, 3rd edition (London: MacMillan & Co., 1888), V.1.

14 Jevons, *Theory of Political Economy*, V.3.

15 Alfred Marshall, *Principles of Economics*, 8th edition (London: MacMillan & Co., 1920), II.III.5.

16 Marshall, *Principles of Economics*, II.III.5, note 33.

17 The title of this section is a quote from John Locke, *Two Treatises on Government*, in *The Works of John Locke, A New Edition*, vol. 5 (London: Thomas Davison, Whitefriars, 1823), p. 116, and from Hanna Arendt, *Vita Activa*, p. 99.

18 Martin Seel, *Versuch über die Form des Glücks* (Frankfurt: Suhrkamp, 1999), pp. 142–50.

19 I take this distinction between work and labour from Arendt, *Vita Activa*, ch. 3.

20 Aristotle, *Politics*, 1254b25.

21 Karl Marx, 'Lohnarbeit und Kapital', in *Karl Marx/Friedrich Engels Werke*, vol. 6 (Berlin: Dietz Verlag, 1961), p. 397. See also Friedrich Engels, 'Einleitung zu Karl Marx' Lohnarbeit und Kapital', in *Karl Marx/Friedrich Engels Werke*, vol. 22 (Berlin: Dietz Verlag, 1977). A more literal translation would be *labour-force*, but the term should not be confused with the modern concept of *labour force* which, in English as in German, denotes the group of people employed by an enterprise or a country's working-age population. As is clear from the quotations above, the classical and neoclassical economists did not distinguish between *work* and *labour* in the same way, a point for which they were chided by both Karl Marx and Friedrich Engels in his introduction to Marx's article. Nor did Marx make such a distinction; Marx equated work with labour, thus denying the creative aspect of work. See Karl Marx, *Das Kapital, Band 1*, in *Karl Marx/Friedrich Engels Werke*, vol. 23 (Berlin: Dietz Verlag, 1962), p. 192.

22 Marx, *Das Kapital, Band 1*, p. 596.

23 These basic insights about the division of labour are already found both in the Bible (e.g. Gen. 11.6) and in the writings of the Greek philosopher Xenophon, *Cyropedia*, trans. H. G. Dakyns, rev. by F. M. Stawell (London: MacMillan & Co., 1897), VIII.2.5–6.

24 *Karl Marx/Friedrich Engels Werke*, vol. 6, p. 421.

25 Smith, *Inquiry*, V.1.178.

26 Smith, *Inquiry*, V.1.181.

27 Richard Whately, *Introductory Lectures on Political Economy*, 2nd edition (London: B. Fellowes, 1832), VIII.1.

28 *Karl Marx/Friedrich Engels Werke*, vol. 6, pp. 399f.

29 Studs Terkel, *Working People Talk About What They Do All Day and How They Feel About What They Do* (New York: Pantheon Books, 1970).

30 Terkel, *Working People Talk*, p. xi.

31 Report of a Special Task Force to the US Secretary of Health, Education, and Welfare, *Work in America* (Boston: MIT Press, 1973), p. xv.

32 Whately, *Introductory Lectures*, VIII.24.

33 There is a possibility that the amount of labour an individual is willing to sell decreases if the wage rate increases beyond a certain threshold. This is called an *income effect* and happens if the increase in income resulting from the wage increase leads to an increase in the individual's desire for more leisure rather than more consumption goods.

34 *Karl Marx/Friedrich Engels Werke*, vol. 6, pp. 21ff. and Engels, 'Einleitung zu Karl Marx' Lohnarbeit und Kapital', pp. 208ff.

35 Walter Y. Oi, 'Labour as a Quasi-Fixed Factor', *Journal of Political Economy* 70 (1962), pp. 538–55.

36 See Tiffany McDowell, Dimple Agarwal, Don Miller, Tsutomu Okamoto, and Trevor Page, 'Organizational Design – The Rise of Teams', *Human Capital Trends* (2016), available at https://dupress.deloitte.com/dup-us-en/focus/human-capital-trends/2016/organizational-models-network-of-teams.html, and Lluís Cuatrecasas Arbós and Jordi Olivella Nadal, 'Shop-floor Work Organization in a Lean Factory: Some Indicators', Group Technology Cellular Manufacturing Conference, Groningen, 2006.

37 David Pardey and Tom May, *Motivation and Rewards*, Institute of Management and Leadership Research Paper (London: ILM, 2014), pp. 20ff.; James O'Toole and Edward E. Lawler III, *The New American Workplace* (New York: Palgrave Macmillan 2006), pp. 127ff.

38 See Pardey and May, *Motivation and Rewards*, p. 5, and O'Toole and Lawler, *The New American Workplace*, p. 55.

39 In their follow-up study to *Work in America*, James O'Toole and Edward E. Lawler III find that dull routine jobs are left mainly in what they call 'low cost operators', many of which are large-scale retail stores and in industries such as food processing. The authors compare these to 'global competitor corporations' and 'high involvement companies' which offer more challenging and interesting work conditions (*The New American Workplace*, pp. 10ff).

40 E.g. Jeffrey Pfeffer, *What were they Thinking?* (Boston: Harvard Business School Publishing, 2007).

41 For reviews of the empirical evidence, see G. Douglas Jenkins, Atul Mitra, Nina Gupta, and Jason D. Shaw, 'Are Financial Incentives Related to Performance? A Meta-Analytic Review of Empirical Research', *Journal of Applied Psychology* 83 (1998), pp. 777–87, and Barbara R. Bucklin and Alyce M. Dickinson, 'Individual Monetary Incentives: A Review of Different Types of Arrangement Between Performance and Pay', *Journal of Organizational Behavior Management* 21 (2001), pp. 45–137.

42 Samuel Bowles, *The Moral Economy: Why Good Incentives are no Substitute for Good Citizens* (New Haven, CT: Yale University Press, 2016), p. 39.

43 Bowles, *The Moral Economy*, p. 9.

44 Adam Grant and Jitendra Singh, 'The Problem with Financial Incentives and What to do about Them', *Knowledge@Wharton*, 30 March 2011, available at www.knowledge.wharton.upenn.edu.

45 Alfie Kohn, 'Why Incentive Plans Cannot Work', *Harvard Business Review* (October–September 1993), available at https://hbr.org/1993/09/why-incentive-plans-cannot-work.

46 For empirical results on this, see Sunkee Lee and Philipp Meyer-Doyle, 'How Performance Incentives Shape Individual Exploration and Exploitation: Evidence from Micro-data', *Working Paper Series* 2015/25/STR, Fontainebleau: INSEAD, and Gary Charness and Daniela Grieco, 'Creativity and Financial Incentives'. Mimeo, 1 April 2016, available at http://econ.qmul.ac.uk/Documents/176140.pdf. See also Daniel Pink, *Drive: The Surprising Truth About What Motivates Us* (New York: Riverhead Books, 2009), ch. 2.

47 Institute of Leadership and Management (ILM), *Beyond the Bonus: Driving Employee Performance* (London, undated), and Pardey and May, *Motivation and Rewards*.

48 Douglas McGregor, *The Human Side of Enterprise* (New York: McGraw Hill, 1960), pp. 10, 16.

49 McGregor, *Human Side of Enterprise*, p. 61.

50 Pink, *Drive*, Part 2.

51 Daniel Ladley, Ian Wilkinson, and Louise Young, 'The Impact of Individual Versus Group Rewards on Work Group Performance and Cooperation: A Computational Social Science Approach', *Journal of Business Research* 68 (2015), pp. 2412–25.

52 George A. Akerlof, 'Labour Contracts as Partial Gift Exchange', *Quarterly Journal of Economics* 97 (1982), pp. 547–69. The point in this argument is that employees are not paid based on individual performance. In their 'When 3+1 > 4: Gift Structure and Reciprocity in the Field', *Management Science* 62 (2016), pp. 2639–50, Duncan Gilchrist, Michael Luca, and Deepak Malhotra report that when employees' compensation has a gift element in the sense of an unanticipated raise before they start their work, their productivity increases. They interpret the higher productivity as being in reciprocation of the wage gift. In contrast, higher wages that were anticipated and paid did not raise productivity.

53 See e.g. Kenneth J. Arrow, 'Gifts and Exchanges', *Philosophy and Public Affairs* 1 (1972), pp. 343–62.

54 For simplicity, we assume that prices are constant so that the purchasing power of the wage is not eroded by inflation. Labour demand is derived from the profit maximization of the employers under the assumption of declining marginal productivity of labour, i.e. the contribution of the last worker or work hour to a firm's output falls as the firm's total employment rises.

55 Obviously, I do not wish to claim that non-Christians generally do not have intrinsic motivations for work. The distinction between non-Christians and Christians here serves to make the example illustrative. A similar argument would hold for other types of intrinsic motivation.

56 Anne Case and Angus Deaton, 'Mortality and Morbidity in the 21st Century', Brookings Papers on Economic Analysis Conference Drafts (Washington, DC: Brookings Institution), March 2017, available at www.brookings.edu/bpea-articles/mortality-and-morbidity-in-the-21st-century; Charles Murray, *Coming Apart: The State of White America 1960–2010* (New York: Crown Publishers, 2013). For a literary account of the developments documented by this research, see J. D. Vance, *Hillbilly Elegy: A Memoir of a Family and Culture in Crisis* (New York: Harper-Collins Publishers, 2016).

57 Of course, I do not claim here that this is the only factor contributing to the decline of this part of the American society. Other factors, especially globalization, may have contributed too.

58 For an excellent introduction, see Michael U. Krause and Thomas Lubik, *Modeling Labour Markets in Macroeconomics: Search and Matching*, Federal Reserve Bank of Richmond Working Paper 14–19 (Richmond, VA: Federal Reserve Bank of Richmond, 2014).

59 Such a basic right is not to be confused with right-to-work laws that exist in many US states and affirm the right of workers to be employed without joining a labour union. A basic right to work was guaranteed by the socialist constitution of the German Democratic Republic until 1989.

12

The Problem of Meaning and Related Problems: Four Voices in a Pastoral Theology of Work

CHRIS R. ARMSTRONG

This chapter is written from a pastoral point of view, seeking both to provide ministers with some historical resources for addressing the 'work lives' of those they serve and to address every working Christian directly in a 'pastoral' voice. The presenting problem it addresses is simple but devastating: *Can we find God's purpose and presence in our work in the 'secular' world?*

This question is personal for me. After a Christian conversion at the age of 22, I spent eight years in the business world – wondering what purpose God might have for me in that work. At last I did what so many do who ask the same sort of question. I decided that if I could employ myself in a job that was 'obviously spiritual', I could answer the burning question of work's meaning once and for all.

I therefore turned to graduate work in church history, then teaching in an evangelical Protestant seminary. There, I again and again heard mature students (the average age of today's seminarians is in the thirties) say this: 'I used to work in the world, where I could find no purpose or presence of God in my work. Then I heard a call to ministry.' By 'ministry' they meant *God's* work. *Church-paid* work. Work in which this question of God's purpose in their daily activities could finally be answered.

I felt there was something wrong with this narrative, but I didn't know what. After all, I had pretty much taken the same path. Sure, in my early work in the business world I had benefited from 'marketplace ministries', which concentrated on helping workers be good disciples and evangelists in their workplaces. But I don't remember learning anything from them about why God would care about what we did *in the work itself*.

In short, my evangelical Protestant formation had failed me. Even the parts of it that had addressed work perpetuated a deeply unsatisfying dualism: the sacred was over *there* (in church, evangelism, mission) and the secular over *here*, in the places where the world's work got done. What did the church tell us about those places? You should work to support yourself and your family. You should be a shining example of Christian ethical probity. You should be extra nice to your co-workers, because they might ask you what was different in your life and you could lead them to Christ. And if you worked hard and climbed the ladder, you should send some money back over to the 'sacred' side, where the *important* stuff happens.

This sort of advice leaves us with a profoundly unsatisfying and disappointing portrait of the activities that take up most of our waking hours, one that implies God's purposes and presence are *simply not to be found* in the essential activities of our work. We may bring 'sacred' or 'spiritual' activities, habits, or attitudes *to* that work; and we may do 'sacred' or 'spiritual' things *with* the money we earn at that work; but *none of these have anything to do with the actual activities we are being paid to carry out.*

If you doubt this, consider how a secularist employer would see the Christian dos and don'ts listed above. Would they see any of them as relevant to what you are being paid to do – that is, to the part your particular job plays in helping the organization produce the goods or services that earn the profits that keep the lights on and the workers employed?

After a lot of searching, I have reluctantly concluded that American Christians of my generation have largely given up on finding any spiritual meaning in our work. In fact, we've stopped looking for God *anywhere* in our ordinary material and social lives, because we just don't know how to find him there. We've bought the lie that there's something called 'the secular world', void of God's presence. Absent a Christian understanding of work, little keeps us from becoming what so many of our best secularist workmates already are: either workaholics idolizing our own accomplishments, or time-servers working for the weekend and retirement.

I want to suggest that when we find people struggling with the larger question of spiritual meaning in worldly work, if we dig a bit, we'll find other questions at the nub of their discontent. This chapter will take up four of these, looking to four thinkers in the Christian tradition for answers.

Question 1: Does time dedicated to working in the secular world endanger our souls? That is, is there an inherent tension or contradiction between the 'worldliness' of work and the 'spirituality' of faith?

I will start now – and end later – by drawing on a source many readers will consider strange, idiosyncratic, and perhaps even useless: medieval Christianity. Some readers may know that medieval Christians co-opted the term 'vocation' for monastic or priestly callings (what Os Guinness calls 'the Catholic distortion'). They may have a sense that the spiritual life, for medieval folks, was held in infinitely higher regard than the material.

This is true, to a point: how could an earthly life of typically no more than 30 to 40 years compete with the eternity that awaits us? Yet, as I intend to show, medieval Christendom gives us important theological resources for thinking about ordinary work.

As the ancient period began winding down, the theologian whose influence would become definitive in the medieval and early modern West, Augustine of Hippo, distinguished two spheres of human endeavour: the 'contemplative life' and the 'active life'.[1] The contemplative life brings the soul together with its God. The active life draws us into service to others – for example, farming, trading, raising families. While Augustine declared both of these good, he held the contemplative life in higher regard – and the church followed him in this.

But a century or so later, along came the monk-pope Gregory the Great (540–604), whom Jean Leclercq called the 'spiritual father' of the medieval period, as Augustine was its theological father. Unlike Augustine, Gregory did not insist on the supremacy of the contemplative over the active life – but the insight was hard won.

Born into a wealthy family and educated in grammar, rhetoric, law, and letters, Gregory was well prepared for public service, and in 573 he served as prefect of Rome, the highest civil position in the land, overseeing the city's police force, food supply, and finances. But the work left Gregory unsatisfied. His heart was troubled.

Gregory's family had been pious: his mother and two of her sisters are regarded as saints in the Roman Catholic Church, and his lineage included two popes. Young Gregory had read and meditated on Scripture, developing a 'love of eternity' that made him yearn for a life of devotion to God. As prefect, however, such full-time devotion seemed impossible. 'While my mind obliged me to serve this present world in outward action,' he wrote, 'its cares began to threaten me so that I was in danger of being engulfed in it not only in outward action, but, what is more serious, in my mind.'[2]

After a one-year term of office, Gregory made a decision that he described as a conversion: he would escape from 'the things of the world' as from a doomed shipwreck. He took vows of obedience, poverty, and celibacy, and entered the monastic life of daily disciplines, prayer, and Bible reading. For Gregory, the monastery offered relief from the never-ending details of administration, the lot of the leader. He expected to live out his years in its cloisters, given over completely to the contemplative life.

But his idyll was not to last. Three years later, in 578, Pope Benedict I called Gregory out of his happy seclusion to become one of the seven deacons of Rome, an office carrying heavy administrative duties. These he fulfilled with distinction, so that when plague took the life of Pope Pelagius II in 590, Gregory was unanimously chosen to succeed him.

It was not an auspicious time. The violent incursion of Germanic tribes; cycles of famine, drought, and plague; and the flight of the old Roman aristocratic class to protect their lives of privilege thrust the newly elected Pope Gregory I into managing supplies and troop movements, negotiating with terrorists, and administering public charity. Under Gregory, the church took a giant step towards its medieval status as the agency most responsible for the society's general welfare.

How hard it now became for the new pope to find even a few minutes for his beloved devotion and prayer! To a friend he wrote, 'I am being smashed by many waves of affairs and afflicted by a life of tumults, so that I may rightly say: I am come into deep waters where the floods overflow me' (Ps. 69.2).[3] Gregory now had to confront the defining issue of his life: the question of the relationship between the contemplative and the active life. The contemplative life was focused on the eternal; the active life was lived amid the world's distractions. This was the 'secular' life (from the Latin *saeculum*, which meant something like 'this present generation'). Gregory was torn between the eternal and the temporal, between that which lasts and those things that are passing but ever pressing.

The biblical story that came alive for him on this matter was that of Rachel and Leah. In that allegorical way of reading Scripture that seems odd today but was standard-issue then, Gregory saw 'Rachel' as the contemplative life: beautiful but infertile – and at first, completely unattainable. As Gregory wrote to the Empress Theoctista upon his elevation to the papacy, he had been 'coupled in the night ... to the fertile Leah' – that is, the life of active ministry.

In the biblical story, 'Jacob begins with Leah, attains Rachel, and returns to Leah.' It was something like this that Gregory discovered while leading in turbulent Rome. How could life with the productive Leah and the beautiful Rachel be combined?

Working from clues in Augustine, John Cassian, and others, Gregory forged a remarkable synthesis between the active and contemplative lives. He concluded that 'activity precedes contemplation, but contemplation must be expressed in service to one's neighbour'.[4] In order to become truly spiritual, one must move not only away from the distractions of the flesh to reach the spirit, but also back from the heights of the spiritual life to the practical concerns of bodily life.

In other words, Gregory concluded that these two modes of life were not as mutually exclusive as he and the church had taught. Each strengthens the other in a never-ending cycle: the contemplative life equipping us for the active life, and the active life grounding us in acts of love to our neighbours, to keep us from floating off into spiritual pride and irrelevance.

Now, too, he came to see those who lived the active life – marked at its best by such ordinary physical and spiritual ministries as feeding the hungry and caring for the sick, teaching the ignorant and humbling the proud – as *better* equipped to experience the contemplative life than those who absorbed all their hours in study and meditation. Remarkably for his time, Gregory insisted that a married cleaning woman might well attain to greater spiritual heights than a cloistered monk. There was, in other words, no 'sacred–secular divide' in the mind of this definitive teacher of the early medieval period.

Of course, Gregory never stopped insisting on prayer and contemplation as crucial for every Christian. But he added that one could never remove oneself from the life of active charity to others. In his *Pastoral Rule* and other works, he taught generations to follow how they could find intimacy with God in the midst of busyness. While in tension, action and contemplation could serve and enrich each other. No wonder the Western church put his writings into the hands of every newly consecrated bishop for nearly 1,000 years!

To us today, the 'mixed life' taught by Gregory might seem cliché: *of course* we must serve others to grow in grace. *Of course* we must recharge our spiritual batteries in order to serve others effectively in a world that 'knows not God'. But Gregory went beyond these simple ideas to a kind of sacramental unity very unlike the sacred–secular divide that characterizes the church today. He insisted that when we commit and engage in our worldly vocations, everything in our experience can become an instrument of God's direct, special communication to us: the material goods that sustain us; our sometimes-stressful relationships with our co-workers; even the dull, drumming repetition of trivial toil.

Of course, recognizing the Lord's voice in these experiences requires that we foster and practise discernment – a virtue that until then had belonged almost exclusively to the monk, nun, and priest. But Gregory came to believe that *any person* could attain spiritual discernment.

One notable way the active life helps us to discern the voice of God, Gregory added, is through the experiences of suffering to which it exposes us. Too often today we accept the 'Disney narrative' of work and vocation: 'Follow your heart, and you'll find what you're made to do – and achieve fulfilment by doing it for the rest of your life.' We have, in other words, no theology of *suffering* in work. This monk-pope – battered constantly not only by the external miseries of war, pestilence, and famine, but also the very personal trials of constant ill-health – turned for wisdom to the book of Job. In his extensive pastoral commentary on that book, Gregory worked out a theology of suffering not as an absolute evil, but rather a special case of God's personal communication to his beloved people.

The sufferings of the active life, Gregory taught, come not from God's good will but from the devil; but God keeps the devil on a short leash and turns to our good what our Enemy intends for our destruction. Battered by the storms of the active life, we are forced again and again beyond our own resources, into a deeper dependence on God. Thus, through suffering in the world, we reach heights and depths of contemplative union with him inaccessible apart from all the brokenness and distraction and frustration of action in the world. Working in the world, we find ourselves wracked with compunction ('holy sorrow') at the sin that confronts us both there and in our own soul. Work is not a rose garden of fulfilment but brings us something more precious. Through it, Gregory taught, the attentive layperson may develop the holy discernment, spiritual integrity, and unruffled tranquillity that once was thought to belong only to the monks and nuns in their cloisters.

Gregory's insights are still fresh, of course, everywhere that Christians continue to struggle for their souls in the worldly arenas of their vocations. He shows us that we may commit ourselves to ordinary labour in 'worldly' careers, content that God works through our work when we serve others – as through the ordinary actions of the parable of the sheep and the goats. Medieval faith did not always remember this insight, tending to return to the old elevation of the monastic life above the ordinary life. This was one reason Martin Luther found himself, in the sixteenth century, needing to recover the godliness of bakers baking and tailors sewing and fathers changing their infants' diapers.

On Luther, more later. But now another question arises in a complex, post-Christian economy full of real, fallen people – including bosses and corporate leaders motivated by other things than service to humanity.

Question 2: Does attending to the virtues needed for the working life (e.g. industriousness, self-control, service to others, obedience to rules and leaders) reduce us to drones or pawns in exploitive structures of modern work? Does becoming a good Christian worker mean sacrificing prophetic autonomy for security, placid labour for social conscience?

During the live opening ceremony of the 2012 London Olympics, before millions of worldwide viewers, England's pastoral island paradise rose slowly into view from below ground, to the wafting strains of British composer Edward Elgar. But suddenly the paradise was shattered.

A group of belching smokestacks arose, accompanied by violent drumming and harsh music. The Industrial Revolution had arrived. Legions of lock-step labourers under the command of black-coated factory owners overran the green land. TV commentators gleefully quoted poet William Blake, describing how the Industrial Revolution's 'Satanic mills' had brutalized the landscape and crushed workers. The ceremony's creator, they told viewers, had titled this section 'Pandemonium', after the capital city of hell in Milton's *Paradise Lost*. This picture has many roots in English history, from Blake himself to J. R. R. Tolkien's *The Lord of the Rings*, where villains with minds 'of metal and wheels' oppress the peoples and blast the landscape.

What, then, of the English church? Did they simply fall in line as willing dupes of the crushing injustices of the new industrial era? In 1949, with the devastating power of the arms pouring forth from the military-industrial complex still echoing in the world's ears, French philosopher and historian Élie Halévy wrote a history of England that charged just this. Halévy argued that some of England's most devoted Christian citizens – John Wesley and the Methodists – simply capitulated, like sheep and slaves, to the worst of the Industrial Revolution, perpetuating its abuses when they should have stood against them.

Methodism was born in the late 1730s, when the commercial virtues of the old Puritans and the new capitalist habits of long-term investment began to build the commercial machine that would drive Western economic growth in the centuries to come. This was the time of nascent industrialization, which aggregated human labour into factories, removing it from the town-based communal settings of homes and shops and catapulting it into the large-scale settings of cities, whose rapid growth resulted, especially in the century after Wesley, in terrible social problems. Like a great landslide, the revolution swept away centuries of solid economic and social ground, leaving Western workers battered and bewildered. Even in Wesley's time, abusive treatment of workers provoked strikes and riots.

In response to these upheavals, Halévy argued, middle-class Methodist leaders led their working-class devotees to seek spiritual, rather than temporal, solutions to the difficulties they faced – insisting their converts work faithfully for their bosses, turning their minds from the oppressive conditions in which they worked and towards their eternal destinies.

This influential portrait of the movement is flawed in several important ways that go to the heart of the John Wesley's theology of vocation.

While Wesley (1703–91) claimed that Christians ought to preach repentance often and politics rarely, except when necessary to defend the king, he was actually not shy about expressing his political and economic opinions. Those opinions were typical of an upper middle-class, Oxford-educated clergyman, but that did not mean he was unconcerned about the problems of English society. One of his responses was to issue scathing indictments of those who profited from others. His tract 'Thoughts on the Present Scarcity of Provisions', for instance, claimed that the poor were hungry because of the influence of 'distilling, taxes, and luxury'.[5]

He also tried to help. Wesley's system of organizing believers into classes and bands within the Methodist 'societies' not only discipled them in spiritual growth but distributed relief funds collected from society members. He established a medical clinic and maintained the pharmacy himself. He founded tuition-free schools for poor children, one in his own home, and a house for widows and orphans, with whom he regularly ate his meals. He spent almost all his own personal wealth to ameliorate the conditions of poor workers, encouraging his followers to do the same.

His biggest impact on his people, though, came through his teachings. In many respects, Wesley had the sensibility of a pious businessman: a melding of the devout Anglicanism of his father; the hard-working, strictly disciplined Puritanism of his mother; and the broad cultural engagement of his Oxford education.

Out of this background, Wesley taught a salvation that was not just a 'way to heaven' but also a 'way on earth': get the heart in order, and good, ethical actions will follow – in the marketplace as well as the church, home, and public square. He emphasized that there were many 'means of grace', many spiritual disciplines to practise to grow in Christlikeness. His most common list of those means of grace included works of piety: prayer, searching the Scriptures, fasting, the Eucharist, and 'Christian conferencing' (meeting together as believers). But he also included works of mercy: feeding the hungry and clothing the naked – whether through acts of charity or, more often, simply working to support one's family and create value for others – were spiritual disciplines for Wesley, not only social acts.

In other words, true holiness for Wesley was not a matter simply of what goes on inside the heart: it must be externalized in service to others through works of mercy and even honest business practices, such as refusing to lend money at unreasonable rates or to borrow when the ability to pay back is uncertain. The heart and soul of Wesley's vocational teaching was his refusal to abstract spiritual lives from material lives. So he provided a pattern of 'this-worldly asceticism' not just applicable to prayer closets or churches. He taught that holiness healed and redirected disordered 'tempers', and he encouraged his people to live in ways marked by integrity and authenticity. As their hearts were transformed, their work soon followed.

Although he was deeply concerned about the love of money becoming an idol, damaging people's relationships with God and others, Wesley was not averse to promoting economic work in the secular world as a means to promote human thriving. With his focus always especially on the poor – settled and working as well as indigent and destitute – he insisted that Methodists educate themselves by, for example, learning new skills as well as a new and sanctified way of living in the world. He taught that industry was a positive good, and that when well handled by Christians, money could become food for the hungry, drink for the thirsty, clothing for the naked, rest for the traveller, support for the widow and the orphan, defence for the oppressed, health for the sick, even life for the dying.

In short, Wesley's teachings encouraged both sober, responsible working virtues and an ethic of love and social responsibility. Personal holiness meant little without an accompanying social holiness ('faith without works was dead'). A changed heart, he believed, could restore the individual dignity of human beings created in the image of God – and that restoration of individual lives could in turn restore society. In other words, Wesley's theology of human dignity and virtue laid a firm Christian foundation for the virtues of the workplace and the economic sphere.

In addressing the needs of the poor, Wesley did not rail against capitalism, though he did preach against its abuses. Instead, he insisted that the truly Christian person was also a flourishing person – that is, someone largely happy and content in all his or her ways. Seek first the kingdom of God, and all these other things – our worldly lives, our work – will follow after in their proper order. The best way to flourish economically and socially was not to change an economic system, but rather to put all else second to the gospel, and let its transformative influence suffuse every area of our lives and work.

Wesley thus attended not only to his followers' *material* embodiment, but also their *social* embodiment. The movement's true dynamism was to be found in its network of small groups and meetings. Rank-and-file members understood themselves to be owners and leaders of the movement's institutions – class meetings, Sunday schools, annual conferences. On any given Sunday, the great majority of Methodist pulpits were occupied by local lay preachers 'on the plan' – that is, preaching every few weeks, but still labouring in their secular vocations as well.

In this, the movement's leadership reflected its membership. Early Methodism flourished most among the new working and middle classes. Nearly 60 per cent were skilled craftspeople – people who enjoyed relative independence and sought decency and self-respect in their work and social lives. These artisans and entrepreneurs were beginning to emerge from their formerly lowly status in the ancestral class system – in which, for example, priests in the Church of England were members of the upper class. Their newly discovered mobility, attained through industry, frugality, and other ordinary working virtues, gave them the confidence to question and challenge the Anglican religious establishment. Such people naturally gravitated to the fervent, warm-hearted, and freeing message of Wesley's 'born-again' religion and its free, democratic organization in small groups and mutual aid societies.

In other words, Wesley's Methodists resembled sturdy, self-reliant English workers more than the cowed factory slaves Halévy and other twentieth-century labour historians took them to be. Even famous Methodist sermons preaching responsibility and decrying drunkenness – sermons attacked by later historians as simply creating docile, sober, industrious factory men – were usually not imposed from above. Most arose from below as Methodists, finding that responsibility had transformed their own lives, preached it to others.

Methodism itself was in many ways entrepreneurial, and so it shouldn't surprise that it enjoyed good relations with business such as the mining companies of Cornwall. The Wesleyan message, meetings, and organizations gave confidence to the people working in the mining businesses, helping those who led the businesses to do so in ways that made their communities healthier. Numerous mine captains were also Methodist preachers who communicated to their communities the powerful messages of respectability and self-improvement, thus helping to ensure that Methodism became the most relevant religious institution for labourers and the working class – far more so than the established Church of England. Through their religion of social as well as personal holiness, Wesleyans found ways to create meaningful and rewarding work that helped to ensure that community needs were met.[6]

Not surprisingly, working-class Methodists quickly began ascending the economic ladder, and this brought them new opportunities for action and influence. Even in Wesley's own lifetime signs abounded that the values of his movement were assisting members temporally as well as spiritually – so much so that Wesley had to remind them on occasion that his famous advice to 'earn all you can' and 'save all you can' had a third component, 'give all you can'. As they gained the material and social blessings that the Gospels had taught them to expect when they 'sought first righteousness', they needed to reach down and help those still struggling.

Behind this independent activism and social mobility lay Methodism's emphasis on the role of each person in his or her own salvation – the Arminian teaching that, though no one can be saved without 'prevenient' grace, they must also respond to this grace and allow it to transform them along the lines of Paul's exhortation to the Philippians: 'Work out your own salvation with fear and trembling. For it is God which worketh in you both to will and to do of his good pleasure' (Phil. 2.12–13).

'True Christianity, when applied by a faithful Christian labourer', said the early nineteenth-century Methodist theologian Richard Watson, was to turn darkness 'into light, confusion to order, shamelessness to character, squalidness to decency, prodigality to frugality, improvidence to foresight, and sloth to industry'.[7]

Though motives of past actors are hard to discern, it seems clear that Methodist societies attracted many of their worshippers precisely through their offer of a more purposeful, disciplined way of life. Workers responded

to the Methodist message at least in part because they found the industriousness and financial prudence preached by the movement to be a solid
means for self-improvement and material success. At some times, when
faced with injustice, Methodists did resist the new industrial order. But at
many other times, they embraced it – *for Methodist reasons.*

Even while we may recognize the truths in the story of Wesley and the
early Methodists – that to be a good worker need not mean capitulating to
oppressive systems; that the virtues required for work can be an important
part of our development as Christians, oriented towards a higher flourishing for ourselves as well as others – we cannot turn a blind eye to the evils
of modern economic and working life. This raises a third, sharper question, with which many modern Christians struggle as they ask whether
work in the secular world can have any Christian meaning.

**Question 3. How can we do our work faithfully while also pushing back
against those parts of organizations and systems that are corrupted
(injustice, immorality, work that harms rather than helps) and accepting
the sacrifices this can entail?**

To think that we can live the life of work according to the fruit of the Spirit
(and as we abide in Christ) without coming into conflict with the Spirit
of the Age (pride of life, lust of the eye, etc.) is foolishness. The life story
of Charles Sheldon, who pastored in a time when economic recession and
unemployment loomed in many people's working lives, meshes with the
famous story he wrote – *In His Steps* – to raise this question.[8] The setting
is near the end of the 1800s, Sunday morning, in the comfortable upper
middle-class 'First Church' in the fictional Midwestern town of Raymond.
Halfway through the service, a tired, sick homeless man walks into the
church, up the aisle to the front, and begins to speak. He wonders aloud
why there is so much trouble and misery in the cities when Christians
living in luxury sang about consecrating themselves entirely to God, but
never seemed to reach out to help. 'It seems to me there's an awful lot of
trouble in the world that somehow wouldn't exist if all the people who
sing such songs went and lived them out. I suppose I don't understand', he
concludes. Then he adds: 'But *what would Jesus do?*' Then the homeless
man collapses, the pastor brings him home, the man lingers and dies. And
the next Sunday the pastor, deeply affected, challenges his congregation
to bind themselves by a solemn declaration to live by the homeless man's
four-word question: 'What would Jesus do?'

Thus begins one of the most popular books of the early twentieth century. As the novel unfolds, we observe how this pledge changes the lives
of those who take it, especially in their workplaces. Each time they enter a

serious situation or face a momentous decision, they speak this same question as a prayer. They ask not for some Kantian categorical imperative, but for direct guidance from the Holy Spirit: What would Jesus himself do were he *them, now, in this job, or this social situation, responsible to these people?* And discerning the answer, they act accordingly. The courage in this is undeniable. The novel records great personal and professional cost, incredulity, dismissal by others, and loss of social status.

In His Steps is one of the most-read novels of all time. Its author was the American Congregational minister Charles M. Sheldon, a man well worth knowing even today. During the 60 years after its publication in 1896, Sheldon's novel sold more copies than any other book in the United States after the Bible: more than eight million. Though it is no literary masterpiece, and its ideals and programmes may seem naïve and unrealistic to us today, *In His Steps* speaks wisdom to today's faith and work movement – as does the life of its author, a model for sacred–secular integration.

We might expect the author of such a novel to have been an impractical dreamer – a man who spent most of his time in his study, thinking up stories. But this is far from the truth. Sheldon, whose life stretched from the Civil War to the Second World War (1857–1946), grew up in Dakota Territory, in a log cabin he helped his preacher father build. From the time he could hold a hammer, young Charles loved the daily toil of the homesteading life, and this birthed a lifelong affection for folks who worked with their hands. In words reminiscent of modern-day TV host Mike Rowe, Sheldon expressed wonder over 'the stupidity of those who regard physical toil as something to be avoided as a burden and even a disgrace'. Labouring on his parents' farm had taught him, he said, 'the dignity and joy of work with our hands'.[9]

As a minister of the gospel, Sheldon combined the progressive theology of the social gospel with a warm-hearted, Christocentric attention to individual salvation. Though this lively holism was typical of the mainline Protestantism of his era, it would soon be torn asunder by the liberal–fundamentalist schisms of the 1920s. The legacy of that divisive age has been a church divided into two camps: one serving the Great Commission to evangelize and make disciples through powerful preaching and event-based ministry, and the other serving the Greatest Commandment to love God and neighbour through social action at home and abroad. Today, no American Christian who cares about the meaning of the gospel for material and social life can afford to ignore the testimony of the pre-schism Protestant church. Likewise, no Protestant leader formed in the last decades of the nineteenth century better exemplifies that time's unified attention to souls *and* human flourishing than Charles Sheldon.

From his first day in his first pastorate in sleepy Waterbury, Connecticut, Sheldon poured his efforts into meeting not only the spiritual but also the material and social needs of his congregation and their town. His people must have suspected this was not your garden-variety pastor when Sheldon launched into his new ministry by 'boarding around', as he called it. 'Starting on Sunday he would go home with a family, eat dinner with them and spend most of the afternoon with them; and then after the evening church service he would return and visit until bedtime.' He would sleep in the hotel room where he had boarded since arriving in town, then take his lunch and dinner with the family and stay for the evening, helping around the house and amusing the children with magic tricks. In this way, he lived week by week with 45 different families of his parish's 175-member church.

There was nothing, it seemed, that Sheldon wasn't prepared to do to meet the practical as well as the spiritual needs in his community. He planted a vegetable garden on church property and sold the produce for the church. He helped promote neat and attractive housing, small-business assistance, and a good local newspaper. He took up a collection for a town hearse. He launched a drive to create a town library. He worked with a doctor to address a serious typhoid epidemic, discovering that the cause was the closeness of the town's pigpens to its wells. Unfortunately, a conservative element in the church felt that all this attention to the quotidian needs of the community was highly irregular in a pastor. They began blocking his efforts, and just two years into his pastorate, in 1889, Sheldon felt hemmed in enough that he resigned.

His next stop was Topeka, Kansas, where he took over a small Congregational mission church that met in a small room over the local butcher shop. In his first sermon, he pledged to preach always 'a Christ for the common people. A Christ who belongs to the rich *and* to the poor, the ignorant *and* the learned, the old *and* the young, the good *and* the bad. A Christ who knows no sect or age, whose religion does not consist alone in cushioned seats, and comfortable surroundings, or culture, or fine singing, or respectable orders of Sunday services, but a Christ who bids us all recognize the Brotherhood of the race, who bids throw open this room to all.'[10] This social angularity discomfited some in his new flock, and the ways he put it into practice would put him at odds with some of his older members throughout his 50-year ministry there, even as he galvanized the church's youth.

Soon Sheldon was confronted in a personal way with the human situation that would spur him to write his famous book: the destitution endemic to the working classes. As in the book, a tramp came to Sheldon, and the minister had to send him away empty-handed. The incident bothered him enough that he felt he must do *something* about the conditions of the day.

By the 1890s America had slid into desperate times. It had started in the 1870s, Sheldon's formative teens and twenties. This was the beginning of the 'Gilded Age', in which industrial capitalists bankrolled corporations that, by the end of the century, would combine into monopolies with an iron grip on the means of production and a tendency to overlook the humanity of their growing workforce. Long hours in poor conditions, child labour, and pitiful wages kept the working poor in a perpetual state of subsistence. Many of the poorest were immigrants and blacks – the scorned, feared, 'indispensable outcasts' of industrial America. This class began, soon enough, to lash out. In 1877 wage cuts were announced in Baltimore and Ohio, and a wildcat strike spread, causing riots and looting, suppressed by vigilantes and militia.

The living conditions of the working poor were made infinitely worse by the state of city politics. The bosses of city wards and their political machines amassed support and money by helping some to find jobs, others to explain away minor crimes, and so forth. Having gained power, these corrupt governments failed to ensure even minimal standards of fresh water, sewers, transportation, and other infrastructure. Thus this urban corruption combined with low wages and cyclical unemployment to keep many workers in near-unliveable conditions.

Americans of the genteel classes were aware of what was going on but not inclined to intervene. The dislocation, bewilderment, and suffering visited on the dispossessed by mechanization, urbanization, greed, and corruption seemed unimaginable – and for the most part, despite their appetite for sensational reports of urban squalor, the more fortunate seem to have preferred not to imagine it.

In the 1890s all of this worsened as economic depression returned. Thousands began losing their jobs, and they usually could not find other employment – much like the broken-down hobo character of *In His Steps*. Rather than coming to the workers' aid, however, the comfortable Christian majority either ignored the growing ranks of the unemployed and indigent or blamed them for their supposed laziness.

The young minister, however, decided to see for himself what the unemployed were experiencing. With his congregation's blessing he left the pulpit, put on his oldest clothes and set out in search of work. 'He tried stores and factories, coal yards and flour mills' with no success. 'He walked into every store (except for the tobacco shops and theaters, of whose business he disapproved) on Kansas Avenue, Topeka's main business street ... and was turned down at every door.' Sheldon kept this up for nearly five days, without being recognized. Finally, 'he saw a crew shoveling snow from the Santa Fe railroad tracks, and asked the foreman if he could help them without being paid. The bemused foreman agreed.'[11] With a borrowed shovel, he went to work and kept at it for the rest of the day. The next morning, he happened on a job unloading a car of coal, which he finished by noon, earning 50 cents.

The experience moved him, and he preached eight sermons on its basis. But the effects of the poor economy and unfair labour practices stretched beyond the unemployed, so Sheldon set out on a new experience. This time he targeted social groups he felt could show him both the problems and the solutions facing Americans of all walks of life during that volatile time. In a new version of his 'boarding around' practice, he ate, talked, worked, and slept for one week each with people from eight different Topeka social groups: streetcar operators, college students, blacks, railroad workers, lawyers, physicians, businessmen, and newspaper men.

At every stop and in many workplaces, Sheldon confronted the effects of the fall. *In His Steps* portrays workers pushing back against this fallenness in their own places of work. The editor of the town paper decides not to run reports of a prize fight and discontinues the Sunday edition, at great cost to the business. The supervisor of a rail yard discovers fraud in the rail company and reports it, at great expense to himself, as he is demoted down the ranks. A leading merchant redesigns his business to give his employees more say in its operations and a share in its profits. Various characters, including a young seamstress and a young carpenter, put their skills to work in a 'settlement house', a turn-of-the-century social-gospel institution founded to provide health care, education, and other material and social services to the urban poor. A wealthy businessman closes a lucrative saloon on his property and gives the land to the settlement house. At every step, Sheldon both acknowledges the injustices that can be perpetuated in all work sectors and offers models for confronting them, while not pulling punches on the sacrifices such actions may require.

The novel is perhaps overly formulaic, and at times naïve and idealistic, as Sheldon himself (and indeed many liberal progressives of his age) could also be. But there is something captivating and deeply human in their pages. We find here the insight and warmth of a minister who 'boarded around' with the families in his town, tramped the streets with the unemployed and fought for the dignity of his African American neighbours, even when to do so was unpopular with many in his congregation. There is something incalculable in a story told from such a heart as this, and it is a story that suggests many answers to the question of this section.

Certainly, the concern for redemptive Christian action in our ordinary spheres of work that was taken up in various ways by Wesley, the early Methodists, the holiness movement, and Sheldon and the social-gospel movement show us one way faith and work can be integrated. It is admittedly a very powerful way. But if faith can find a place in our work *only* where injustices are being corrected, oppressive systems and structures challenged and changed, and broken people healed, then we are still left with a fourth and final question.

Question 4. Where is God in our actual work – its positive intent, the value it seeks to create through goods and services? How can life in the material world actually connect with life in the spirit – that is, how can it bring us closer to God?

The sixteenth-century Reformer Martin Luther gets us partway to an answer to this question. In reaction to late medieval excesses, including the 'Catholic distortion' of vocation noted above, Luther taught that every legal and moral employment in the marketplace, the home, and the civic sphere is a vocation from God. It is through our ordinary work that God supplies the needs of others, whether or not they name the name of Christ. So yes, in that sense, our work has a larger meaning: we become in effect the hands of God for his provision to our neighbour.

However, drawing on Augustine's distinction between the City of God and the City of Man, Luther placed strong limits on the *spiritual meaning* of work done to serve what later theologians called God's 'common grace' to the world at large. In reaction to strains of works-righteousness in late medieval Christian thought, Luther felt he had to insist that no kind of earthly work had any relation to that crucial, spiritual task in our lives: our preparation for eternity, our progress in sanctification and salvation. All is grace; all is the work of God; none is our work; whatever little righteousness we might grow into (and he was sceptical as to the extent of such righteousness) belonged properly not to us, but to Christ.

Intensified into the Reformed tradition by Luther's contemporary Ulrich Zwingli, this dismissal of any engagement of the body in spiritually significant activities – this nervousness about the 'outer', physical life as spiritually irrelevant (at best) or dangerous (at worst) – has continued to weave its way through Protestant piety ever since. Protestants have not much expected our 'active lives' to advance us in our salvation – as Gregory had suggested it can – except as our involvement in secular employments reveals to us our sin and drives us back to prayer (which, as we've seen, Gregory also affirmed). Missing in Luther is that other, sacramental dimension Gregory affirmed: that in those employments, if we have but ears to hear and eyes to see, God *does* meet us, and *does* touch us through his grace.

What modern Protestants need, then, is a thinker who shares our modern vantage-point, but who has adopted and absorbed the sacramentalism of Gregory and his era. We need someone improbable, who is both a scholar of medieval faith and culture, and a clear and convincing communicator of medieval wisdom in the church of today. Fortunately, we have such a person in C. S. Lewis.

C. S. Lewis has many sides: beloved children's book author; lay theologian and apologist; scholar of medieval literature; central figure in a modern Christian literary movement that also included J. R. R. Tolkien, Charles Williams, Dorothy L. Sayers, and such earlier influences as G. K. Chesterton and George MacDonald.

Two things are true about Lewis in his impact on readers today: first, many still experience him as a spiritual mentor – a transformative influence in their quests to live well for God in this world. Second, whether these modern appreciators of Lewis know it or not, his greatest usefulness is not as a lone modern genius, but as a conduit to earlier wisdom – the wisdom of 'old books', as he once put it.[12] Thus Lewis provides a fitting conclusion to this chapter, which has looked back in history in search of guidance for our work today.

The facts of Lewis's life are easily summarized: born in 1898 in Belfast, the son of a lawyer and a cultured, linguistically gifted mother who died when he was nine, Lewis read voraciously and omnivorously from his earliest years. By the age of eight, he was writing stories about 'dressed animals' with his brother Warren. In his teen years, learning classics under the Irish schoolmaster William T. Kirkpatrick, he learned to appreciate the quest for truth not as an idle intellectual exercise, but – in the ancient and medieval tradition – as a search for what is real and true in the world, *so that we can live better.*

As he says in his testimony-cum-memoir *Surprised by Joy*, for Lewis this search was marked, early and repeatedly, by experiences of deep longing and yearning for something beyond the bounds of this world.[13] This longing he called simply 'joy'. The paradox was that though these experiences pointed to something transcendent and immaterial, they always came through the most vivid, material, sensory images – distant green hills, a toy garden in a biscuit-tin lid, powerful images of 'Northernness' from Norse myths. These pointers to the *metaphysical* were thus simultaneously profoundly *physical*. 'For me,' he later wrote, 'reason is the natural organ of truth; but imagination is the organ of meaning.' And when such experiences finally led him to God, he called himself an 'empirical theist' who 'arrived at God by induction'.[14]

So what did Lewis's imagination find in our medieval Christian heritage that can help us with our questions about finding meaning in our work? For Lewis was more than a medieval *scholar*. He was a medievalist in his *imagination*, in his *intuitions* about life, and in his *practices*. The medieval era he loved was an era in which the very character of the Western world – every institution, custom, or practice that touched human material and social bodies – *reinforced* the link between the material and social world and the divine.

In various descriptions of the medieval world view, Lewis shows us the medieval view of the material world as charged with the spiritual, 'tingling with anthropomorphic life, dancing, ceremonial, a festival not a machine',[15] 'a world of built-in significance'.[16] A medieval night watcher would see 'a world lighted, warmed, and resonant with music'.[17] Lewis also *shows* us this world of vibrancy and wonder. In his science fiction novel *Out of the Silent Planet*, the protagonist, Ransom, peers out of the window of a spaceship to see – not the black void of space, but a pulsing, glowing matrix of glory. This matches a description Lewis once gave of the medievals' vision of the cosmos, which borrows phrasing from fourteenth-century Italian poet Dante: 'Each [celestial] sphere', that is, each planet and heavenly body, 'is a conscious and intellectual being', moved by 'intellectual love' of God'.[18]

As alien as such a view of the world may seem to us – maybe just rank superstition, in fact – there is a coherent 'theo-logic' to this view of things:

- **First,** the medieval person understood – based on the scriptural account of the creation – that the material world is not evil; nor is it (as we moderns are more tempted to believe) spiritually irrelevant, for it all was made by God and bears his imprint.
- **Second,** the medieval person *also* understood that the material world cannot hold the *ultimate* end and fulfilment of human life. Where do we find that end and fulfilment? As Augustine, Boethius, and all who followed insisted, only in God himself.
- **The middle way** medievals hewed between the gnostic and the material-istic error about the material world was that *because of God's action in first creating, and then indwelling it, and then continuing to love and care for it,* the world must be shot through with the truth, goodness, and beauty of the Trinity itself. It must be a place of God's presence and glory, for those with eyes to see and ears to hear.[19]

The theological term for this vibrant medieval understanding of the material world is *sacramentalism*. This is a linked set of beliefs that, first, the outward and visible can convey the inward and spiritual; second, all creation is in some sense a reflection of the creator; and thus third, God is present in and through every square inch of his world, waiting to be discovered.

The world sacramentalism of the medieval era was rooted in the central-ity of the incarnation of the second person of the Trinity in the man Jesus of Nazareth. The great church historian Jaroslav Pelikan has shown us that the incarnation was the central preoccupation of medieval faith, at least in the 'high' and 'late' medieval periods, stretching roughly from AD 1000 to 1500.

During that period, medieval art, theology, church life, and private devotion all focused on the incarnation. The Gospel accounts became their 'canon within the canon'. The puzzle of why he had to come and die was their great theological obsession. And in the midst of it all came the insight that bubbled and frothed and entered into every part of their lives. This was the realization that by taking on human flesh and human senses, experiencing our temptations, suffering as we suffer, and then dying and rising, conquering even death itself, God in Christ *raised the dignity of what it means to be human.*

Quite contrary to modern stereotypes of barbarism and otherworldliness, medieval people affirmed our human lives (our eating, drinking, working, marrying, getting sick, being healed, and eventually dying) as transcendentally *important.* Each of these elements of our lives, they understood, is intimately related to our identities as divine image bearers of God and the redeemed of the Lord. The church could, and did, speak to every nook and moment of human life.

In an age so shot through with incarnational and sacramental awareness, faith and work – faith and everyday life – could never be separate. God was met at every turn. Lewis channelled to his modern readers a medieval sacramental awareness of not only our *material* embodiment, but also our *social* embodiment: 'There are no ordinary people. You have never talked to a mere mortal ... It is immortals whom we joke with, work with, marry, snub, and exploit ... Next to the Blessed Sacrament itself, your neighbour is the holiest object presented to your senses. If he is your Christian neighbour he is holy in almost the same way, for in him also Christ ... is truly hidden.'[20] This could easily be a passage from Benedict's *Rule.*

A Christian age that believed such things could not also believe that to be Christian is to be somehow 'spiritual, but not religious', as many say today. Having bought modern Enlightenment portraits of medieval stupidity and superstition, we have missed the powerful cultural generativity of this 'incarnationalism': medieval Christians invented the hospital, created the breathtaking artistry of the Gothic cathedrals, and pioneered modern Western science through a new institution: the university. These are three huge modern work sectors – health care, the arts, and higher education – each underwritten by this same lively, incarnational sacramentalism.

Two medieval Christians who applied this sacramental view directly to ordinary work were the fourteenth-century German Dominican friars Meister Eckhart (*c.*1260–*c.*1327) and Johann Tauler (*c.*1300–61). Along with other German mystics of their day, Eckhart and Tauler affirmed a non-monastic call of God. For them, not just monastics but ordinary working folk could achieve the highest title of traditional monasticism, 'friend of God'. They kept alive Gregory's understanding of the symbiotic relationship between action and contemplation, acknowledging that at times external work is more useful than internal.

For example, Eckhart says, 'If one were in [a state of mystical] ecstasy, even if it were as high as that of Paul, and knew that beside him there was an infirm man who needed a bowl of soup from him, it would be better for him to abandon his ecstasy and serve the needy man.'[21] This is not just a momentary concession. 'We are brought forth into time', wrote Eckhart, 'in order that our sensible worldly occupations may lead us nearer and make us like unto God.' Thus 'one can gather nettles and still stand in union with God.'[22]

Tauler criticized those who believed the work of the businessperson who 'knows all the secrets of commerce' to be a spiritual obstacle: 'It is certainly not God who has put this obstacle.'[23] Rather, the working life of active service is simply a different way of serving and knowing God. This work, too, is a calling, and the person who obeys it 'with single-ness of purpose' is truly on the way to God.[24] Thus the door to 'calling' was opened, centuries before Luther, to the common working person. Despite the medieval appropriation of the word 'vocation' by clergy and monastics, Gregory's legacy of the united, sacramentally understood con-templative-active life was sustained.

What Lewis in fact discovered as a professional medievalist, and then wove into all his fiction and popular religious writings, was a faith-driven culture that, because it raised up the humanity of Christ, affirmed the most prosaic and seemingly 'secular' parts of our lives as places of divine significance. One is reminded of the wonderful image of domesticity in the beaver family portrayed in Lewis's *The Lion, The Witch and the Wardrobe*, so like the convivial, rustic life of Tolkien's hobbits in the Shire: their love of pipes and parties and meals (and more meals). Or his strange novel *That Hideous Strength*, which is from one end to the other a defence of the ordinary virtues of embodied life: work, sexuality, household life, and all.

In his letters, too, you can often find Lewis celebrating the sacred in the materiality of our ordinary life and work. In one delightful letter to a woman who has clearly been expressing her discouragement at the drudg-ery of domestic life, Lewis said of housework:

> It is surely in reality the most important work in the world. What do ships, railways, mines, cars, government etc. exist for except that people may be fed, warmed, and safe in their own homes? As Dr Johnson said, 'To be happy at home is the end of all human endeavour' ... We wage war in order to have peace, we work in order to have leisure, we produce food in order to eat it. So your job is the one for which all others exist.[25]

As he signed his letters, he liked to use of himself that very embodied moniker St Francis of Assisi had used for himself: 'Brother Ass'. Of his own ageing and increasingly malfunctioning body: 'I have a kindly feeling for the old rattle-trap. Through it God showed me that whole side of His beauty which is embodied in colour, sound, smell and size.'[26]

What we find in Lewis, in short, is a medieval-inflected, sacramental, incarnational, earthy, and *practical* theology of life and work. 'Every created thing', he once wrote, 'is, in its degree, an image of God, and the ordinate and faithful appreciation of that thing a clue which, truly followed, will lead back to Him.'[27] If this is true, then *work* is a kind of sacramental space where one can – if one will – meet God. In a wartime talk to a group of Oxford students about the vocation of being a student, he pushed back against the modern tendency among Christians to dismiss ordinary work as somehow non-spiritual:

It is clear that Christianity does not exclude any of the ordinary human activities. St Paul tells people to get on with their jobs ... Christianity does not simply replace our natural life and substitute a new one; it is rather a new organization which exploits, to its own supernatural ends, these natural materials ... All our merely natural activities will be accepted, if they are offered to God, even the humblest, and all of them, even the noblest, will be sinful if they are not.[28]

What would it mean if we learned from Lewis this sacramentalism of daily work? How would our approach to our daily work change?

Notes

1 Augustine, *City of God*, XIX.19.

2 Gregory, *Moralia in Job*, Dedicatory Epistle to Leander, as quoted in Robert Markus, *Gregory the Great and His World* (New York: Cambridge University Press, 1997), p. 9.

3 Gregory, letter to Anastasius, Patriarch of Antioch, as quoted in John Moorhead, *Gregory the Great* (London: Routledge, 2005), p. 3.

4 Carole Straw, *Gregory the Great: Perfection in Imperfection* (Berkeley: University of California Press, 1988), p. 20.

5 John Wesley, *The Works of the Reverend John Wesley*, ed. John Emory, vol. 6 (New York: J. Emory and B. Waugh, 1831), p. 277.

6 David Wright, *How God Makes the World A Better Place: A Wesleyan Primer on Faith, Work, and Economic Transformation* (Grand Rapids, MI: Christian Library Press, 2013), p. 92, and his sources.

7 As quoted in Brian W. Gobbett, 'Inevitable Revolution and Methodism in Early Industrial England: Revisiting the Historiography of the Halevy Thesis', *Fides et Historia* 29, no. 1 (1997), pp. 34–5.

8 Charles Sheldon, *In His Steps: What Would Jesus Do?* (Chicago: Advance Publishing Company, 1897).

9 In Timothy Miller, *Following in His Steps: A Biography of Charles M. Sheldon* (Knoxville: University of Tennessee Press, 1987), pp. 7, 17.

10 Miller, *Following in His Steps*, p. 23.

11 Miller, *Following in His Steps*, pp. 24–5.

12 To say this is only to repeat Lewis himself. To the Cambridge University audience gathered to see him installed as their Professor of Medieval and Renaissance Literature in 1953, he insisted that if he was to have any usefulness to them, it would be as a sort of living dinosaur: a man born out of time whose whole vocation was to revive for this age the 'discarded image' of the old Christian West. The 'old books' reference here is to his preface to his friend Sister Penelope's translation of Athanasius's *On the Incarnation*.

13 C. S. Lewis, *Surprised by Joy: The Shape of My Early Life* (New York: Harcourt, 1955).

14 Lewis, unfinished MS precursor to *Surprised By Joy*, called by Walter Hooper the 'early prose Joy' and quoted in Andrew Lazo here: www.firstthings.com/web-exclusives/2013/08/c-s-lewis-got-it-wrong.

15 C. S. Lewis, *English Literature in the Sixteenth Century, Excluding Drama* (Oxford: Oxford University Press, 1973), p. 4.

16 C. S. Lewis, *The Discarded Image: An Introduction to Medieval and Renaissance Literature* (New York: Cambridge University Press, 1964), p. 204.

17 Lewis, *Discarded Image*, p. 112.

18 Lewis, *Discarded Image*, p. 115.

19 For an extended account of the roots of this belief, see Hans Boersma, *Heavenly Participation: The Sacramental Tapestry* (Grand Rapids, MI: Eerdmans, 2011).

20 C. S. Lewis, 'The Weight of Glory', in *The Weight of Glory* (New York: HarperCollins, 1976), p. 46.

21 In Karl Holl, 'The History of the Word Vocation (*Beruf*)', trans. H. F. Peacock, *Review and Expositor* 55 (April 1958), p. 141.

22 In Paul Marshall, *Callings: Spirituality, Work and Duty in Sixteenth and Seventeenth Century England* (unpublished manuscript, 1993), p. 24.

23 In Marshall, *Callings*, p. 25.

24 In Holl, 'The History of the Word Vocation', p. 142.

25 C. S. Lewis, letter to Mrs Johnson (16 March 1955), in *The Collected Letters of C. S. Lewis*, vol. 3, *Narnia, Cambridge, and Joy*, ed. Walter Hooper (New York: HarperSanFrancisco, 2007), p. 580.

26 C. S. Lewis, letter to the 'American Lady' (26 November 1972), *Letters to an American Lady*, ed. Clyde S. Kilby (Grand Rapids, MI: Eerdmans, 1967), pp. 110–11.

27 C. S. Lewis, in his commentary on *Arthurian Torso, Containing the Posthumous Fragment of the Figure of Arthur*, by Charles Williams (Oxford: Oxford University Press, 1948), p. 116.

28 C. S. Lewis, 'Learning in War-Time', in *The Weight of Glory*, p. 54.

13

The Marketplace as Common Ground
for Serving Others

SAMUEL GREGG

Though often regarded as one of the more prominent critics of the society that began to emerge in the wake of the Industrial Revolution, Karl Marx understood the revolutionary transformation associated with commercial society. What Marx portrayed as the new capitalist order was, to his mind, infinitely preferable to the feudal-mercantile society that preceded the growing dominance of a commercially oriented middle class.

The attraction of Marx's theory is its apparent concurrence with shifts in the dominant modes of economic production that have occurred over time. The difficulty is that this is too simple an explanation. It fails to account not only for observable facts in the history of economic life, but also changes in the way that people have thought about the production and consumption of materials. This includes practical insights such as that of the Scottish Enlightenment philosopher Adam Smith's attention to the manner in which the specialization of labour facilitated greater efficiency in the production of goods, alongside a web of supporting ideas about the nature of human beings, the demands and consequences of human liberty, and the character and purposes of different institutions that have evolved over time.

Consider, for instance, the expression 'free exchange'. This necessarily implies that a commercial society depends upon more than just the exchange of goods and services. It demands a *free* as opposed to a *coerced* exchange. The word *free* indicates in turn that the economic processes that characterize commercial society presuppose a certain understanding of human beings that differs from the view of humankind promoted by, for instance, Marxist and other deterministic visions of human life. Markets and commercial society thus embrace dimensions that go beyond the economistic visions of Marx and his disciples.

One of those dimensions is the insight that market orders, far from being narrowly focused on the autonomous individual, involve a high degree of attention to others beyond oneself, some of whom we may never meet. This chapter focuses on the fact that commerce, trade, and open markets depend heavily upon a willingness to establish lasting and mutually bene-ficial relations between people. While the model of service embodied by markets may not be that of altruism or even the self-giving that is required by Christianity, there are many ways in which market relations promote lasting and healthy relationships between individuals and groups that, in many respects, constitute a form of service, often in unanticipated ways.

Premodern Traditions of Commerce

The Europe pre-dating the great sixteenth-century religious schism is often regarded as dominated by an essentially communal mindset. Cary Nederman has indicated that while medieval Latin Christendom could not be described as collectivist, the phrase 'communitarian' best summarizes the nature of the prevailing social, economic, and political order.[1] The Western European feudal system was based upon a web of mutual obli-gations that different social groups such as the nobility and the peasantry were held to owe each other. While various forms of commerce existed in this period, all these activities and institutions were meshed in what the political theorist Antony Black calls the widespread diffusion of corporat-ist values within rural areas, villages, and towns.[2]

By *corporatist* Black has in mind the prevalence of particular ideas about the social order that flowed in part from Christianity's emphasis upon brotherly love, friendship, and mutual assistance. According to Black, it was the medieval guilds found in every village and town throughout Europe that gave particular form to such notions and spread them through-out society. Terms associated with the life of guilds such as *fraternitas*, *confraternitas*, and *bruderschaft* evoked notions of brotherhood, while phrases such as *communio* and *consortium* spoke of comradeship and fellowship.[3] They also indicated a range of concrete obligations that guild members owed each other. In practical terms, membership of a guild determined who could and could not engage in certain occupations or produce certain goods and services, and thereby effectively constituted what would be regarded today as 'closed shops'.

Corporatist-communalist ideals were seen as ostensibly promoting the well-being of one's neighbour. That makes it all the more significant that these ideas were challenged in the same historical period by the emergence of concepts from within Christian belief that were to help define com-mercial order. Black holds that this 'complex of ideas' was present in Europe at least as early as the thirteenth century. He summarizes them as:

First, personal security in the sense of freedom from the arbitrary pas-sions of others. And freedom from domination in general. This involves freedom (or security) of the person from violence, and of private property from arbitrary seizure. But these ... can only be maintained if legal process is credible and successfully enforced as an alternative to physical violence, in settlement of disagreements, and in redressing wrongs committed by violence. This leads to the notion of legal rights (whether or not so called), both in the sense of the right to sue in court on equal terms with everyone else – legal equality – and in the sense of claims, for example, to property, recognized and upheld by the law.[4]

This attention to *liberty* appears to have flowed primarily from Christianity's distinctive stress upon freedom. Thomas Aquinas emphasized, for instance, that, unlike animals, people could only acquire what they needed through using their 'reason and hands' freely and creatively.[5] At an even deeper level, the Christian accent upon humans being freed from the burden of sin, not to mention its insistence upon the reality of free choice, underlined the idea that human beings were, by God's grace, free. Paul spoke of everyone being called 'to liberty' through Christ.

While there is a way of discussing this in Christian theology that focuses upon humankind's interior liberation from sin, the conviction that all people were called to freedom had profound political, social, and economic implications. Though Christianity affirmed that social groups, law, and the secular authorities had legitimate roles to play in shaping the social order, it avowed that there were limits to what these bodies and even the church could do when it came to influencing people's exercise of their freedom. In the words of the medieval theologian John of Salisbury, though virtue and ultimately communion with God and other people was the proper and natural end of man, people could not achieve this 'without liberty, and the loss of liberty shows that perfect virtue is lacking'.[6]

Having emphasized that human freedom implied limits to the power of secular and religious authorities, it is hardly surprising that one of the great institutional expressions of these limits and a prerequisite for a commercial society – *private property* – also received much attention in the Middle Ages. Following Aristotle, Aquinas outlined three reasons why appropriation of property to particular owners is morally licit and even necessary. First, people tend to take better care of what is theirs than of what is common to everyone, since individuals tend to shirk a responsibility which is nobody's in particular. Second, if everyone were responsible for everything, the result would be confusion. Third, dividing up things generally produces a more peaceful state of affairs, while sharing common things often results in tension. Individual ownership, then – understood as the power to manage and dispose of things – is justified.[7]

This explanation is attentive to what Christianity stresses as the effects of sin upon human beings. Aquinas's argument assumes that it is generally unreasonable to expect fallen human beings to own things in common for long periods of time. Sin, Aquinas implies, limits our capacity to be other-regarding in an altruistic sense. Aquinas appears conscious of the fact that each individual's *self-interest* and its workings cannot be ignored in any reflection upon the social order.

One implication of this attention to the importance of private property was that it suggested that, subject to the demands of law and natural justice, people could *freely exchange with others* what they privately owned. Certain rights concerning the free trade of privately owned goods thus began to receive formal legal recognition in twelfth- and thirteenth-century civil law. By the thirteenth century, the willingness and legal authority to buy and sell different forms of property had become so widespread in England and facilitated such low-transaction costs in the exchange of goods as well as relatively easy capital-formation that the historian Alan Macfarlane has described this society as 'an open, mobile, market-orientated nation'.[8] This was especially true of towns, where those who became residents were generally able to enter into business partnerships, contracts, and exchanges without requiring the local lord's agreement.

With the moral validity of freely buying and selling goods within society becoming a given fact of economic life in towns and cities, it was inevitable that the concept of *contract* became widespread in these societies. The idea of contract was already well established in Roman law and was implicit to the nature of many feudal obligations. With the spread of private ownership and free exchange in medieval Europe, it became more widely understood that fulfilment of promises, as well as legal provision to enforce unreasonable failures to perform promises, was a prerequisite for ensuring that services and goods would be delivered in return for payment.

Last, we should recall that the idea of *civility* was also associated in the minds of some medievals with the growth of trade and commerce. Another of Aquinas's likely disciples, Ptolemy of Lucca, stated that business affairs in cities needed to be conducted with politeness, gentility, and 'a certain civility'.[9] By this was meant that people in urban commercial settings needed and therefore tended to treat each other as formal equals (regardless of social or economic status) under the law and a certain degree of kindness and gentleness, even if their primary contact was through business transactions.

Many of these ideas concerning liberty, exchange, property, contract, and civility were presented by Renaissance Christian humanists as increasingly characteristic of the commercial cities of their time. It was common for Renaissance writers to portray self-made and entrepreneurial individuals who pursued personal gain in a way consistent with Christian morality and the law as among the city's greatest treasures.[10]

Leonardo Bruni of Arezzo (1369–1444), for example, penned essays linking the persistence of commercial liberty with rule of law and civility. 'The magistrates', Bruni wrote, 'are set up for the sake of justice ... lest the power of any person should surpass that of the laws in the city.'[11] He also described the people of Florence as a commercial people who were 'industrious, liberal ... affable, and above all urbane'.[12] Mario Salamanio (1450–1532) advised the readers of his *De Principatu* that just as contractual arrangements were the basis for business partnerships, so too were contracts also 'the means by which the state is arranged and preserved'.[13] He thus employed a legal concept increasingly used to facilitate ease and predictability in commercial life to define the character of the state and implicitly the limits of its powers. A contemporary of Salamanio, the Italian humanist Brandolinus (1440–97), emphasized that the prevalence of liberty and rule of law in many Italian city states was central to the emergence of a spirit of free enterprise and the encouragement of commercial interactions across Europe:

> Our citizens enter into commerce and partnerships freely with all nations, open up the whole world for their own gain, and come to the aid of all men with their industry [*industria*] and skills [*artibus*]; and all nations from everywhere flow together into our cities as into markets common to all peoples [*communia gentium emporia*].[14]

Markets and a New World

The emerging world of Christian humanism eventually was shattered by the religious wars that shook Western Europe. The commercial ways that encouraged positive interactions between people, however, persisted.

Mercantilism did become the dominant mode of economic life as absolutist governments began to establish a grip over much of Protestant and Catholic Europe. But it is also true that previously unimaginable commercial possibilities emerged. Smith once described the discovery of the Americas and of a passage to the East Indies via the Cape of Good Hope as two of the most important events recorded in human history. In terms of their significance for the expansion of commerce throughout the world, Smith did not exaggerate. The gradual conquest and settlement of the New World by Spanish adventurers, not to mention the Dutch and Portuguese expansion into Africa and South East Asia, transformed Western Europe's economic life, especially in the Netherlands, Italy, and the Iberian Peninsula. International trade expanded at an unprecedented rate.[15]

Many early modern Christian thinkers generally regarded commercial activity as morally indifferent.[16] Others, however, ascribed positive moral characteristics to trade and commerce. The economic historian Henry Robertson records that the Jesuits Francisco Suarez and Luis de Molina were unashamed promoters of the social benefits of enterprise and the expansion of trade.[17] Another late Scholastic, Domingo de Soto, even portrayed commercial activity as evidence of civilizational development:

> Mankind progresses from imperfection to perfection. For this reason, in the beginning barter was sufficient as man was rude and ignorant and had few necessities. But afterward, with the development of a more educated, civilized and distinguished life, the need to create new forms of trade arose. Among them the most respectable is commerce, despite the fact that human avarice can pervert anything.[18]

In other late Scholastic texts, one finds awareness that there was something new and energetic about this expansion of commerce. Bartolomé de Albornóz described commercial activity as 'the nerve of human life that sustains the universe. By means of buying and selling the world is united, joining distant lands and nations, people of different language, laws and ways of life. If it were not for these contracts, some would lack the goods that others have in abundance and they would not be able to share the goods that they have in excess with those countries where they are scarce.'[19] Likewise in Mercado's manual, we encounter a sense of wonder concerning the commercial life of Seville, where a 'banker traffics with a whole world and embraces more than the Atlantic, though sometimes he loses his grip and it all comes tumbling down'.[20]

In other parts of Europe, important intellectual developments were occurring that would further stimulate the emergence of commercial society. This is especially true of the seventeenth-century English philosopher John Locke. Articulating many of the ideas outlined above, Locke integrated them with the concept that a person's work could be viewed as something that could be bought and sold; he even went so far as to describe a person's labour as their property.[21] This made it possible to speak of a labour market in which people could *freely* sell their labour to others or purchase the labour of others in the form of wages. An important effect of these ideas was their provision of a stronger moral and legal basis for labour to escape the confines and regulations of the guilds and other labour-restricting organizations, thus facilitating a freer market in labour, a high degree of occupational mobility, and a greater capacity to choose how we serve others.[22]

Another idea much associated with Locke that proved vital for commercial society was that of *tolerance*. While Locke had much to say on subjects such as private property, his most significant contribution to commercial society may have been his anonymously published *Letter Concerning*

Toleration (1689). Like others of his time, Locke evoked the death and destruction that had flowed from the intolerance showed by Protestants and Catholics alike during Western Europe's religious wars. For Locke, one way of resolving this issue was through what he called 'toleration'. This embraced many facets, but at the heart of Locke's argument was the notion that the state should refrain from interfering in the religious beliefs of its subjects, save when these religious beliefs lead to behaviours or attitudes that run counter to the security of the state and the legitimate demands of public order.

On one level, Locke's understanding of toleration could be viewed as a logical extension of the civility that medieval and Renaissance writers associated with commercial activity. Being polite to others with whom one disagrees about, for instance, religious questions is surely implicit in the idea of civility. In practical terms, the gradual acceptance of tolerance allowed people to travel for trading purposes without fearing that those with whom they exchanged goods and services would denounce them to the public authorities for the particulars of their faith or politics. The Britain of Locke's time was, of course, a far from religiously tolerant country. Nonetheless, the demands of commerce appear to have contributed over time to the spread of a de facto toleration of religious differences throughout England. Voltaire commented upon this when visiting London in the middle of the eighteenth century. Though he stressed the established Church of England's political dominance, Voltaire remarked in his *Philosophical Letters* upon the tolerance encouraged by commerce:

> Go into the Exchange in London, that place more venerable than many a court, and you will see representatives of all the nations assembled there for the profit of mankind. There the Jew, the Mahometan, and the Christian deal with one another as if they were of the same religion, and reserve the name of infidel for those who go bankrupt.[23]

Markets, Service, and Otherness

This background helps to explain how it was that a good number of thinkers were, by the eighteenth century, regarding markets as a place that allowed people to benefit themselves and others, albeit often indirectly.

Echoing the Anglo-Dutch philosopher Bernard Mandeville, Adam Smith famously wrote, 'It is not from the benevolence of the butcher, the brewer, or the baker, that we expect our dinner, but from regard to their own interest.'[24] But while Smith affirmed Mandeville's view that the pursuit of self-interest facilitated greater independence of action as people pursued their interests in increasingly creative ways, he parted with Mandeville's radical individualism by noting that it also meant that people were increasingly *interdependent* upon each other. In Smith's vision of commercial society, no man could be an island – the liberty to pursue one's self-interest created reciprocity as people engaged in mutually beneficial exchange: something that was enhanced by the increasing specialization of labour which drove commercial society.

But it was not simply that Smith believed that commercial society was materially superior to its predecessors. He and other Scottish Enlightenment thinkers – the majority of whom were believing Christians (and some even ministers of the Church of Scotland) – affirmed that the expansion of trade and the increase and spread of wealth provided increasing numbers of people with more resources and time to deepen their knowledge of the finer things of life and the study of more abstract subjects. At a more general level, they observed that as more and more people acquired substantial property and business interests, they had a greater interest in the prevalence of rule of law.

Then there was the way commerce changed the manner in which people thought about each other. In a point reminiscent of Voltaire, Scottish thinkers stressed that, while the significance of a person's social status, religion, or nationality could never be obliterated, commerce encouraged more people to see others in a new light – as consumers, producers, owners, customers, and clients – and pay less attention to their differences. Commercial society thus encouraged people to see themselves as individuals who cooperate with each other voluntarily rather than as members of groups who adhere to caste or tribal patterns of social interaction.

Here Adam Smith's reference to the 'invisible hand' perplexes some. But it is simply a metaphor for the idea that through allowing people to pursue their self-interest, unintended but beneficial social consequences for others will follow. As individuals pursue profit, they unintentionally add to the sum total of the wealth in society, unintentionally allow people from different nations to come to know each other, unintentionally promote civility and peace, unintentionally allow others to benefit from more and better jobs, and unintentionally contribute to technological development.[25] Moreover, it is precisely because increasingly large numbers of people in commercial society are able to accumulate sums of capital that exceed their immediate needs and acquired responsibilities that they begin to develop opportunities to be generous to others.

Despite this, the pursuit of self-interest by individuals and groups alike remains perhaps the most controversial moral-cultural feature of commercial societies. When twentieth-century economic historians such as R. H. Tawney portrayed the age of commerce as the age of acquisitiveness, they associated the pursuit of self-interest with the indulgence of greed, the effective endorsement of depravity, and a type of ruthlessness when it comes to achieving the ends chosen by individuals. Such observations rarely account for the fact that the 'self' is capable of being other-regarding and even critical of his own behaviour. Nor do they acknowledge that every self is enveloped in a web of relationships, ranging from the contractual to the familial and communal, all of which moderate and check our acquisitive instincts. It is even possible to speak of a reasonable self-love. When Aquinas underlined the imperative of people pursuing virtue, he did so because he regarded this as a natural result of people engaging in a reasonable form of self-regard. This is, for Aquinas, a reasonable love of self.[26]

Creativity and Trust

This is connected to something else about market economic orders that underscores the ways in which commercial society encourages us to be attentive to others: entrepreneurship. Private initiative rarely occurs unless considerable incentives exist to encourage people to exercise it. At the same time, this creativity is not limited to one choice or one action on the part of one individual. It invariably involves building upon the creative choices and insights of people living now and those long dead. This collaborative creativity can occur informally or in a more structured environment such as a business. The creativity that flourishes in commercial society is thus rarely that of an isolated individual. It is invariably social in character.

But while a society may embody great resources of creativity, commercial development is equally dependent upon a more commonplace moral quality with a highly social character. For all its reputation for rugged individualism, free markets are very reliant upon the element of trust. In commercial terms, 'trust' refers to an aspect of a relationship between two or more parties in which a given situation is mutually understood and commitments are made towards different actions designed to produce one or more desired outcomes. The trust required in free markets extends to faith in people as well as a confidence that certain rules will always, save in exceptional circumstances, be followed and that certain institutions such as courts will follow consistent patterns of behaviour.

In pre-commercial societies, trust was not unknown. Nevertheless, it tended to remain relatively weak outside families and to be grounded in expectations attached to different social roles. In feudal society, there was a strong sense that clergy, nobles, and commoners would fulfil various responsibilities ascribed to them by customary and feudal law. While this qualified as a form of trust, it was more limited in scope and application than the type of trust essential for commercial society. Loyalty and trust in pre-market orders might well be expanded to a broad concept of family of the type that existed in the Scottish Highland clans or even some of the banking houses of Renaissance Italy. Outside these confines, deep suspicion of the stranger is often the rule.

The emergence of commercial society requires an extremely widespread diffusion of the willingness to trust others, even total strangers, and to make and keep promises. The legal philosopher Roscoe Pound did not exaggerate when he wrote, 'Wealth, in a commercial age, is made up largely of promises.'[27]

Trust is essential to a medium as characteristic of commercial society as the forming and fulfilment of contracts. While legal guarantees secure some protection against unreasonable failure to fulfil the contract, the contract itself is unlikely to come about unless there is a minimum of trust. When people make a contract, they are engaging in a commercial convention and a recognized legal practice. Such an activity presupposes a basic exercise in promise-making in which we make a reasoned choice to commit ourselves to perform certain actions while relying on others to bind themselves to doing particular things. Contracts are in fact null and void without such prior commitments. They therefore enlist our willingness to trust others and to merit their trust.[28]

If commercial society required that all agreements receive formal contractual endorsement, its ability to prosper would be limited. By necessity, trust in market orders extends far beyond what is formally endorsed by commercial law. Most economic exchanges do in fact involve making promises which carry only minimal and sometimes no legal weight. Most things are bought and sold in commercial society without extensive checks that the goods and services being exchanged are in fact what the buyers and sellers believe them to be. There is a prevailing expectation that, in most situations and most of the time, people will do what they said they would do and there will generally be little need to have recourse to legal remedies.

Once Again, Civility

The giving and receiving of trust assumes a certain willingness to treat others in particular ways until they prove that they are unworthy of such trust. It thus involves behaving towards others in a certain manner – not necessarily in the way that people interact with close friends, but certainly in a manner best described as *civil*.

While figures such as Adam Smith and his friend the Presbyterian minister and Moderator of the Church of Scotland, William Robertson, drew upon the Aristotelian and Christian attention to the importance of a virtuous citizenry in describing the content of commercial society, they emphasized that the type of virtues developed often depended upon the culture in which people lived. 'In general,' Smith wrote, 'the style of manners which takes place in any nation, may commonly be said to be that which is most suitable to its situation.'[29]

In market orders, civility is no longer associated with an inherited social caste. It effectively moves away from a small group and embraces increasing numbers of people as levels of wealth rise across society. In commercial society, many people have for the first time the possibility of having sufficient means to be generous, to learn to defer immediate gratification, to follow lives marked by graciousness, and to abstain from rude or coarse behaviour. It is precisely, as Smith remarked, because every person 'becomes in some measure a merchant'[30] in commercial society that commerce leads increasing numbers of people to acquire habits of order and economy. In his lectures on jurisprudence, Smith commented that 'When the greater part of people are merchants, they always bring probity and punctuality into fashion, and these therefore are the principal virtues of a commercial nation.'[31] People experience a sense of what Tocqueville called 'real sympathy'[32] with others in commercial society precisely because the set social roles of pre-commercial society have broken down. They may not be ready to sacrifice themselves quickly for each other, but people are careful with each other. 'It makes no difference', Tocqueville wrote, 'if strangers or enemies are in question.'[33]

Moreover, having attained a certain degree of wealth, many people in commercial society find themselves able to spend time and energy on activities ranging from patronage of the arts, philanthropy, and the pursuit of hobbies previously perceived as the preserve of aristocracy. The irony is that civility in commercial society often begins as a means to the end of material prosperity. But this prosperity allows more people than ever before to engage in activities that, while often bringing them little or no personal monetary gain, are regarded as reflective of man's higher aspirations to truth, goodness, and beauty: the truly civilized man.

Part of the vision of civility in commercial society involves people refraining from using violence to achieve their ends. In the pre-commercial world, war was perceived on the part of figures ranging from Alexander the Great to Napoleon as the path to greatness and glory. By contrast, commercial society thrives upon and inculcates the value of peace. Though commercial societies have engaged in war, they do tend to accord higher worth to peace than did their predecessors. War is generally disruptive to free trade, the forging of commercial links, and society's overall material well-being.

Considerable incentives thus exist for commercial societies to avoid war. 'Peace is the natural effect of trade', Montesquieu writes. 'Two nations who traffic with each other become reciprocally dependent; for if one has an interest in buying, the other has an interest in selling; and thus their union is founded on their mutual necessities.'[34] Tocqueville underscored the manner in which commerce undermined incentives for war when observing:

> The ever-increasing number of men of property devoted to peace, the growth of personal property that war so rapidly devours, mildness of mores, gentleness of heart, that inclination to pity which equality inspires, that cold and calculating spirit which leaves little room for sensitivity to the poetic and violent emotions of wartime – all these causes act together to damp down warlike fervour.[35]

Commercial society's aversion to the use of force is not confined to the sphere of war and foreign relations. It also applies to relations between people within a commercial society and the desire to minimize conflict within this society. As Smith explained, it was not a coincidence that as commercial relations developed between towns and rural areas, 'order and good government, and with them, the liberty and security of individuals became more pronounced among the inhabitants of the country, who had before lived almost in a continual state of war with their neighbours, and of servile dependency upon their superiors. This, though it has been the least observed, is by far the most important of all their effects.'[36]

The emergence of free markets also creates particular incentives for the value that many began – albeit slowly and not without significant regressions – to attach to something we have already mentioned: tolerance. Commercial society's emergence and continued growth is very dependent upon a high degree of openness to new ideas and endeavours. A society that closes itself to concepts and investment from people whose political and religious beliefs differ from the dominant culture places itself at a potential economic disadvantage from those communities open to such people. Moreover, many of the tools, institutions, and mechanisms of commercial society depend upon people distancing themselves from assuming hostile positions towards people with differing views.

As modern commercial societies began to assume their present form during the seventeenth and eighteenth centuries, wealth became far more mobile, as did banking and trading practices. Businesses became less family-oriented and thus far less uniform in their linguistic, ethnic, and religious composition. Even the language of commercial society – capital, profit, loss, property, markets – though rooted in the Western tradition, has shown a remarkable capacity to transcend cultural and religious boundaries. The mediums of credit and money were able to communicate, as A. J. Conyers points out, certain human needs, wants, and desires across the very same boundaries. With the growth of joint-stock companies, there were increasing numbers of people who had financial interests in enterprises and organizations that engaged in commerce across a variety of areas with different cultural, political, and religious traditions. In short, the spread of markets brought people from notably different backgrounds into contact with one another through their mutual pursuit of wealth. With good reason, therefore, Montesquieu declared:

> Commerce is a cure for the most destructive prejudices; for it is almost a general rule, that wherever we find agreeable manners, there commerce flourishes; and that wherever there is commerce, there we meet with agreeable manners. Let us not be astonished, then, if our manners are now less savage than formerly. Commerce has everywhere diffused a knowledge of the manners of all nations: these are compared one with another, and from this comparison arise the greatest advantages.[37]

The desire for free trade necessitates links across regions, oceans, and national boundaries. Through engaging in trade, people are forced to encounter the traditions and habits of others, a process that often leads to people comparing and learning more about their respective customs and practices. As Tocqueville stated:

> Trade is the natural enemy of all violent passions. Trade loves moderation, delights in compromise, and is most careful to avoid anger. It is patient, supple, and insinuating, only resorting to extreme means in cases of absolute necessity. Trade makes men independent of one another ... it leads them to want to manage their own affairs and teaches them how to succeed therein. Hence it makes them inclined to liberty but disinclined to revolution.[38]

Conclusion

Neither peace, tolerance, nor civility is sufficient for commercial society, let alone a world characterized by deep Christian commitments. Nevertheless, taken together and integrated with trust, creativity, and self-interest rightly understood, they do promote other-regarding relations. Moreover, they need not exclude other, more communal habits of choice and interaction. Altruism is not something foreign to commercial order. Free markets have helped create the material basis for altruism to occur on a scale unprecedented in history. But this should not blind us to the many ways in which market orders rely upon and encourage other-regarding qualities such as trust and civility. To be sure, these are not enough for a community or even entire societies if they want to embody the commitments required by Christian belief and practice. But nor should we underestimate just how much market economies take people in many instances beyond the confines of radical individualism and help them develop a genuine knowledge and concern for others.

Notes

1 See C. Nederman, 'Freedom, Community and Function: Communitarian Lessons of Medieval Political Theory', *American Political Science Review* 86 (1992), pp. 977–86.

2 See Antony Black, *Guild and State: European Political Thought from the Twelfth Century to the Present* (London: Transaction Publishers, 2003), p. xvii.

3 This paragraph draws upon Black, *Guild and State*, pp. 13–19.

4 Black, *Guild and State*, p. 32. See also C. W. Bynum, 'Did the Twelfth Century Discover the Individual?' *Journal of Ecclesiastical History* 31 (1980), pp. 1–17.

5 Thomas Aquinas, *Summa Theologiae*, ed. T. Gilby (London: Blackfriars, 1963), I-II, q.95, a.1. Hereafter ST.

6 John of Salisbury, *Policraticus*, vol. 2, ed. C. Webb (Oxford: Typographeo Clarendoniano, 1909), p. 217.

7 See ST, II-II, q.66, a.2. Aquinas states that the *use* of things is a different matter. In regard to use, one is not justified in holding things as exclusively one's own (*ut proprias*) but should rather hold them as common, in the sense that one must be ready to share them with others in need. For Aquinas, private property is the normative way of realizing this principle of common use, but it is not absolute.

8 See A. Macfarlane, *The Origins of English Individualism: The Family, Property and Social Transition* (Oxford: Oxford University Press, 1978), p. 163. See also John F. McGovern, 'The Rise of New Economic Attitudes – Economic Humanism, Economic Nationalism – During the Later Middle Ages and the Renaissance, A.D. 1200–1500', *Traditio* 26 (1970), pp. 217–54.

9 Ptolemy of Lucca in *De Regimine Principum*, bks II–IV, in Thomas Aquinas, *Opuscula Omnia Necnon Opera Minora*, vol. 1, *Opuscula Philosophica*, ed. J. Perrier (Paris: Cerf, 1949), bk II, ch. 8. *De Regimine Principum* is a continuation of an earlier unfinished work (probably by Aquinas) to which Ptolemy began adding approximately half way through Book II. Books III and IV are entirely by Ptolemy.

10 See Quentin Skinner, *The Foundations of Modern Political Thought*, vol. 1 (Cambridge: Cambridge University Press, 1978), p. 74.

11 Leonardo Bruni, *Laudatio Florentinae Urbis [Eulogy to the City of Florence]*, ed. H. Baron, *From Petrarch to Leonardo Bruni* (Chicago: University of Chicago Press, 1968), p. 259.

12 Bruni, *Laudatio*, p. 263.

13 Mario Salamonio, *De Principatu*, ed. M d'Addio, *Pubblicazioni dell'istituto de diritto pubblico dell'Universita di Roma*, vol. 4 (Milan: Giuffrè, 1955), p. 28.

14 Aurelius Brandolinus, *De Comparatione Reipublicae et Regni ad Laurentium Medicem Libri Tres*, in *Irodalomtörteneti Enlekek*, vol. 2, *Plaszorszagi XV Szazadbeli Iroknak*, ed. A. Jenö (Budapest, 1890), pp. 123–4.

15 See *Economic Thought in Spain: Selected Essays of Marjorie Grice-Hutchinson*, ed. Laurence S. Moss and Christopher Ryan, trans. Christopher K. Ryan and Marjorie Grice-Hutchinson (Aldershot: E. Elgar, 1993).

16 See Alejandro Chafuen, *Faith and Liberty: The Economic Thought of the Late Scholastics* (Lanham, MI: Lexington Books, 2003).

17 See Henry Robertson, *Aspects of the Rise of Economic Individualism: A Criticism of Max Weber and His School* (Clifton: A.M. Kelly, 1973).

18 Domingo de Soto, *De Iustitia de Iure* (Madrid: IEP, 1968), VI, q.II, a.2.

19 Bartolomé de Albornóz, *Arte de los Contratos* (Valencia, 1573), VII, 29.

20 Tomas de Mercado, *Summa de tratos y contractos*, ed. R. Sierra Bravo (Madrid: IEP, 1975), p. 10.

21 See John Locke, *Two Treatises of Government*, ed. P. Laslett (Cambridge: Cambridge University Press, 1967), pp. 305–7.

22 See Black, *Guild and State*, p. 155.

23 Voltaire, 'On the Presbyterians', *Philosophical Letters*, trans. Ernest Dilworth (New York: Macmillan Publishing Company, 1961), letter six.

24 See Adam Smith, *Glasgow Edition of Works and Correspondence of Adam Smith*, vol. 2, *An Inquiry into the Nature and Causes of the Wealth of Nations*, ed. R. H. Campbell and A. S. Skinner, revised edition (Oxford: Oxford University Press, 1979), I.ii.2.

25 Many theologians associated with the Jansenist movement in seventeenth- and eighteenth-century Catholicism spoke about a type of self-interest being integral to many acts of charity. The theologian Jean Domat insisted, for example, that: 'The fall of man not having freed him from wants, and having on the contrary multiplied them, it has also augmented the necessity of labour and commerce, and of ties; for no man being sufficient of himself to procure the necessities and conveniences of life, the diversity of wants engages man in an infinite number of ties, without which they could not live. This state of mankind induces those who are governed only by a principle of self-love, to subject themselves to labour, to commerce, and to ties which their wants render necessary. And that they may reap advantage from them, and persevere in them both their honour and the interest, they observe in all those intercourses, integrity, fidelity, sincerity ... We see, then, in self-love, that this principle of all the evils is, in the present state of society, a cause from whence it derives an infinite number of good effects ... And thus we may consider this venom of society as a remedy which God makes use of for supporting it ...' Jean Domat, *Lois Civil dans leur ordre naturel, le droit public, et legum delectus*, Nouvelle édition (Paris, 1713), p. xx.

26 See ST, II-II, q.44, a.8, ad.2, q.26, a.5. As John Finnis notes, if a person is truly a friend to himself, then he should want a superabundance of the goods of reason and virtue for himself. Moreover, Finnis adds, given that the goods of reason and virtue are goods for any human being, and that they include friendship and every form of harmony between persons, then this reasonable self-love helps to facilitate the realization of moral goods common to all. See John Finnis, *Aquinas: Moral, Political, and Legal Theory* (Oxford: Oxford University Press, 1998), p. 113.

27 Roscoe Pound, *An Introduction to the Philosophy of Law* (New Haven, CT: Yale University Press, 1954), p. 236.

28 For a more detailed treatment of this subject, see Samuel Gregg, *On Ordered Liberty: A Treatise on the Free Society* (Lanham, MD: Lexington Books, 2003), p. 101.

29 Adam Smith, *Glasgow Edition of Works and Correspondence of Adam Smith*, vol. 1, *A Theory of Moral Sentiments*, ed. A. L. Macfie and D. D. Raphael, revised edition (Oxford: Oxford University Press, 1979), V.2.13.

30 Smith, *Wealth of Nations*, I.iv.1.

31 Smith, Adam Smith, *Glasgow Edition of Works and Correspondence of Adam Smith*, vol. 5, *Lectures on Jurisprudence*, ed. Ronald L. Meek, D. D. Raphael, and Peter Stein, *Glasgow Edition of Works and Correspondence of Adam Smith* (Oxford: Oxford University Press, 1978), (B), 539.

32 See Alexis de Tocqueville, *Democracy in America*, vol. 2, ed. J. P. Mayer, trans. G. Lawrence (London: Fontana, 1994), p. 562.

33 Tocqueville, *Democracy*, vol. 2, p. 564.

34 Guy de Montesquieu, *The Spirit of Laws*, ed. David Wallace Carrithers (Berkeley: University of California Press, 1977), bk 20, ch. 2.

35 Tocqueville, *Democracy*, vol. 2, p. 646.

36 Smith, *Wealth of Nations*, III.iv.4.

37 Montesquieu, *Spirit*, bk 20, ch. 1.

38 Tocqueville, *Democracy*, vol. 2, p. 637.

14

Poverty, Justice, and Work

MICHAEL MATHESON MILLER

To write about the relationship between poverty and work can be precarious: first, for fear of being associated with those who believe poverty is simply a result of laziness, or second (and perhaps worse) for fear of being associated with the callous man faced with a poor person in need who responds with a sneering, 'Get a job.' While there are cases of poverty resulting from laziness, lack of virtue, or simply because of bad luck or tragedy, this is not the primary issue for the majority of poor people throughout the world – people who often work much harder and longer hours than many wealthy people (especially those of us who think and write about poverty).

To avoid any association with equating poverty with laziness or lack of virtue, we can go so far as to avoid talking about work altogether. This would be unfortunate because a rich, biblical understanding of work can have profound effects on how we think about poverty, specifically the issue of inclusion for the poor in institutions of justice which enable people to participate in networks of productivity and rise out of poverty.

In this chapter I argue that a biblical vision of work, which sees labour as positive and essential for human flourishing, orients our thinking about poverty towards creating the conditions for justice and inclusion for the poor in a way that the dominant model of humanitarianism does not. When we consider poverty through the lens of a biblical vision of work, poverty is no longer seen primarily as a problem to be solved from the outside through large-scale plans or social engineering, but more an issue of creating the conditions for people to work and develop and exercise their capabilities. A biblical understanding of work places the human person at the centre of the economy. Rather than being a problem to solve, the poor person is recognized as the protagonist of economic activity and ultimately the solution to poverty.

The first section provides an overview of the Jewish and Christian understanding of human work. As this has been addressed in more detail in previous chapters, I only touch a couple of aspects. The second section briefly outlines some of the philosophical problems which underlie the current model of humanitarianism, as well as how by treating poor people as objects, humanitarianism tends to undermine the dignity of work and overlook the foundational issues of justice and inclusion. The third and final section connects a biblical understanding of work and the idea of human flourishing with the foundational institutions of justice and economic inclusion. This involves access to justice in the courts, the importance of clear title to land, and the ability to engage in exchange and trade without undue burden. Here, the Jewish and Christian traditions have much to offer, and I will offer a few examples for further reflection.

A Biblical Vision of Human Work

Work is Good

A common misconception about the Christian understanding of work is that work is a punishment for sin – something required in this fallen world, but not integral to our original nature. This is not surprising when we think of God's declaration to Adam about the 'sweat of your brow' and the lived experience of work (even when we find it rewarding) as painful, tiring, and sometimes pure drudgery. Yet when we consider the larger picture, we see human work portrayed in Genesis as good and indeed as a reflection of the *imago Dei*. Most important, God's mandate to work comes *before* the fall. Rather than being a punishment, Genesis depicts work as a central part of Adam's vocation. God places Adam in the garden and tells him to be fruitful and multiply, to guard and till, and to subdue the earth and fill it (Gen. 1.22; 2.15).

Some readings of Genesis present Adam and Eve pre-fall as a type of Rousseauian 'noble savage' neither fully reasonable nor consciously aware of themselves.[1] Yet this reading is problematic on several levels and does not do justice to the full rationality of Adam in the garden. First, and most obvious, God gives Adam instructions to work and a command not to eat the fruit of the specific tree. He also implicitly gives Adam the responsibility to teach Eve this commandment. All of these actions – guard, till, be fruitful and multiply, teach, and obey – imply reason and freedom in full consciousness and are a manifestation of human nature as reasonable and free. A non-rational, or even partially rational, semi-conscious being would be unable to follow these directions,[2] much less convey them to the woman. Most important, neither would be culpable for great sin when they disobeyed.

Right from the beginning, then, Adam is not a type of 'noble savage' who does not fully become himself until he sins, but rather a fully human person endowed with reason, freedom, and moral agency. This is important in considering work because reason and freedom are necessary conditions for the capacity to engage in human work (with its interior dimension) and to be creative and apply one's intellect to physical matter to transform the world and participate with God in perfecting and completing his work of creation.[3]

Work and Human Nature

When we think about human nature, we tend to focus on reason, freedom, and our eternal destiny. But work also is an important element of how we live and flourish as persons. While we often recognize our creativity and ability to produce gratuitous works of art and music as a reflection of God's image, normal labour can be seen as secondary and instrumental, and almost an obstacle to our freedom, pleasure, and the highest human experiences of worship, love, and leisure in its fullest meaning.[4] There is something to this: we are not, after all, made for labour alone, but ultimately for rest in the Lord. A central theme of the Bible from Genesis and Exodus to the Psalms and the letter to the Hebrews stresses the importance of the Sabbath and how we are called into rest with God. It is rest that in fact makes us (and our work for that matter) more fully human.[5] Without a Sabbath, without authentic rest, every day is the same and we live, as it were, an almost animalist existence.

The Sabbath rest, when we can worship and engage in authentic leisure, not only orients us to worship but also dignifies us. Work is not our highest purpose: we are not made for the sixth day, but for the seventh. To idolize work or view us as merely workers dehumanizes us and reduces us to cogs in a machine.[6] Any economic system that does not recognize the importance of rest and set aside a time for worship is failing in justice. Yet so is an economic system that does not create the conditions wherein persons can exercise their talents and skills, develop and build businesses, and provide for their families. Work is not the end of man, yet at the same time it is through work that men and women can live out their vocations and provide service to others.

The idea of work as secondary also rings true because the human person gains neither his or her dignity nor their right to exist based upon whether they can exercise their capacity to work well or not. This same concept also applies to reason and freedom. A child who does not yet have the full use of reason, or an elderly or sick person who has lost the capacity to exercise her reason, still has dignity and a right to life. In the same manner, an elderly person who is no longer productive or a disabled person who cannot work does not have any less dignity or inherent value than a highly productive person. Nevertheless, we see that while work and productivity do not define a person or give them value, the Genesis narrative makes clear that our ability to work is somehow a vital part of who we are, how we develop, and how we reflect God's creativity.

Another reason one could view work as a secondary element of our nature is because one could argue that work is merely a manifestation of reason. It is reason which distinguishes us from the lower animals, who also labour in their own way. It is true that we could not engage in specifically human work without our capacity to reason and our self-awareness as personal subjects, yet this could be applied to all our human abilities including love and worship, and we would be reticent to say that these things are *merely* derivative and extrinsic to our experience as persons.

So while work is not the source of our dignity and while reason and freedom are indeed essential characteristics of our personhood and our reflection of the *imago Dei*, it is telling that in the creation narrative our reason is made manifest not by God telling us 'to be reasonable' but in man's ability to guard and till the garden, to fill the earth and subdue it, that is, to create, invent, and apply our intellect to transforming matter. We 'learn' about and experience our rationality through our capacity to work, just as we first learn about and experience God through his creation of the world.

External and Interior Dimensions of Human Work

Another aspect of human labour that is important for a proper understanding of the relationship between work and human flourishing, and why work must be a central element in our thinking about poverty and economic development, is the interior dimension of work.

Human labour is not only valuable for what it accomplishes – that is, for its utility, creation of goods and services, and contribution to economic growth. There is more than instrumental value at play. Human labour is also valuable for its impact on the subject who works. In his philosophical works before becoming Pope John Paul II, Karol Wojtyła explains these two dimensions of work as the 'transitive', that is, what work accomplishes on the outside (external), and the 'intransitive', that is, what happens to the worker as person on the inside (interior). While we understandably focus on the external nature of work, it is in the interior dimension where the deepest meaning of work is to be found. Work helps us develop as persons, helps build virtues, helps us live out our vocation as creative and social beings, and through this interiority work – if properly ordered – can convey spiritual benefit to ourselves and through our work we can participate in God's work of sanctifying the world.

This is not to say that work has no utility or benefit, nor is it to suggest that a job providing no benefit to others is equally valuable to one that does. The man who sews up a basket in the morning and takes it apart in the afternoon simply so that he can say he worked is not providing equal value to a woman who cleans a room, tends a garden, builds a home, or invents a medicine. The external and the interior are deeply connected, yet it is the interior (intransitive) impact of work and the attitude towards it that have a more profound impact on our souls. Does our work create resentment or anger, do we turn it into an idol, a source of domination over others, or do we see it as an opportunity for cooperation with others and God?[7]

Ultimately the external dimensions of our work will fade away: the buildings we build will crumble, the products we sell will be thrown away and disintegrate, the things we write will be forgotten, the dishes we clean will be dirtied again. Ecclesiastes puts it starkly: 'Vanity of vanities, all is vanity. What does man gain by all the toil at which he toils under the sun?' (Eccl. 1.1–2).

What remains as it were is the interior dimension of work, which can have profound spiritual significance on our immortal souls. Even the most seemingly insignificant jobs or suffering that comes from the drudgery of work, when offered to God can effect our sanctification. Biblical scholar Gary Anderson, in his book *Adam and Eve in the Jewish and Christian Imagination*, writes that Adam 'was reduced to an animal by virtue of his transgression. But in taking on this new condition as a means of penance rather than just enduring it solely as a punishment, Adam was on the road to deification.'[8] Early Christian monks in Syria also saw their work as imitating Adam and saw work as a penance and a medicine for their souls in reparation for sin. 'Where moderns see signs of pathological self-denial, ancient Christians saw the tokens of a life lived after the pattern of Christ (*imitatio Christi*).'[9]

Thus, work plays an important role in human flourishing, and everyone – rich and poor alike – is called to participate in it. A humanitarianism wishing to provide goods to the poor without factoring in the interior subjective dimension of work can easily descend into seeing poor people as simply problems to be solved instead of protagonists called to participate in society and their own story of development.

Work and Human Flourishing

In summary, the biblical understanding of work is a positive one. Work is not something to be avoided or idolized, but something to be done properly in accord with reason and truth. Just as we are called to exercise our reason and freedom for the good and beauty and not to abuse it for evil, so too is work to be done well – neither used for an evil, abused by the workaholic or the exploiter, for whom productivity and wealth are the highest end, nor avoided in a manner that instils laziness and disorder.

Each of these is an obstacle to human flourishing. When it comes to laziness, let us here not first think of the poor, but of the idle rich who are often spiritually worse off than the poor and whose disengagement from work becomes an occasion for all kinds of mischief and evil.

In contrast to many pagan understandings (and some aristocrats and intellectuals in Christian Europe) that view servile work as something for slaves or the lower classes, a Jewish and Christian view sees all work, including work with one's hands as well as study, as dignified. The Talmud speaks of both intellectual work and agricultural and other manual labour as worthwhile and beneficial for human beings.[10] This view influenced the rule of St Benedict, the father of Western monasticism, and his focus on 'ora et labora', a combination of prayer, study, and manual labour that had tremendous influence on instilling a positive view of labour, as well as the development of modern accounting and management practices that played a key role in the economic growth of the West.[11]

Understanding work as a fundamental good for the person and indeed essential to human flourishing allows us to avoid both the faults of humanitarianism, which focuses on the short term at the expense of work and flourishing, and the crude materialism of crony capitalism or socialist industrialism that reduces people to cogs in a machine who exist simply for the good of the state or GDP. Instead, viewing the person as a subject, created in the *imago Dei* with creative capacity, and recognizing work as integral to human flourishing changes the way we think about poverty, charity, and economic development. It shifts our focus from what *we can do* to the more pressing question of *what do poor people need in order to create prosperity in their own families and communities*? This raises foundational questions about access to the institutions of justice and the problems of exclusion and inclusion for the poor. Here too the Scriptures and Jewish and Christian traditions have much to offer, but before addressing these issues in the third section, we need to consider how humanitarianism undermines the biblical vision of work.

How Humanitarianism Undermines the Role of Work

Before moving into the institutions of justice I think it is important to briefly address some of the underlying elements of the dominant model of humanitarianism and poverty alleviation that permeate large domestic and multinational aid agencies, charities, and NGOs. One can get a general sense of this dominant model by looking at the mission statements of most large agencies and the United Nations Millennium Development and Sustainable Development Goals.[12] What I want to focus on here, however, are not the various policies but the underlying philosophical assumptions of this dominant viewpoint.

While humanitarianism has many facets, the underlying assumptions of the dominant model of how society thinks of poverty have four primary characteristics, all of which lead us to miss the important role of work in human flourishing and poverty alleviation:

Social Engineering

The first problem is one of technocratic social engineering. This is not unique to poverty, as it influences everything from city planning to education. A social engineering approach to poverty views poverty fundamentally as a problem to be solved from the outside by experts.[13] This approach developed in the years following the Second World War and the end of colonialism with the view that by injecting large sums of money into the developing world for projects and infrastructure, developing nations could make a quick leap into industrialism.

One of the classic examples of this is large-scale foreign aid.[14] The idea of using foreign aid is understandable; poverty is a big problem, and foreign aid is a big solution. Yet if we look at its effects over time, there is no real correlation between aid and economic development. More importantly, as Peter Bauer argues, such aid has delayed the development of business and politicized economics, and created a permanent political class.[15] When Bauer made these arguments in the early 1980s he was an outlier. Though his views are still rejected by the establishment, in the last decade a number of books have affirmed Bauer's critiques. The 2015 Nobel laureate Angus Deaton reiterated Bauer's arguments, while adding some of his own in *The Great Escape*.[16]

More important for our topic than the data about aid is the flawed view of work that comes from a social engineering approach to poverty. On the one hand, this view misses the implication of everyday work and business for economic development, while on the other it reduces individual workers to statistics in a large external plan. Both these tendencies undermine the dignity and personal dimension of human work and its role in promoting sustainable development.

Humanitarianism v. Charity

The second problem is that we have replaced charity with humanitarianism. Superficially, the two can appear similar, although in fact they are significantly different in both motivation and meaning. Charity comes from the Latin word *caritas*, meaning love, which is understood in the

Christian tradition as seeking the good of the other. That is, to love is to will the other person's good and promote integral human development, while keeping the eternal destiny of the person in mind.

Humanitarianism, however, is a hollowed out, secular form of Christian love that focuses on providing comfort and solving the immediately apparent problem. It sounds more 'realistic' and 'concrete' as opposed to Christian love, which is concerned about the soul and human flourishing. Yet on further reflection, humanitarianism has limited horizons and undermines the dignity and long-term integral development of people and communities. It misses the fundamental human and personal dimension of the people we are supposed to be helping.

By focusing on the immediate, humanitarianism confuses an emergency situation with a chronic one. Perhaps the easiest way to explain this is to think of the first time a person from the United States or Europe visits a poor country and experiences poverty. We see a poor family living in a small hut with a leaky roof and a dirt floor, and this cries out to us as an emergency. But it is an emergency for *us*. For the people who live in poverty, it is a chronic problem.

Ultimately, humanitarianism puts the emphasis on the expert and technician who will drop in to solve the problems of the poor. One detects the close relationship with social engineering and how both focus on outside solutions instead of creating the conditions for poor people to engage in highly productive work and create prosperity themselves.

Sentimentality

Closely connected to humanitarianism is the problem of sentimentality, which creates in us strong feelings about the situation of poverty, though often divorced from the concrete reality of the persons we are trying to help. We see poverty and naturally are moved and feel strong feelings to help. This is good, but if it is not guided by prudence and seeing a situation as it really is, this can cause harm. We must not be indifferent to suffering, like the rich man was indifferent to the poverty of Lazarus. Yet neither must we replace authentic love with sentimental humanitarianism. It is not enough for us to have strong feelings. Those feelings must be guided by the truth of the situation and the truth about the human person who is not a problem to be solved, but a person to be engaged. As Benedict XVI summarized powerfully, 'When charity is separated from truth, it degenerates into sentimentality.'[17]

Sentimentality is not the same as an authentic response of charity which keeps the subjective dimension of the person in focus. Thus when it is combined with social engineering, sentimentality can lead quickly to policies that undermine human dignity and liberty. The most obvious and notorious of these are large-scale population control and eugenic programmes that include abortion and forced sterilization.[18]

Objectification

The most profound problem with the dominant view of development and poverty alleviation – and in many ways both the origin and the consequence of social engineering and humanitarianism – is that we tend to objectify the poor. In our desire to help those in need and in an authentic emotional reaction to extreme poverty, we have tended to treat poor people like objects – objects of our charity, pity, and compassion – instead of treating them like subjects and the protagonists in their own story of development. I am not suggesting this is necessarily intentional or malicious. Part of it is the normal struggle of the human condition and the result of the fall, where we objectify other people for our own benefit. Just as we objectify persons when we reduce them to an object of gratification by isolating their sexual values from their personhood or reduce them to an object of utility when we exploit people for their labour, we do the same with people in poverty when we use them as a means to feel good about ourselves and our awareness, and it can be harder to recognize because we feel that we are doing good.

Each of these four characteristics, because they encourage us to see the solution to poverty as coming from the outside, leads to a devaluing of the importance of work. This happens, first, because the problem and the solution seem so big that individual efforts seem insignificant. Second, paradoxically, because of the imposed model of social engineering, there is a reticence to talk about work because it feels like imposing labour on someone. But this devaluing of work that comes from the humanitarian social engineering model distracts from the question of what poor people need to create prosperity in their own families and communities.

We often hear (doubtless well-intentioned) religious leaders, political leaders, and politicians claim that what poor nations need is more aid and charity. Richard Sterns of World Vision has claimed that if Christians were more generous we could raise 52 billion dollars a year and over 20 years raise 1,040 billion dollars and we could eradicate extreme poverty.[19] While this type of rhetoric can inspire generosity and action – and we should be generous – giving aid and assistance will not end poverty because the main reason people are poor is not because they lack material things, but because they are excluded from institutions of justice. The main question is not how we can solve poverty, but what it is that people need in order to create prosperity in their own communities. It is to this that we now turn.

Inclusion for the Poor: Work and the Institutions of Justice

The Peruvian economist Hernando de Soto has argued that the developing world does not lack entrepreneurs, or intelligent, motivated people who desire better lives for their families.[20] The question is why do entrepreneurs not emerge in the developing world like they do in the United States, Europe, or the Asian Tigers? After all, these places used to be poor as well. We often ask why there is poverty, but forget to ask why there is wealth and how it was created.

Entrepreneurship, economic development, and the wealth of nations are complex topics. There are many reasons for poverty, but one area that is often neglected in the dominant humanitarian model but which is linked closely to the issue of work and human flourishing is the institutions of justice that create inclusion for poor.

These institutions include things such as clear titles to land, the ability to own private property, basic access to the courts, rule of law, and ability to participate in the formal economy and free exchange.[21] These too are complex issues, but here the Jewish and Christian traditions not only have much to say, but are in many ways the primary sources of these ideas in the West.

The institutions of justice are linked closely to the question of work because they create the conditions for building businesses, engaging in entrepreneurial activity, and high levels of productivity to create prosperity in their own countries, communities, and families. A biblical vision of work that places the person at the centre of the economy orients towards helping the poor not only with charity and assistance in emergencies, but in creating access and inclusion so people can flourish on their own.[22]

One can debate the relative merits of wealth and prosperity for culture and our souls, and there is no doubt that the prosperity we experience in the West comes with serious spiritual challenges. Yet so does poverty, especially when it is the result of exclusion.[23] It is easy for us in the West to romanticize the simple life, but real poverty negatively impacts human flourishing, prevents the development of cultural pursuits, and can create the conditions for envy, anger, and desperation. Poor people often feel stuck, as Herman Chinery Hesse, a Ghanaian software entrepreneur put it bluntly, 'in a hole with all your skills and talents, and that is simply the way it is'.[24] This type of poverty is an obstacle to human flourishing and highlights the importance of the institutions of justice that those of us who live in wealthy countries can often take for granted. Let us briefly consider three of these institutions of justice.

Clear Property Title

The lack of clear property titles is a serious problem throughout the developing world. In some countries 50 to 60 per cent of the land has no clear title. Without a clean and secure title, people's land can be easily taken, seized, or expropriated quickly and with little or no compensation. This is especially a challenge for poor rural farmers who can be viewed as an obstacle to industrialization, or the widow and the orphan who often lack social influence and contacts. Widespread lack of clear title creates serious problems for economic development for the poorest people in society. It also creates disincentives to engage in productive work. Without clear title, people are stuck in low-productivity jobs. This is because if people do not know who owns the land they live on, they will not take risks, they will not build a business or even plant a vineyard or an orchard (which require capital investment and take years to produce), because at any time the land could be taken away from them, after they put in all the work to make it productive and valuable. Millions of people are stuck in subsistence, low-productivity work, not because they lack motivation or skill, but because they are *acting rationally* – why would anyone build a business when it could be taken away from them? You cannot build an economy and create incentives for higher-level work and innovation without private property.

While I can only touch briefly on it in this chapter, it is important to recall that the idea of private property and its importance is not simply a modern concept. It is found in the Scriptures and has always been a part of the Jewish and Christian traditions.[25] Private property is presupposed in the Decalogue, and there are clear penalties and requirements for restitution found in Exodus. We see the importance of clear title all the way back in Genesis 23 when Abraham is insistent that he wants to buy a plot of land to bury his wife, Sarah. Violations of private property are condemned by the Prophets, and private property is presupposed for both charity and sacrifice.[26]

Additionally, we see how the Jewish and Christian traditions have always connected private property to the family and to passing down culture and religion. One of the key reasons for private property is the creation of space for families to live out their freedom and responsibilities. While many Christians may not be aware of the deep connection between private property and the family, socialists from Robert Owen to Marx and Engels to the Frankfurt School and other modern iterations understand this very well. All of them recognize private property, family, and religion as the three primary obstacles to their social reform. Ultimately all things belong to God, we are stewards, and private property is not an end itself but a means to human flourishing.

Christianity has much to say about the institutions of justice. The Christian understanding of private property is part of a larger vision of justice that undergirds political and economic liberty, and it is important that we do not think of these as simply modern categories.

Justice in the Courts

The lack of property rights for the poor is just the tip of the iceberg. It is part of a larger pattern of them not enjoying what many of us take for granted: access to justice in the courts, or what development economists call the rule of law.

The topic of justice is complex, but there are two main problems facing poor people. First, the poor enjoy little to no access to justice in the courts, and second, the poor tend to face exclusion from the formal economy. Let us consider each in turn. According to the Research Foundation for Governance in India, there is a backlog of about 31 million cases that will take 320 years to be resolved. On average it takes close to 20 years for justice to be served, and the cost of litigation is often extravagant, so the poor cannot afford it, and this gives the wealthy and connected unfair advantages. If you are poor, illiterate, a widow, or an orphan, you are generally excluded. This is a violation of justice and the biblical injunction of equal justice regardless of one's economic or social standing.

Notice that this challenges both the elitist crony capitalism that gives preferential treatment to the rich and well connected, as well as a number of social justice approaches that argue that the poor should get special treatment because they are poor. Leviticus 19.15, for example, makes it clear that justice requires impartiality and no favour.

The lack of a generally just system of rule of law whereby the poor can get their court case heard without undue economic burden is a serious obstacle to economic development and human flourishing, and a related problem is the difficulty poor people face when trying to participate in the formal economy.

Poor people are often locked out of the formal economy. While they can engage in little unofficial businesses, many poor people find it quite difficult and expensive officially to register their business in the formal economy. Sometimes we talk about the informal sector as the 'black market', which invokes images of gangs and violence. This is not what is happening in most of what is more properly called the 'extra-legal' sector throughout much of the developing world. These are small (and some medium) sized businesses that are producing and selling normal goods and services. The reason they are not officially legal is because it is too difficult and expensive to register their legitimate business, not because they are doing anything immoral or criminal.

This exclusion from the formal economy combined with difficulty in getting one's court case heard means that when there is a dispute of land or contracts or payment, there is no simple method of resolving the dispute. Thus, again, people act rationally and only engage in very small production and trade because they don't want to take larger risks without clear justice and rule of law.

Another problem with both clear title and exclusion from the formal economy is that even if one were willing to take a risk and expand one's business, it is quite difficult to secure a loan or access to other financial and insurance services. In summary, being outside the formal economy creates enormous barriers that those of us who live in the developed world never consider.

Hernando de Soto did a study to illustrate the problem. He set up a small sewing machine shop just outside of Lima, Peru, and enlisted four law students for the purpose of going out to register the business. They had to take public transportation, just like a poor person, and they had to fill out all the forms and pay all the fees with no access to a lawyer, just like a poor person would do. Working 6 hours a day, it took 289 days to officially register the business. De Soto explains that this is when he realized that if one is poor, the law and the legal system could be real obstacles to progress and development.[27]

Peru is not atypical. Similar problems exist in other countries, as well. The Heritage Index of Economic Freedom reports the following:

- Ghana: The business start-up process takes two weeks, but obtaining necessary permits takes over 200 days and still costs over twice the level of average annual income.[28]
- India: Launching a business takes more than 25 days on average, and licensing requirements cost almost ten times the level of average annual income.[29]
- Nigeria: Obtaining necessary permits still takes more than 100 days and costs over 30 times the level of average annual income.[30]
- Brazil: On average, it requires over 100 days to incorporate a company, and obtaining necessary permits takes 400 days.[31]

Just as with private property, there is a strong correlation between ease of starting a business and wealth and poverty.

Freedom of Exchange

The final institution of justice I'd like to discuss is freedom of exchange. This can sound surprising because we often think that competition hurts the poor – and sometimes it can, especially when it is rigged in favour of the wealthy or when crony capitalist arrangements come in the form of aid or charity through government grants or the work of NGOs. However, when we listen to entrepreneurs, small businessmen, and farmers in the developing world, we hear a different story. They often speak of their desire for access to markets and a chance to compete.

Free exchange is not perfect, but perhaps counterintuitively it is especially important for the poor. Why? When governments get involved in regulating industry and handing down complex rules regarding the economy, they almost always favour big business and powerful interest groups who employ highly paid lobbyists and lawyers who live in the capital city and can influence legislation and policy.

The ones who get hurt are smaller producers, the poorest of the poor, who lack the political, economic, and social contacts to navigate these complex systems. What ends up happening is almost always some type of crony, oligarchic capitalism that is unfair and further locks out the poorest. In Kenya, for example, coffee growers cannot sell directly to the market – they have to sell at a set price to a government board, which then sells to the market.

There is a common narrative that free exchange is a modern invention of intellectual liberalism and individualism and that is opposed to Christian thinking. This is not historically the case, though. While these are very complex topics in intellectual history, free, competitive market economies existed long before the rise of modern secular liberalism. Just as Jewish and Christian thought has addressed the dignity and value of work and the importance of private property, it has recognized the work of merchants and traders, while always warning of the dangers of wealth and avarice. Complex issues around the topic of exchange, trade, and banking have been addressed by Jewish and Christian theologians, both Protestant and Catholic, since the medieval era. Again: free economies are not modern inventions, but existed in the medieval and Renaissance worlds in northern Europe and the Italian city states.[32] Medieval and Renaissance Florence is a prime example of a free market economy prior to the rise of modern individualism and liberalism.[33]

Moral Ecology

What the poor need most is inclusion, justice, rule of law, and a clear framework in which to operate. These things are hard to build, and while politics plays an essential role, politics alone cannot solve this problem. There must be moral and spiritual transformation – a hungering for justice and the prudence and persistence to cultivate it effectively.

These institutions of justice do not arise out of nowhere and cannot be sustained in a moral and cultural vacuum. This is no simple task, but just as the institutions of justice arose from a biblical vision and centuries of Jewish and Christian reflection and practice, the church has a role to play developing a healthy moral ecology. This is because it is from love of neighbour, desire for justice, and the recognition of the dignity of the person and the family that these institutions develop.

Conclusions

There will always be poverty and suffering that will require human love. We will always have the need for almsgiving, and economic development alone will not solve all our problems. There will always be poor people who cannot help themselves and need our care. We must care for the widow and the orphan in their distress, and we must not be indifferent like the rich man was to Lazarus.

But for the majority of the world's poor, the problem is not one of charity, or even redistribution: the problem is that the poor lack the institutions of justice that would enable them to create prosperity for their families and their communities. Here a biblical vision of justice and charity, connected with a biblical vision of work and its role in human flourishing, can help orient our thinking about poverty in a way that is rooted in the human person, who is a subject not an object, and the protagonist of his and her own story of development. A biblical vision of work puts the issue of poverty and development in proper perspective: that while humankind is created in the *imago Dei* and this includes work, we are not made for work but for rest and worship. It is only in a proper relationship of work, rest, and worship that we can become what we were made to be.

Notes

1 Leon Kass, in his wonderful book on Genesis, tends to take this type of Rousseauian approach (*The Beginning of Wisdom* (New York: Simon & Schuster, 2003), p. 60). Specifically related to work, Marx for example views primitive man in a semi-conscious state wherein he becomes human through work (see Erich Fromm, 'The Nature of Man', available at www.marxists.org/archive/fromm/works/1961/man/ch04.htm). This, however, creates a logical problem for Marx, since he argues that only man can work, and so it would be impossible to become man through work. This is addressed in John F. Crosby, 'Evolutionism and the Ontology of the Human Person: Critique of the Marxist Theory of the Emergence of Man', *Review of Politics* 38, no. 2 (April 1976), pp. 208–43.

2 Except of course the command to be fruitful and multiply, which applies to all animals and plants and could be a question of instinct. Because of our rational-

ity and our subjective nature, our command to be fruitful and multiply – though a strong drive – is not simply instinct, but must be guided by our rationality and the recognition of ourselves and the other as a subject to be respected and not merely used for pleasure or generation of life.

3 Paul also uses this imagery of working with God in 1 Cor. 3.9 when he writes we are 'fellow labourers with God'.

4 See Joseph Pieper's insightful book on work, worship, and leisure: *Leisure, the Basis of Culture* (San Francisco: Ignatius Press, 2009).

5 For an interesting book on the importance of rest, see Abraham Heschel, *The Sabbath* (New York: Farrar, Straus & Giroux, 1951).

6 This is why Josef Pieper notes that 'labour day', a holiday celebrating labour, misses the fundamental relationship between work and worship. See his *In Tune with the World: A Theory of Festivity* (South Bend, IN: St Augustine's Press, 1999).

7 This theme is developed more fully in Mark Greene, *Fruitfulness on the Frontline* (Grand Rapids, MI: InterVarsity Press, 2014).

8 Gary Anderson, *Adam and Eve in the Jewish and Christian Imagination* (Louisville, KY: Westminster John Knox Press, 2001), p. 153.

9 Anderson, *Adam and Eve*, p. 154.

10 'If a person has no work to do, what should he do? If he has a dilapidated yard or field, he should go and occupy himself with it' (*Babylonian Talmud*, Avot D'Rabbi Noson 11:1).

11 See *The Rule of St Benedict*, available at www.holyrule.com/index.htm. I address this is in a bit more detail in my 'Jewish and Catholic Sources of Private Property', in *One and Indivisible: The Relationship between Religious and Economic Freedom*, ed. Kevin Schmiesing (Grand Rapids, MI: Acton Institute, 2016), as well as in a forthcoming book on poverty and justice that will be published by Crossroad in 2018.

12 Available at www.un.org/millenniumgoals/ and https://sustainabledevelopment. un.org.

13 For some critique of the so-called experts, see Thomas Sowell, *A Conflict of Visions* (New York: Basic Books, 2007); Nassim Nicholas Taleb, *AntiFragile* (New York: Random House, 2012) and *Fooled by Randomness* (New York: Random House, 2004); and William Easterly, *Tyranny of Experts* (New York: Basic Books, 2013).

14 It is important to reiterate that poverty is quite complex. There is no single solution, and good people can disagree. In this section, I discuss some complex things in a cursory manner in order to give a general context and concrete illustrations. For example, foreign aid (government-to-government transfers) is a complex topic about which numerous studies have been written. My point in using it here is as an illustration of an underlying problem of social engineering.

15 See P. T. Bauer, *Rhetoric and Reality: Studies in the Economics of Development* (Cambridge, MA: Harvard University Press, 1984) and *Equality, The Third World, and Economic Delusion* (Cambridge, MA: Harvard University Press, 1981).

16 Angus Deaton, *The Great Escape: Health, Wealth, and the Origins of Inequality* (Princeton, NJ: Princeton University Press, 2013), especially ch. 7. See also William Easterly, *The Elusive Quest for Growth* (Cambridge, MA: MIT Press, 2001), *The White Man's Burden* (New York: Oxford University Press, 2006), and *Tyranny of Experts* (New York: Basic Books, 2013); and Dambisa Moyo, *Dead Aid* (New York: Farrar, Straus & Giroux, 2009).

17 Pope Benedict XVI, *Caritas in Veritate*, available at http://w2.vatican.va/

content/benedict-xvi/en/encyclicals/documents/hf_ben-xvi_enc_20090629_caritas-in-veritate.html.

18 www.thenewatlantis.com/publications/the-population-control-holocaust.

19 See Richard Stearns, 'The Gospel as a Virus', *Q Ideas Conference*, available at http://qideas.org/videos/the-gospel-as-a-virus/.

20 See Hernando De Soto's important book, *The Mystery of Capital: Why Capitalism Triumphs in the West and Fails Everywhere Else* (New York: Basic Books, 2000). This book is important and worth reading for anyone concerned about justice for the poor. There are some philosophical weaknesses in his reliance upon postmodernists to explain property and representation, and he does not sufficiently address the influence of the Hebrew Bible and the Jewish and Christian traditions on the development of private property and rule of law, but nevertheless, De Soto addresses the important effects of private property and clear title for poor communities.

21 The Nobel laureate Douglass North addressed these institutions of justice in great detail in a number of works including *Understanding the Process of Economic Change* (Princeton, NJ: Princeton University Press, 2005). Others who have written about these institutions include Peter Bauer, Hernando de Soto, and William Easterly; David Landes in *The Wealth and Poverty of Nations* (New York: W.W. Norton, 1999); and Daron Acemoglu and James Robinson in their book *Why Nations Fail* (New York: Crown Business, 2012). One weakness of the Acemoglu and Robinson argument is that they take a narrow view of culture instead of recognizing institutions as a product of culture. For the relationship between culture and institutions, see Rodney Stark, *The Victory of Reason* (New York: Random House, 2005). Lawrence E. Huntington and Samuel P. Huntington, *Culture Matters: How Values Shape Human Progress* (New York: Basic Books, 2000).

22 These ideas are found throughout Jewish and Christian sources, but one of the clearest is the medieval Jewish theologian and philosopher Moses Maimonides and his '8 Levels of Charity', according to which the highest level is to help a fellow Jew build a business of his own. www.chabad.org/library/article_cdo/aid/986711/jewish/Matnot-Aniyim-Chapter-10.htm.

23 I am not speaking of the voluntary decision for evangelical poverty of a monk or nun or a family who decides to live with stark simplicity.

24 See the documentary film, *Poverty, Inc.* (Acton Media, 2014), directed and produced by Michael Matheson Miller.

25 See my 'Private Property, Religious Freedom, and Economic Development', in *One and Indivisible*. I also recommend the lectures by Professor John Bergsma at Acton University that can be found at http://university.acton.org/.

26 See 2 Samuel 2.23–24 where David insists that he buys land and cattle from Araunah the Jebusite in order to offer a thanksgiving sacrifice to God.

27 See De Soto, *The Mystery of Capital*, ch. 2. See also *Poverty, Inc.*

28 'Heritage 2014 Index of Economic Freedom', available at www.heritage.org/index/pdf/2014/book/index_2014.pdf, p. 218.

29 'Heritage 2014 Index of Economic Freedom', p. 240.

30 'Heritage 2014 Index of Economic Freedom', p. 340.

31 'Heritage 2014 Index of Economic Freedom', p. 134.

32 See Robert S. Lopez, *The Commercial Revolution of the Middle Ages: 950–1350* (New York: Cambridge University Press, 1976).

33 See, for example, Richard Goldthwaite, *The Economy of Renaissance Florence* (Baltimore: Johns Hopkins University Press, 2009).

Afterword

GABRIELA URBANOVA

You have just finished what I trust has been for you a very enriching and exciting journey through *Work: Theological Foundations and Practical Implications*. I hope that you, like me, found this journey not only fulfilling, but also intellectually and practically challenging. At the heart of this book, the thread that connects each chapter is a clear desire on the part of each contributor to effect real change by building a bridge from *knowing* that our daily lives and the work that fills it are meaningful to *acting* in accord with this reality.

The church cannot afford for any Christian to ignore the call to build this bridge from knowledge to practice. Why? The unified message present throughout this volume is relevant in a specific way to the life of every follower of Jesus. Researchers in London recently concluded that the average person in the West spends 92,210 hours working over the course of a lifetime. This is *12 years*. This makes the consideration of work an indispensable topic among Christians. If we are true to our calling to *perform work as an act of love*, just how deeply can we change our society?

When we recognize our work as a calling from the Lord, it should be clear that our work should mirror the kingdom. We should see service to the Lord as the top priority of our labour, and as such, understand that through our work we are practising love of neighbour and given the privilege to use our work to improve the lives of others and the world in which we live. The reality is that God can use *me* in ways I cannot foresee to bless those close to me and those I will likely never meet when I surrender my whole life, including my work, to the cause for which I was created and gifted. If such a tremendous opportunity exists through the seemingly mundane, there can be no doubt that it is the Holy Spirit that works with and through us to make this priority a reality.

My home, the Slovak Republic, has been a free society for just a little more than 25 years. From 1948 to 1989 my people were occupied by an oppressive Communist state that actively represented the complete antithesis of a free and open society. Today, Slovakia has what is considered a free economy, but those 40 long years of Communist rule took a toll on us. It is not just that this system controlled the production and exchange of goods, the labour market, and many other facets of public and private life. This system corrupted the way we as a society think about ourselves and our work. Despite the ironic root of the system's name, it conditioned us to think individualistically. We missed the relational and missional aspects of our work because we did not serve others – we served the State and the Party.

The echoes of this poisonous system still persist. We build high walls between houses. We've forgotten to share and engage with others because we still think that we have nothing to share with our neighbours. We enjoy many of the benefits of a free market system, but many of us still do not understand the responsibilities. All microeconomic data indicates that Slovaks need not think of themselves in need of constant help from others, but recognize that we have something to share. Our work in a free and open society gives us the means to be a blessing to others, but it was the soul-crushing efficiency with which the Communist occupiers purged the society of Christian influence that still blinds us to this reality.

The culture from which I come, I think, causes the lessons of this volume to impact me in a special way. There is not a doubt that there is a material aspect to work. In 2 Thessalonians 3.10 the apostle Paul clearly reminds us of this: work is linked to provision. But as John Taylor so aptly explains early in this volume, it is not just *our* provision but the provision for others through our support of the church that is to be one of the fruits of our labour. Work allows us to demonstrate love and concern tangibly, but it can also lead to the valuation of a person on the basis of what he can produce, in effect turning him into a slave who serves a master who is not his creator. We engage in work for ourselves, yes, but without forgetting the relational aspect of our work that impacts the broader society. It is crucial, therefore, for Christians who are to be the light for the world, to show different attitudes and the highest moral standards.

How then shall we work and create relationships? Exactly as we read in Chapter 13: by 'creativity and trust'. This activity, as Greg Forster points out in Chapter 9, goes 'beyond the walls of the local church'. But by what power do we fulfil this mission? By cooperating with God in our work, as Miroslav Volf tells us in Chapter 6.

These principles will help us to fulfil his calling: *to perform work as an act of love.* Sure, the challenge is difficult, but it is one that is well worth the effort. How do you answer this calling?

Name and Subject Index